SOCIAL WORK PRACTICE

SOCIAL WORK PRACTICE

RONDA S. CONNAWAY
and
MARTHA E. GENTRY

College of Social Work
University of Kentucky
Lexington

PRENTICE HALL, Englewood Cliffs, New Jersey 07632

Library of Congress Cataloging-in-Publication Data

Connaway, Ronda S.
Social work practice.

Bibliography: p.
Includes index.
1. Social service. I. Gentry, Martha E. II. Title.
HV40.C657 1988 361.3'2 87-14972
ISBN 0-13-819558-7

Cover design: Diane Saxe
Manufacturing buyer: Carol Bystrom

Printed in the United States of America
10 9 8 7 6 5 4 3 2 1

ISBN 0-13-819558-7 01

Prentice-Hall International (UK) Limited, *London*
Prentice-Hall of Australia Pty. Limited, *Sydney*
Prentice-Hall Canada Inc., *Toronto*
Prentice-Hall Hispanoamericana, S.A., *Mexico*
Prentice-Hall of India Private Limited, *New Delhi*
Prentice-Hall of Japan, Inc., *Tokyo*
Simon & Schuster Asia Pte. Ltd., *Singapore*
Editora Prentice-Hall do Brasil, Ltda., *Rio de Janeiro*

Dedicated to

Grace White and Leone Renn

CONTENTS

PREFACE

This book is a comprehensive introduction to social work practice. It provides information, assumptions, and knowledge to answer three broad questions. First, what are general categories of social worker activity, their historical contexts, and contemporary usage? Second, to what general social goals and specific practice objectives are these activities directed? Third, what knowledge and assumptions do social workers use when engaging in planned change in each of these categories of practice activity?

This is a book about the breadth of social work practice—what all social workers should know about practice in our profession. It is, then, about generalist practice. Such a focus invites important, even skeptical questions. What is meant by generalist practice? Why is another book about it needed? How does this one differ from others? Given the profession's move to specialized practice, is attention to generalist practice needed? Who needs to learn about it? We respect these and related questions about our purpose and approach and invite you to join us in exploring answers to these issues whether or not you share our conclusions.

WHAT IS GENERALIST PRACTICE?

Generalist practice is defined here as a constellation of social worker role sets designed to respond inclusively and flexibly to a broad range of client systems consistent with the goals and functions of the profession. It is not simply a combination of methods such as casework, group work, and community organizing. It is not simply those activities that are common across different fields of practice such as child welfare, health services, and economic security. It is a broad set of social work practice responses to social issues, which has characterized the historical core of our profession's change mandate.

Generalist practice depends upon an inclusive rather than exclusive theoretical framework, which captures the profession's most prized perceptions about social systems, about the sources of social difficulties, about how change occurs, and about how social workers can influence change processes. It relies on general problem-solving activities and occurs in many different places. It is influenced by positions social workers hold, the client systems with which they work, and professional values social workers espouse. It is the foundation for all practice. All social workers need to know about generalist practice even though their own practice may emphasize a narrower range of problems and highly specialized procedures.

Generalist practice requires a frame of mind from which social workers attempt to connect their practice to broad professional values, purposes, and issues. Their practice is guided by a commitment to relate specific instances of client-system problems to social policy initiatives. It relies on a worker's ability to connect client-system objectives with appropriate change strategies rather than fit those objectives to a favored strategy. It emphasizes the critical place of research to both inform and evaluate worker activities. This frame of mind leads social workers into unlikely, nontraditional, and often unexpected practice settings and opportunities.

ANOTHER GENERALIST TEXT?

Yes, another one! We appreciate your skepticism if you have asked this question; you deserve a reasoned response, which describes the route we have taken and some choices we have made. In the 1960s we were part of a lively group of colleagues at Washington University working on a conceptualization of practice. Under the leadership of Peggy Wood and along with Hans Falck, Bill Gordon, Margo Schutz Gordon, Dorriece Pirtle, Mary Schulte, and others; we tried to locate ways to overcome artificial conceptual boundaries that fragmented practice education. The profession and professional education were in ferment. The National Association of Social Workers had been established from several special interest groups and the Council on Social Work Education had revised the framework for curricula to eliminate the Basic Eight and traditional methods as organizing themes. These influences and those of the civil rights movement, the War on Poverty, and protests against the war in Vietnam required us to perceive our practice world differently.

In this context, the historical themes in practice constantly interacted with our own experiences in practice and teaching. Later, at the University of Kentucky, our focus was teaching for practice where social workers must be flexible, self-directed, and responsive to a range of client-system issues and service delivery characteristics. We asked how social work's historical mission and themes persisted in contemporary practice to make us one profession and not many. What about that history did student social workers need to know to carry practice into the future and defend and improve it? What might social work become with a comprehensive theoretical framework, a clear focus on the connections between practice purposes and practice strategies, and problem-solving strategies considered in a social role and client-system context?

We have answered these questions in a particular way, which is not currently reflected in other books about generalist practice. Briefly, this is what we do: First, we present a theoretical framework for practice. It contains three major parts—explanations of client systems, explanations about change, and explanations about social worker actions. We present this framework using concepts and assumptions about wholes, parts, and relationships, similarity and difference, dynamics of change, and constellations of worker activities. This framework is consistent with our history and the main themes in social work literature. It is presented in an integrated, comprehensive way.

Second, problem solving in practice takes place in and is influenced by a context. This context is comprised of features of agencies and positions, client-system characteristics, and worker characteristics. We present a way for social workers to identify critical agency and position influences on various stages of problem solving and how some of their own characteristics may affect what they do.

Third, we identify and present detailed conceptualizations of six social worker role sets—broker, advocate, social reformer, educator, clinician, and mediator—as major categories of social worker action. Each is examined historically and matched to one general client-system goal. The strategies available in each role set are identified and described. Guidelines for differential assessments and strategy choices are given.

Fourth, the ways these role sets may occur and be combined in actual practice are elaborated in a chapter that gives five client-system examples. This chapter also shows how the theoretical framework guides practice choices.

Fifth, we discuss some issues for social workers of the future. These are evaluating practice, a dual focus requiring renewed emphasis on social action, limits of professional status, directions for specialized practice, and new practice arenas.

GENERALISTS AND SPECIALISTS

Social work's need for specialized practice knowledge and procedures is obvious. Our world is complex and social work's purposes and activities in it are based on an ever-expanding knowledge base about the sources of and ways to resolve social difficulties. We must find ways for social workers to keep up with this knowledge and translate it into informed, effective change efforts.

Is generalist practice, then, outmoded, unnecessary, or unimportant? Our response is a firm, no. Generalist practice is the foundation that captures the purposes, goals, and broad action categories for the profession as a whole. It is what all BSW graduates need to know about social work. It is what persons coming into graduate programs from other fields without advanced standing need to know about social work—what concerns us and what we do about these concerns. It says to both the undergraduate and beginning graduate student: Social work is not only using strategies for therapeutic or educational purposes, but also for mediation, advocacy, and social reform purposes.

This book is directed specifically to these two groups. First, it is for upper level undergraduates who have had: (1) an introduction to social work (its history, usual service locations, values, and ethics); (2) an introduction to basic techniques of relating to and working with people who are in difficulty, and (3) an introduction to beginning concepts in human behavior, the social environment, and social policy. It is designed to be used in interventive strategy courses and as background content for practicum placements. It also is designed to thoroughly prepare students for advanced standing in graduate programs.

Second, this book also is directed to beginning graduate students without advanced standing who come from other educational and career backgrounds. It provides an introduction to central themes in our practice history as well as basic information about social work purposes, frameworks, and practice activities. There are no prerequisite courses at this level, but concurrent enrollment in human behavior and social policy courses might be helpful.

This book may be useful in other ways. We hope doctoral students learning how to conceptualize practice may use it. If so, we further hope and expect they will modify and extend our work. Persons responsible for staff development and in-service training should find the problem solving and six role set chapters useful in their work. Finally, this book identifies a broad research agenda important to undergird our practice.

BEFORE YOU BEGIN

This is not a book about how to practice. Rather, it is a book about how to think about practice. We are committed firmly to the idea that raising expectations and standards for thinking clearly about practice will improve its quality and ultimately benefit those we attempt to help. We trust the ability of our colleagues in education and practice to teach specific techniques and procedures that derive from our approach in actual practice.

Chapter One

INTRODUCTION

This book is designed to answer the question, what does a social worker do? We answer this question by identifying the major purposes or goals of social work practice and the general strategies social workers use to achieve them. While not all social workers need to use these strategies in all of their practice, all social workers should know them, be able to distinguish them from each other, and know when and where they are appropriate to use.

This is not a how-to book that helps you learn specific techniques such as how to conduct an interview or serve as group leader or conduct a community meeting. Those techniques are better taught and learned through films, video tapes, and practice sessions where an expert social worker can observe and talk directly with you. Instead, this book presents social work strategies such as bargaining, public disclosure, campaign and contest, social skills training and moderating. We introduce you to social work strategies, the goals to which these are directed, and the knowledge and assumptions used in engaging in change.

This journey into the breadth of social work practice will not be easy. We ask you to think critically and to analyze issues and problems. We ask you to learn how to ask and answer questions systematically. We urge you to see research as part of practice. And we ask you to give up any personal bias you have about your favorite part of practice, at least temporarily, so that you can learn about and appreciate the whole. You are not expected to become instantly an expert social worker. Nor are you asked to be a particular kind of social worker who can do everything for everyone or solve every problem. But when you have finished reading this text, we think you will understand how broad and complex social work is, appreciate its challenges and opportunities, and recognize the major options for helping others.

WHAT IS SOCIAL WORK?

Social work is one human service profession whose general purpose is to prevent and remedy problems that interfere with social functioning. These problems are many but may include such issues as poverty, discrimination, inadequate access to resources, personal deficiencies and maladies, and interpersonal difficulties. Social work's arena includes anything which happens to and among persons that threatens survival, creates loss of opportunity for personal and interpersonal development, or interferes with persons' capacities to cope. Other professions such as medicine, vocational rehabilitation, and law share concern for the same arena and we often work in concert with them to solve social and individual problems.

Three main concepts characterize social work and help distinguish our activities from those of others. First, social workers are concerned about wholes, parts, and the relationships between these. They do not try to solve any problem by focusing on one person or problem alone but always by placing that person or problem in a social context. Second, social workers try to understand, explain, and predict how change comes about. We do not see the world in static terms but look for ways to understand the dynamics of change. Finally, social workers have a special appreciation for similarity and difference. We expect to find and look for ways persons and social problems are alike, but we also anticipate and appreciate diversity and difference.

Our practice has been shaped and molded by historical events. Throughout its history social work has attempted to stand for and promote important social values. All people have the right to participate in making decisions that affect them. All people have the right to basic life necessities including protection. All people have the right to grow, develop, and achieve. All people have the responsibility to contribute to the well-being of others consistent with their ability to do so. All persons have the right to live in a just society characterized not only by equity but by equality. Our special concern is any person, group, or community without sufficient power to solve its own problems.

These values help social workers choose the social problems, issues, and people we are concerned about and attempt to help. They have influenced our general purposes or aims, which are to:

1. Prevent and remedy distress and promote utilization of resources in individuals, families, households, groups, and communities.
2. Promote and establish policies, programs, and services required for basic survival needs and for enhancement of human potential.

As a constellation of helping behaviors directed at achieving these general purposes, social work uses knowledge from other fields as well. It is sanctioned by society, primarily through support to social institutions where we work, to provide resources, enhance opportunities, and control some social problems. Because we work in many different institutions, our social mandate is not as easy to locate as mandates of other professions such as education or medicine. Occasionally we may reject some portion of our mandate when it appears to be contrary to our values. Social work is expected to help solve social problems even though there is not always agreement in society as to the best or preferred solutions for these problems.

GENERALIST SOCIAL WORKERS

Social work developed first as a method of helping individuals and families and as a way of organizing services for the poor in urban communities. Methods of working with small groups were established later. These three methods came to be known as social casework, community organization, and social group work. This way of organizing social work knowledge and activities, called the *methods* approach, assumed that the goals and activities of the three groups were distinct.

At another time social work was described in terms of problems commonly found in the locations or fields where we practiced. This *fields of practice* approach assumed, for example, that social workers in child welfare and medical work, engaged in some similar activities but also experienced important differences because they practiced in different institutions and attended to different problems.

In recent years social workers have organized their knowledge and activities by using the terms "generalists" and "specialists." These terms have been used in two different ways. First, generalist denoted what is common to all social work no matter where it is practiced or what methods are used, while specialist meant its unique features in certain locations and with particular problems. Second, the terms have referred to the level or complexity of practice. In this use generalist means basic knowledge and activities of beginning social workers, and specialist refers to more complex knowledge and activities of social workers with advanced skills.

This book is about six major practice roles, rather than methods or fields of practice or levels of competence. Furthermore, this book conceptualizes the focus of our helping activities as client systems rather than individuals, groups, or communities. Client systems are composed of any number of persons to whom our helping activities are directed. Generalist practice is defined as *a constellation of social worker role sets designed to respond inclusively and flexibly to a broad range of client systems consistent with the goals and functions of the profession.* Generalist social workers are expected to: (1) recognize and assist client systems without respect to their size, (2) engage in a general set of problem-solving activities, (3) select and use one or more strategies consistent with client system goal(s), and (4) consistently connect their practice to broader professional values and purposes.

All social workers are constrained in some way by the roles inherent in their agency positions. These role expectations are important, but social workers' role conceptions are equally important and often should be different from expectations of their positions. Therefore, practice as described in this book requires social workers to bring a clear and strong philosophy to their practice which goes beyond what is expected in a particular social work position. This philosophy of generalist practice contains five central ideas each of which is examined further in Chapter 4.

First, social workers are expected to be leaders rather than followers in defining their tasks. Taking initiative and working autonomously requires self-assurance, knowledge and skill, and willingness to take risks on behalf of clients. Second, social workers are expected to define client-system problems in terms of their meaning to client systems rather than according to some definition favored by the agency where they work. Third, social workers are expected to move out of their agencies and take leadership roles in the community on one or more social welfare issues. Fourth, social workers are expected to adopt an attitude of inquiry that questions the efficacy of current solutions to client-system problems. Finally, social workers are expected to adopt a dual focus in practice, which reflects simultaneous concern for specific client systems *and* the larger social problems or issues these systems represent.

TWO GENERALIST SOCIAL WORKERS

What does practice look like when it has these characteristics? A typical day in the practice of two social workers employed in a community mental health center shows how diverse human problems are and how broad is the range of knowledge and skill a social worker needs.

M. Esther Bower

This social worker began seeing clients at 8:30 A.M. and finished her day at 7 P.M. In this time she met with members of six client systems in her office. Client-system problems included anorexia nervosa, marital discord, phobia, loneliness, alcoholism, and teenage conduct disorders. She spent the lunch hour meeting with other social workers to discuss if and how to establish a professional social work group in the area. Her work day concluded with an hour and a half meeting with a radio station reporter to provide the reporter with information needed for a special program on anorexia nervosa.

Bower's work required her to set specific objectives with client-system members, other social workers, and news media personnel; to select appropriate strategies for achieving these objectives; and to carry out these strategies. Her work was not limited to six client systems in the agency. It included professional concern about the total community and the larger problems that might exist there. She used clinical and educator strategies. She joined other social workers in plans that might eventually lead to advocacy and social action.

Dale Smith

During his typical day Dale Smith provided services to three client systems in his office. Principal members of all three systems were diagnosed as schizophrenic. Other serious problems noted in these systems were alcoholism, poverty, inadequate independent living skills, depression, lack of social supports, and poor housing. Smith spent the remainder of his day providing leadership to two groups working on problems associated with mental illness. One of these, a local task force on mental illness, had the goal of improving services to chronically mentally ill persons and their families in the community. The second group was a local chapter of the National Alliance for the Mentally Ill. This group works to develop support for families and friends of long-term mentally ill persons.

Smith's work also required him to set specific objectives with client system members, social workers, other professionals, and members of the community. In working to meet these objectives, he used clinical, educator, broker, and advocate roles. He conceived his professional responsibility as requiring work with community groups to meet the needs of client systems and the larger community. He prepared news releases, chaired meetings, and prepared educational materials, in addition to teaching clients about chemical dependency, helping client-system members to express anger, and providing transportation and other resources.

These examples of two social workers practicing demonstrate that social work is not a simple, uncomplicated profession where we can make do with a few basic skills. Instead, social workers need to be prepared to work with different types of client systems and problems in our communities as well as in our offices, in cooperation with other agencies as well as community leaders and residents, and in taking responsibility both for specific client systems and for community problems. This conception of social work is as old as social work itself and is consistent with our most significant contributions to society throughout our history.

A PREVIEW

Bower and Smith used several different helping strategies. These are called role sets and are comprised of social worker activities and behaviors designed to achieve certain specific client-system goals. The major goals that derive from social work's purposes or aims are to: match persons with resources, protect and secure existing rights and entitlements, establish new entitlements, help people learn social skills and improve role performance, help persons alter internalized effects of system stress, and assist people in reducing or resolving system conflict.

Social work practice occurs in a framework of concepts that makes it social work and not some other profession. This framework contains major propositions and assumptions about human conditions and how change occurs as seen through social workers' eyes. Chapter 3 presents the conceptual framework used in this book.

Social workers and their client systems choose change activities they think will resolve existing problems or prevent the onset of incipient problems and difficulties based on a thorough understanding of relevant client-system information. Making this choice is part of a general problem-solving process social workers use. The process includes identifying characteristics of and the location and nature of client-system problem(s), assessing, selecting goals, contracting with the client system, engaging in change strategies, and evaluating the outcomes of change. These activities occur in and are influenced by a context that includes the agency or location where practice occurs and social worker and client-system characteristics. This problem-solving process and its context are presented in Chapter 4.

Six major social worker role sets are presented in chapters 5 through 10. Each chapter includes the goal of the role set, a brief historical perspective on social work's use of the role, general kinds of problems it is designed to change, problem-solving activities specific to the role, strategies the social worker may choose from to achieve the goal, and practice issues in evaluating role effectiveness. Chapter 5 presents the broker role for client systems where the goal is matching resources to needs. Chapter 6 presents case and class advocacy strategies to protect and secure existing rights and entitlements for client systems. The social action role is described in Chapter 7 and is directed to establishing new entitlements. Education for learning new social skills and improving role performance is presented in Chapter 8. Chapter 9 identifies the clinical role, the goal of which is to alter internalized effects of system stress. Finally, the mediator role, which is directed to the goal of reducing or resolving system conflict, is presented in Chapter 10.

Chapter 11 presents examples that will assist the reader to see how roles occur both consecutively and simultaneously in work with one client system or across a social worker's total work load. Examples include a brief description of client-system problems, the goal of social worker assistance, specific client-system objectives, and social worker strategies. Finally, some practice principles are discussed.

Social work, like all human endeavors, has an agenda of unfinished business as well as opportunities for future development. In Chapter 12 we discuss some agenda items and some opportunities we think important for our profession. It would be more satisfying for us if we could present solutions as well as questions about these issues and opportunities, but we cannot, precisely because they are unfinished business for the whole profession. As you join us as professional colleagues, you will have the opportunity to help shape social work's future. We invite you to share our vision of it, to improve upon what we have proposed, and, above all else, to test the ideas presented throughout this book against your own experience and understanding of social work's place in society.

ACKNOWLEDGMENTS

We appreciate the help and advice of many persons. S. Zafar Hasan, Dean, College of Social Work, University of Kentucky supported our requests for writing time. Our colleagues, Maryrhea Morelock and Marlene Ballard read portions of the text and made critical and helpful comments and suggestions. Members of the Bluegrass Representational Unit, Kentucky NASW Chapter, anonymously provided data on which some examples in Chapter 11 are based. Lillian Milanof, Chapter President, and Buddy Moore of the Chapter Office in Frankfort, facilitated our securing these data. Mary Beth Durnell, Director of Social Services, St. Joseph's Hospital, Lexington, Kentucky, provided an example used in Chapter 6 and Rose Denman, Social Worker, Veterans Administration Hospital, Lexington, Kentucky, provided an example in Chapter 12.

Our colleagues and former students, M. Esther Bower and Dale Smith, understood our request for help and provided descriptions of their practice from which we benefited and which are included in Chapter 1. Ms. Bower is a social worker service supervisor at a children and youth center in Bowling Green, Kentucky. At the time she randomly selected a typical day's practice, she was a social worker therapist with the staff of the Comprehensive Care Center, Bowling Green, Kentucky. Mr. Smith is Continuing Care Coordinator and Psychotherapist, Comprehensive Care Center, Bowling Green, Kentucky. It is our privilege to have had both as students and to know them as professional colleagues.

We appreciate the interest and special assistance of friends located in two libraries—Harriet Ford, Social Work Collection, University of Kentucky and John Garralda, former Director, and Patrick Muckleroy and Frances Jacobson of Western State College of Colorado. We appreciate the help of our graduate assistants Diane Hobson, Laura Kaplan, Millicent Wright, and Lisa Reinig.

Our secretaries, Joyce Rieman and Sharon Hodge, have seen more drafts and revisions than they can count. We appreciate their patience and word processing skills. Martha C. Rudd, Administrative Assistant, changed print heads, short cut intricacies of hard disks, fussed about style, and shepherded manuscript organization. They do not pay such people enough!

We express our thanks to our former students at George Warren Brown School of Social Work, Washington University, the University of Kentucky at the Lexington Campus, in Hazard and at the University of Kentucky Graduate Center at Highland Heights. Their questions and glazed looks forced us to clarify our thinking about social work practice.

DEDICATION

This book is dedicated to Grace White and Leone Renn who shared insights from their long careers in social work education and practice with us in many helpful ways. Their comments and suggestions about Chapter 2 are appreciated. More importantly, each was interested in all our activities whether at the university or in the community. Thanks for such support is not a strong enough word but will have to do. They represent our ties to earlier social work history. We have tried to distill and present the best of that history and those ties and combine it with our experience, so that future social workers will share a vision of what social work can do to create a more just society.

Chapter Two

HISTORICAL PERSPECTIVE

The professional practice of social work is interesting, challenging, and rewarding. Because of its breadth of concern and action, it draws persons of diverse backgrounds, motivations, and interests who use their knowledge and skills in a range of settings, for many different purposes. Given our diversity, however, we may miss discovering and appreciating our unity.

This chapter introduces some of our profession's history. We identify and discuss historical events and themes so you can discover how the part of social work that interests you has developed and fits into the whole. This is neither a comprehensive history nor an analysis of American social welfare. Instead we have selected themes and events in social work and social welfare history to assist you in discovering how the past helped shape both present issues and our profession's future agenda. This chapter also introduces you to our biases—what we think is important about social work and its history and our assumptions and questions about our profession. We hope this short historical journey will support and confirm your enthusiasm for and commitment to the profession.

SOCIAL WORK AND SOCIAL WELFARE

The first paid social workers probably were employed by the Special Relief Department of the U.S. Sanitary Commission during the Civil War (Miller, 1977). This commission, established in 1861 and the forerunner of the American National Red Cross, was one setting for activities which have come to be labeled social work. Some other settings are state social service departments, hospitals, mental health centers, and schools.

Social work and social welfare are not synonymous although events and trends in each influenced the other. ''Social welfare'' refers to all those laws, regulations, policies, agencies, programs, and services designed to support basic life necessities and opportunities. The most far-reaching definition of social welfare usually includes such diverse activities as financial assistance, public education, health programs, legal aid, and commissions to protect citizens' civil rights. Some say, only half facetiously, that subsidies to railroads, airlines, and defense contractors are part of the social welfare system. The general public often uses the term more narrowly to mean ''welfare'' in the most perjorative sense of giving money to persons considered unworthy.

Social work is one profession, along with many others, which helps design and construct the social welfare system and assists persons who use it. When our professional association, the National Association of Social Workers, was established in 1955, social work was defined as follows:

> Social work practice, like the practice of all professions, is recognized by a constellation of value, purpose, sanction, knowledge, and method. . . . It is the particular content and configuration of this constellation which makes it social work practice and distinguishes it from the practice of other professions (Bartlett, 1958; 5).

This means that social work, while practiced in many different settings throughout the social welfare system, is an identifiable professional activity independent of its specific location. Although the form social work takes is a function of where it occurs and the particular problems and issues with which it deals, there is a core of purposes, values, knowledge, and activities that binds us together. This core can be identified, studied, changed, and transmitted systematically to others. Despite differences within the profession, which sometimes make us uncomfortable and confuse outsiders, social workers hold much in common and can be distinguished from other professionals.

One theme in this chapter is what social workers share in common. Against what is shared, we disagree among ourselves about such things as how social and individual problems originate, how to resolve them, and what theories and techniques to use. We work in many different places—mental hospitals, public schools, legislative planning bodies, health and welfare councils, courts and prisons, and youth service agencies. We work with health and disease, rich persons and poor, persons of all ethnic groups, persons in power and those on the margins of society. Given our differences, it is amazing we are one profession rather than many. But our purposes, values, knowledge, and practices bind us together.

BEGINNINGS

Who were our foremothers and fathers and how did they shape today's practice? They were volunteers, paid agents, and professional social workers. They were political conservatives, liberals, and radicals: helpers, planners, and reformers. Some were motivated by religious values and precepts; others relied on theories from science, sociology, and medicine. They participated intimately in a wide array of events and movements aimed at improving conditions for the socially disenfranchised (Breul and Diner, 1980).

Most authors identify the beginning of professional social work with establishment of Charity Organization Societies, the first of which opened in Buffalo, New York, in 1887 (Miller, 1977; Pumphrey and Pumphrey, 1961). These societies gave us three important directions: practice with individuals, organizing community services, and social work education.

COS Movement

Community Organization Societies were founded in many large cities as one way to combat poverty (Lewis, 1977). Societies in the United States were modeled on similar organizations established earlier in England. Societies' philosophy and methods were influenced by religious precepts and by principles, assumptions, values, and practices reported in literature from the London Society. In retrospect it is easy to argue that these organizations adopted invalid assumptions and engaged in questionable and ineffective procedures that did not touch the causes of urban poverty. Nevertheless, friendly visitors, agents, and general secretaries (such as Mary Richmond) developed a philosophy, constructed agencies, designed procedures, and made choices which still influence practice. COS philosophy and practice gave us a case method that focused on individual change through a professional relationship.

Individual Change COS philosophy assumed that significant social problems could be modified by changing individuals who experienced those problems. Although social work has participated in social reform to eliminate social problems by changing social structures, we persist in a strong preference for work with individuals even though many professional goals cannot be met through individual change.

The COS movement was not the only source of this idea. Individualism is rooted deeply in our culture and derives its rationale and support from many sources in Western society. While a philosophy of individual liberty, rights, and responsibility is modified by laws, customs, and social arrangements that protect and sustain the whole society, major emphasis is placed on the individual. Thus persons are responsible for events, behavior, and experience in all but the most unusual circumstances. The COS movement did not invent this idea, but adapted it to the problem of poverty and later to other family problems.

Social work with individuals has been modified, of course, since the early 1900s. Individualism has lost some of its stridency and social work is less identified with specific religious values. We now understand relationships among social systems better and recognize large systems also must be changed. Despite these changes, social work holds fast to some ideas inherent in COS work with individuals and developed further by others in the COS tradition. One of these is the idea that relationship is the vehicle for change.

Change Through Relationship COS volunteers working directly with the poor were prohibited from providing financial assistance (Lewis, 1977). It was assumed clients would change when helped by a concerned, interested person with whom they could establish a fairly long-term relationship. This relationship existed separately from relief provided by or arranged for by an agent who studied each client's situation prior to assigning a volunteer friendly visitor. It was assumed the visitor's encouragement, advice, and role modeling (a more modern term) would result in clients' finding work and solving other problems.

In time, the nature of practice changed in COS agencies. Volunteer visitors were replaced by paid workers. Less emphasis was given to community organizing and more to noneconomic aspects of family problems. Greater attention was paid to training and professional education. The relationship theme survived these changes and emerged with a mystique that persisted until recent years. This theme was one battleground for social workers with different psychological perspectives. Taft (1944) and Robinson (1930) argued for a functional view of relationship while Hamilton (1951) and others examined relationship from a diagnostic perspective.

Relationship as the vehicle for change still is an important practice theme. Contemporary social workers use this idea of mutual connection differently (Collins and Pancoast, 1976; Specht, 1985) and have broadened the scope of theories used to understand and explain it (Reid and Epstein, 1972).

Investigation Another COS activity that persists is the thorough study and evaluation of clients' circumstances as the basis for helping. Although names for investigating and its purposes and procedures have changed, we still assume that social workers' helping should be based on understanding client systems' situations, strengths, weaknesses, and opportunities.

Investigation was made the centerpiece of early social work practice (Lewis, 1977). Specific investigating procedures were given prominence in the writing of COS workers such as Richmond (1917) and their successors (Hamilton, 1940). Richmond "conceived study, diagnosis, prognosis, and treatment planning as separate entities in a chainlike series" (Pumphrey and Pumphrey, 1961; 341) and planned two major books. The first, on study and diagnosis, was published but a second volume dealing with treatment was not written. Social workers did not have a systematic analysis of treatment until Hamilton's 1940 text on casework.

The total process, including investigation, came to be called study, diagnosis, and treatment. This name persisted until the term problem-solving process entered practice and literature much later. Because the first two stages were given such prominence, social workers often were better prepared to assess than to treat, although practice required both.

Despite excesses that led to seeing investigation as an end in itself and arguments about its length, content, and focus, the compilation of extensive case data is a major social work contribution to the human service professions and a practice strength. This is so not because we are more reliable observers, but because we aim for breadth and depth of information about individuals in a social context.

Case Method A case method was developed when focus on individuals, change through relationship, investigation (and later, treatment) were organized into instructions for training new COS volunteers and agents. COS organizers and staff wrote about program philosophy to gain public support and recruit volunteers. Societies had their own journals, contributed to popular magazines, and published in some social science journals (Lewis, 1977).

Early training probably was based both on this written material and compilations of workers' experiences. One can imagine a COS agent explaining the agency's background and the volunteer's role to a new worker. It might have sounded like this: "First, read the agent's investigation. Then, when you think you understand this family's problems, go visit them. You should say you are a neighbor and want to be a friend. Then, see what sort of work they can do and try to help the father get a job!" Simple instructions were expanded and developed and became what we now term in-service training. Very quickly (by 1898) more formal training was established in a summer course in New York and shortly thereafter the first formal university course of study was begun (Bernard, 1977).

In order to train unskilled workers, experienced workers had to organize their observations. Apparently before 1900 they were using the term "case" to refer to clients and "caseworker" to refer to helpers (Briar and Miller, 1971; Pumphrey and Pumphrey, 1961). There is little evidence they used systematic case analysis procedures we use today. However, they probably attempted to locate common themes in cases and worker activities. Training materials had ready audiences in local, regional, and national meetings. As a result, procedures for working with relief cases were adopted rapidly by persons working with other client groups (Briar and Miller, 1971). These procedures, considered more methodical and systematic than uninformed helping, became the bible of social casework. Few procedures were tested; they were treated as articles of faith.

Social workers had a philosophy, a method, and specific procedures. They trained others systematically using an extensive anecdotal literature. Practice (casework) developed rapidly and gained such influence that it threatened to become all of social work. Toward the end of Richmond's career, she is reported to have said:

> I have spent twenty-five years of my life in an attempt to get social casework accepted as a valid process in social work. Now I shall spend the rest of my life trying

to demonstrate to social caseworkers that there is more to social work than social casework (Bruno, 1948; 186–87).

Settlement Movement

The settlement house movement was a second important development in our history. Neighborhood Guild was opened in New York City in 1886, and, by 1910, more than 400 settlements had been established (Davis, 1977). Like other social institutions, settlements have changed since their inception. Many of their practices and philosophic positions, however, persist and can be seen in contemporary multi-service community centers. This movement significantly influenced the direction and character of social work practice.

Early settlement philosophy was similar to some aspects of the COS movement. It assumed that persons of means, education, and community standing owed service to the poor and uneducated, and could make a significant difference in social problems. Both movements attracted well-educated, affluent, and caring people who threw all their energy into the causes they espoused. Zilpha Smith is said to have served as a COS friendly visitor for one family for forty-seven years (Becker, 1977) while Jane Addams continued as head resident of Hull House until her death in 1935 (Farrell, 1977). Social work developed not only an individual case method. The settlement movement gave social work a group and community perspective based on a democratic ideal, which stressed education, research, reform strategies, and decision making as a vehicle for change.

Group and Community Perspective Early settlement workers assisted community residents and tried to solve major social problems by living in a community. They focused on poverty, disease, illiteracy, exploitation, and socialization of immigrants to American culture. It soon became apparent to settlement workers that the problems were more complex than they anticipated.

Settlement workers did not focus on or work with cases; they knew people as neighbors. Settlement workers had the advantage of seeing a whole community as well as its parts. They did not need to learn how to construct a social environment; they saw it every day and felt it, at least partly, in the same ways their neighbors experienced it. They were not sent to see cases but invited neighbors to come for classes, health clinics, and to discuss neighborhood problems. While settlement workers were interested in individuals, they thought about, described, and provided assistance to groups in communities, not cases.

Settlements joined in social reform with such groups as the Young Women's and Young Men's Christian Associations, the Young Men's and Young Women's Hebrew Associations, the National Association for the Advancement of Colored People, and the Urban League. Although the philosophies of these groups differed, they shared concern for the group and community—for residents, neighbors, and members. This focus persists in contemporary neighborhood and multiservice centers. Social work would have become a different, less interesting, and less effective profession without this community theme.

Democratic Ideal A commitment to participation by all neighbors in democratic processes was central to settlement philosophy. This ideal assumes citizens have rights and responsibilities and that society will be more just and cohesive when these are carried out. Settlement workers discovered many impediments to this ideal. New immigrants could not read or write for effective communication. Many did not understand basic democratic premises and processes. The distance between haves and have nots was a gulf maintained by influential administrators, politicians, and business leaders. Community services often were inadequate for safety and public health. Workers were exploited and neighbors were discriminated against because of race, ethnic origin, and religion. These problems widened settlements' agendas beyond the initial plan to offer classes in cooking and sewing and English.

Settlements attracted workers interested in social reform, politics, and social welfare issues in general. Some of these helped form the NAACP, encouraged W.E.B. DuBois, influenced John Dewey, Frances Perkins, and Harry Hopkins; they promoted social change through the Progressive Party (Davis, 1977). The commitment to a democratic ideal shaped philosophy, services, and worker practices by emphasizing education, research, and social reform and by focusing on group decision making as the vehicle for change. These themes are important in contemporary practice.

Education, Research, and Reform Educational strategies were used to achieve neighborhood improvement. One common set of techniques consisted of providing information about, instruction for, and experience in, some new area or task. Research was used as the foundation for social reform. Our earliest comprehensive, reliable information about urban poverty and social problems, for example, came from settlement research (Davis, 1977).

These studies and subsequent published and unpublished reports were platforms for social reform activities. Florence Kelley, for example, documented child labor abuses and used this information to persuade Illinois legislators that reforms were needed. Jane Addams used data from settlement research to paint vivid pictures of social problems (Pumphrey and Pumphrey, 1961).

Social reform involved settlement workers in coalitions aimed at significant social change. Unfortunately, however, social work moved away from social reform to concentrate on individual change and case methods. This shift may have occurred as one way to improve professional status and claim an exclusive domain (Thursz, 1977). We began to recover these earlier commitments to the poor, disenfranchised, and victims of discrimination in the 1960s.

Group Decision Making All social workers explain their helping contacts in some way. COS workers called these contacts relationships and assumed change occurred in them. Settlement workers called them group processes and explained change in terms of these processes, particularly group decision making.

Settlement workers gave group members the opportunity to decide and helped them learn how to participate in deciding. This tradition persists today when a social worker in a youth services agency helps a club decide on the purposes, membership, rules, leadership, and activities. A worker who assists agency board members to decide on the agenda, timetable, and distribution of tasks is another example. The process is used to carry out a group's tasks and provide members with opportunities to learn about themselves and others. Members acquire skills they did not possess and often gain emotional support from other members including the social worker.

Decision making in settlements also included matters external to the group such as agency policy. Groups in membership organizations such as the YWCA participate in deciding agency philosophy, agenda, and procedures. The War on Poverty took the idea further and members also planned, organized, and offered services. While some programs failed for lack of effective leadership, the idea was consistent with our best traditions of membership participation (Gilbert, 1970).

Settlement houses and their successors gave us important practice goals. They helped us discover the group and community as locations for practice and as social systems that require us to practice differently from the COS tradition. They kept us close to people of different races, beliefs, values, traditions, problems, and opportunities. Settlement philosophy reminds us that, "Before there was a profession of social work, there was social work. . . . The first social workers were crusaders whose full-time occupation was social action" (Thursz, 1977; 1274).

Welfare Council Movement

Early social welfare activities were characterized by efforts to coordinate services for entire communities. Persons introduced to social work in the 1980s may find it difficult to identify the welfare council movement's significance since its contemporary activities are not our exclusive domain. Nevertheless, social workers participate in planning, funding, and coordinating services. Some historical themes influence our practice goals and the social welfare context in which we practice.

Service coordination began with structures and procedures for interagency cooperation designed by COS agencies (Lewis, 1977). It was assumed poverty could be reduced if adequate relief were available *and* if it were not wasted by duplication. The best way to prevent duplication was to register everyone on relief at a central bureau or clearinghouse. Registration for relief and other services was common into the 1950s. Even today organizations such as the Resource Office of Social Ministry in Lexington, Kentucky, provide a central location for workers to coordinate financial assistance and avoid duplication.

Efforts to coordinate brought social workers and community leaders together to discuss funding and service delivery issues and to identify problems for which no services were available. Two different community organizations evolved. One, usually called the health and welfare council or the welfare council, plans and coordinates services. The other is a federated fund raising agency such as the United Way or Community Chest. In many cities both organizations exist; often they are united under one board. In some communities a central fund raising group operates without a health and welfare council. Contemporary planning for social needs also is conducted by area planning agencies and by planning units of state agencies.

Three important themes in the welfare council movement continue to influence social work practice. They are efficient use of resources for public accountability, community-professional partnerships, and a conservative philosophy of community problem solving.

Efficiency and Accountability The idea that the public has a right to have its voluntary contributions and public funds used efficiently is a popular notion. COS agencies emphasized that gifts would not be wasted and recipients were worthy. As other groups adopted coordinating functions and practice moved toward greater professional status, efficiency was replaced with the idea of accountability. Realistically, of course, there never have been (and may never be) enough dollars to meet all social welfare needs. Nevertheless, communities and professionals continue to coordinate and plan with stress on avoiding duplication and on accountability.

Practice is influenced by this theme today. When we work in agencies associated with a council, we provide data for planning and coordination. If some of our agency funds come from the community, we must live with its restrictions. While these influences are not necessarily negative, they may have a conservative influence on an agency board, its administrator, staff, and clients.

Community-Professional Partnership Social welfare activities have a long history of partnerships between interested, sympathetic, and influential community leaders and the professionals who provide services. This partnership pattern is designed, in part, to maintain public support for and involvement in social welfare. It is the unusual United Way allocation committee member who does not understand more about needs and programs after a term of service than before. When ministers, lawyers, and business persons serve on planning committees, they learn about problems they might not have known otherwise. In turn, they contribute knowledge and professional skills to social agencies. This partnership helps maintain an ethic of public service which has been a significant feature of social welfare history in this country. Social workers depend upon this partnership for support, funds, knowledge, and skills they do not possess.

Conservative Philosophy The movement to plan and coordinate services frequently has served a conservative role in many communities, a role that continues to influence our practice. Many councils and other planning groups, for example, represented only a certain segment of the community and seldom concerned themselves with citizens of middle or lower class status (Tropman and Tropman, 1977). As a result, the poor and minorities often were ignored.

It is difficult for planning and coordinating groups to move beyond the interests, knowledge, and tolerance of their members. Controversial issues often are not addressed, advocacy is difficult, and social action may be impossible. Early in the women's movement, for example, concern about rape and violence victims was not shown by some councils and funding organizations. These problems were accepted as legitimate and services were funded *after* women's groups planned, organized, and offered services that communities accepted.

A conservative approach has two effects. First, it helps promote continuity. When a group meets the needs of its majority members, takes a conciliatory approach to potential conflicts, and maintains the commitment and support of the community and its leaders, threats to continuation can be deflected. While this may have negative consequences by slowing change and ignoring some community needs, it also has positive consequences. Communities need continuity, which cannot develop without stable and consistent organizational leadership.

But a conservative approach also poses serious problems. Social welfare needs sometimes change rapidly and communities need institutionalized means to respond, which a highly conservative organization may not provide. This is critical where systematic discrimination occurs and in situations of threat to public health and safety in poor housing, insufficient food, and/or medical care. Requirements for council membership or federated funding may smother the most interesting, creative, or important practice ideas. Social workers must not only live with planning and coordinating groups but also help them represent their communities and anticipate social problems and needs.

SOCIAL WORK AND KNOWLEDGE DEVELOPMENT

Practice has been shaped by choices we made in developing our knowledge base as well as by social welfare institutions and movements. Practice was informed by moral and ethical pronouncements and common sense assumptions about human betterment. It was based on ideas and concepts which could not be called formal theories. We were and are doers without a grand, all-encompassing theory to organize, explain, and make predictions about practice. We borrowed concepts and theories from other fields, particularly the social and behavioral sciences, to explain and plan practice. Sometimes social work borrowed thoughtfully with attention to how well these theories met our needs. Often we borrowed hastily and uncritically.

But in both instances, our choices influenced practice history, contemporary issues, and future agenda. Some choices social workers made in selecting knowledge for practice are identified in this section. The discussion of each theory or set of concepts includes a brief assessment of how well our choices met three needs of social work practice.

First, does the theory help us explain one or more client systems? All persons engaged in change activities search for ways to explain the system toward which their efforts are directed. Physicians need ways to explain physical growth, decline, and disease. Educators explain how learning occurs so that they may influence its processes. Psychologists explain how mental and emotional growth occur and factors that interfere with normal development and functioning. Social workers need concepts and theories that explain client systems. Because we are concerned about many different kinds of systems and our goals vary from interpersonal helping to social action, social workers have incorporated many concepts and theories. But not all our choices served practice well.

Second, does the theory or concept(s) help us understand the relationship between the social worker and the client system? We need ways to describe what happens when the worker and client system come together to engage in change. These worker-client system contacts take place in a context that our knowledge choices need to help us understand.

Third, the essence of practice is doing something. Does the theory or concept that contains information and predictions tell us what to do under the circumstances observed in the client system? Practice strategies, techniques, and procedures are needed that are effective in achieving our goals and purposes. As we will discover later, not all theories that explain something also contain information about what to do.

Psychoanalytic Theories

During and immediately after World War I, social work was influenced by psychoanalytic theory and its use in psychiatry. This influence was not on social work alone but on all of society including art, literature, historical analyses, medicine, religion, education, psychology, and, ultimately, on our everyday language. Social work needed a way to explain observations of clients served by caseworkers and in Freudian concepts, we found appealing explanations for many individual problems. Psychoanalytic concepts gave social workers two ideas which "changed the face of casework: (1) behavior is purposeful and determined, and (2) some of the determinants are unconscious and unrecognized by the client" (Briar and Miller, 1971; 13).

Social workers studied psychoanalytic concepts, incorporated them into their work, used them to educate trainees, organized curricula with them, and developed schools of thought around them. These concepts provided social workers a complex and all-encompassing description of individuals, especially ways to explain irrational behavior and resistance to change. The concepts were intriguing as well as seductive. Social workers have understood only recently some limitations of these concepts. For example, it is difficult to identify the change procedures social workers can use based on the theory's propositions about change. These concepts do not, of course, help explain larger social phenomena such as poverty and discrimination (and do not purport to). Thus, for some social work concerns we need to look elsewhere for explanations.

Individuals in Context

Social workers explain individual client systems in a social context. Three main theoretical perspectives have been used. From the work of George Herbert Mead (1934) and Charles H. Cooley (1920), we selected concepts and assumptions to explain relationships between individuals and other persons in their environments. These approaches provided ways to understand socialization processes. They became major fundamental elements for practice with many different client systems and provided a way to rationalize and develop practice for two major purposes—socialization and resocialization (Hartford, 1977).

Lewin's (1947) field theory is a third source of concepts, which helped us explain individuals in a context. His concept of life space placed individuals in an environment characterized by all those elements which in any way influence behavior and help explain the person. This life space concept was used to explain some group processes (Garvin, 1983), ways behavior is determined (Strean, 1983), and some relationships between thinking and acting (Middleman, 1983b). Field theory has been used as part of an ecological perspective to examine relationships between individuals and environments (Laird and Allen, 1983).

Theories such as these, which explain individuals in context, usually have a significant impact on the development of social work knowledge. They have been less useful, however, in providing strategies, techniques, and procedures for changing client systems.

Learning Theories

Beginning in the 1960s, social workers incorporated the newer and more comprehensive work of various learning theorists into practice. Although Edwin Thomas, among others, was criticized for promoting learning approaches, he was one of the first to examine these theories carefully against the needs and values of the profession (Thomas, 1964, 1967). His analyses showed that such theories do not fit everything we need to explain, and our uses of them must be tempered by our values and the requirements of settings where we practice.

Since learning theories are based on certain assumptions about human growth and behavior which were (and possibly are) anathema to many social workers, their use distressed some. Nevertheless, these explanations for some client systems and problems had a dramatic impact on practice and our literature contains many examples of work based on them. One strength of learning theories is that they contain information about how to change behavior as well as how it develops and is maintained.

System Theories

Social and behavior scientists, biologists, and other physical scientists began, probably as early as the 1920s, to develop concepts for explaining and describing units larger than single individuals. These concepts came to be called system theories. They have had such widespread use that almost no field of endeavor, including social work, has escaped their influence.

System concepts help to explain social units such as groups, organizations, and communities. They assist us to explain how groups form, the nature of and influences on interactions in them, and relationships between social units and their environments. They have been used to describe families, school classrooms, agency boards, prisons, neighborhoods, and mental hospital wards. They helped us examine social exchanges, dimensions of task and affect in groups, sources of social influence on behavior, and styles of leadership. It is difficult to find any area of social work that is *not* influenced in some way by system concepts.

We have used the work of Homans (1961), Thibaut and Kelly (1959), Bales (1950), Parsons (1951), and Perrow (1967) among many others. Their work came into our profession primarily through doctoral programs that prepared teachers for graduate and undergraduate programs. As with psychoanalytic theories, our uses of system concepts have not always been careful or precise. We often have used them as shorthand ways to convey an idea without examining its assumptions and implications. Nevertheless, system concepts have been invaluable in helping us organize practice experiences and observations of clients.

Social work has drawn from other theories in addition to these three sets. But these are the major sources that frame what social work has become and help set our future knowledge development agenda.

SOCIAL WORK AND PRACTICE EDUCATION

An organized set of activities and the knowledge and skills people use to perform them do not comprise a profession unless those activities can be collated and transmitted systematically to others. Thus, the evolution of social work education is important in our history and has influenced practice.

Apprenticeship

Early practice education resembled contemporary in-service training or staff development. Charity Organization Society workers drew from personal observations and the success or failure of their change efforts to teach what they knew to others. Often these training sessions were based on specific case examinations, with a trainer discussing what had been done and what had happened or had not happened as a result. In Richmond's day training emphasized social worker processes. Particular attention was paid to the types and extent of information to be gathered on the assumption that more and better data would improve chances for successful intervention.

A central feature of orientation and training was learning through close contact between trainee and a teacher or supervisor (Bernard, 1977). This apprenticeship model became the predominant way new social workers learned to practice. Although social work education expanded the role of formal academic work, learning from an experienced (often expert) practitioner remains a central part of practice education.

Apprenticeship education had both positive and negative influences on social work. Practice wisdom and knowledge were passed to succeeding generations in a personalized way, which usually fit the needs of workers and agencies. Trainees had the benefit of support from supervisors who experienced similar demands, frustrations, and successes. At the same time, invalid assumptions and ineffective techniques were promoted. Precisely because apprenticeship personalizes teaching and learning, it can be a powerful source of valid and invalid approaches to practice—but it is difficult to distinguish them from each other!

Apprenticeship learning may have limited our concerns to populations served by established, traditional agencies. Practice may have focused on remedial goals and conservative helping strategies because we needed to maintain partnerships with agencies to provide learning opportunities. But it also brought textbook descriptions of problems alive in ways which strengthened our capacity to engage in change and describe social problems.

Some issues about apprenticeship have been resolved, but others remain. Universities control field learning experiences and depend upon a unique partnership with agencies to offer these courses. But the shape and form of field learning are not fixed (Schutz and Gordon, 1977). Because knowledge about helping is becoming more highly specialized, further changes in apprenticeships and internships may be necessary. How these issues are resolved will continue to influence practice.

Curriculum Standards

Any curriculum is a product of the school's history, influential deans, directors and faculty, and the university and practice community which supports it. All curricula are based on an ideology of social work. A curriculum contains assumptions about the field, present and future goals for the profession, and significant values students are expected to adopt. A curriculum is designed to introduce and socialize students to this ideology and to teach practice consistent with it.

Contrasting ideologies have developed in social work education's evolution. Some programs emphasized practice with individuals and families in the COS tradition. Others focused on public welfare, economics, and social work roles in administration and social policy development. A few prepared for work in specific agencies. The Council on Social Work Education and its four predecessor associations influenced practice by setting standards for the content and structure of education.

Most standards focus on general goals, values, and assumptions about social work's domain and content students need to learn. Some outline minimum learning opportunities and general structures but do not specify designs, particular ideologies, or content arrangements. Minimum content standards, such as the

Basic Eight before the late 1950s, often reflected the way agencies organized practice. After NASW was formed in 1955, emphasis turned to unifying a disparate practice by locating its common features. The term "generic" returned to our lexicon to denote activities common to all practice regardless of the method or setting. More recently, the term "generalist" has been used to identify common knowledge, values, and activities.

Standards function to assure that all social workers know about and do essentially similar things. They also are statements of preferences formed out of compromises among competing interest groups in practice and education. They evolve in response to trends, perceptions of needs, knowledge available for practice, and contingencies under which educators work. Thus, curriculum standards are one arena for changing as well as maintaining practice emphases and directions.

Levels of Study

Practice has been influenced by the ways social work education arranged content between undergraduate and graduate study. Beginning in 1939 the newly formed American Association of Schools of Social Work set the standard for professional practice as a two-year graduate program (Bernard, 1977). This pattern existed until the 1960s when demand for professionally educated social workers increased, and federal support was available to establish additional undergraduate programs. Subsequently, both the Council on Social Work Education and the National Association of Social Workers recognized undergraduate social work as the first or entry level practice degree.

Recognition of undergraduate professional degrees helped unify social workers and prompted a more inclusive and less elitist view of social work. It helped reaffirm our commitments to goals and purposes beyond those in traditional counseling and mental health activities. Despite these positive outcomes, significant issues remain. How can the integrity of undergraduate liberal arts study be protected while offering adequate professional preparation? How can content and experience be articulated and rationalized more effectively between levels? These are some of the issues in our future agenda which will help mold and shape practice.

SOCIAL WORK AS A PROFESSION

Contemporary practice is understood not only in terms of how it developed within social welfare, the major knowledge sets we use, and how practice education shapes what we do. It also is characterized by nearly sixty years' preoccupation with the question, is social work a profession?

Professional status is important. It helps determine how much we are paid and who recognizes and listens to us when we promote a cause. High status may support our change efforts; it may assist us to obtain scarce resources for client systems. It may help recruit intelligent, sensitive workers into the field. But status may not be the most important issue. We think the issue is: given our values and social concerns, how can we be more *effective* helpers? The focus in this section is *not* whether social work is or is not a profession. Instead, the focus is on two events in the search for professional status and how they shaped practice. These are Abraham Flexner's analysis of social work and the formation of one professional association, the National Association of Social Workers.

Flexner's Answer

Most attention to our status came in response to Flexner's address to the National Conference of Charities and Corrections in 1915. Flexner had completed a major survey of medicine and proposed a design for medical education to improve its quality and make medicine more professional (Austin, 1983). On this basis, he was asked to assess social work's status as a profession. He concluded social work was *not* a profession.

Flexner's assessment was characterized by several logical flaws, which social workers did not recognize, understand, or debate (Austin, 1983). Although Flexner's criteria were those he had applied to medicine, little thought was given to whether they should apply to social work. When different criteria were used later, social work had a positive answer to the question of professional status (Greenwood, 1957).

In the meantime, social workers did those things they thought would make it possible for Flexner to say yes rather than no. The National Social Workers Exchange was formed and developed into the American Association of Social Workers to carry out traditional functions of professional associations. Subsequently, six other professional associations were organized to exchange information, develop practice knowledge, and set standards. Their membership requirements attempted to distinguish what "true" social workers did from the helping efforts of those without similar education and experience. Some of these standards were basic requirements for entrance into practice and were adopted in social work education.

Social workers searched diligently for definitions and domain boundaries. Depending upon one's view, these efforts were appropriate and useful or misguided or the inevitable natural history of an occupational group's attempts to become a profession. Popple (1985) noted that the search for status occurred at a time when only casework had concepts, methods, and procedures in a literature that met Flexner's criticisms. As a result, individual case methods were developed further and other goals and methods, such as social action and advocacy, were deemphasized. Since the late 1950s our search included other methods and procedures and recaptured concern for rights, entitlements, minority groups, and a broader range of client system goals.

Dance to One Tune

The National Association of Social Workers was formed in 1955 from seven separate professional associations, each of which was based on a particular method or field of practice. NASW's purposes are to define what is a social worker, represent its members' interests, and serve society (Beck, 1977). Because NASW drew social workers together from all fields and methods, one of its purposes is to speak for all on matters of common interest. These include personnel standards, salary levels, social legislation, and licensing. Through its journals and other publications, it promotes information exchange and knowledge development.

NASW has changed since 1955 as a result of pressures to become involved in major social issues, to increase access to human services, and to support advocacy and reform. It acted to maintain control over clinical work by establishing a clinical registry, sponsoring conferences, and supporting licensing and third-party payments. Some have been critical of the profession's direction. Richan and Mendelsohn (1973) complained, for example, that we separated ourselves from poor people by emphasizing agency practice. For those who want a radical focus, placing emphasis on professionalism diverts attention away from critical human needs.

Social work's search for status helped unify us. Differences remain, and we do not share precisely the same concerns, use exactly similar methods, or explain our actions in the same ways. But, social work did not splinter and compete for a social mandate. Social work still has much to do. If we can focus on effective helping activities consistent with *all* the profession's goals, our differences will not be so important in the future.

SUMMARY

The evolution of practice in the past hundred years was shaped by many forces and events. Our history is tied in significant ways to social welfare institutions in which practice occurs. From practice based on moral and ethical pronouncements, we sought to identify our practice wisdom and extend it by using knowledge from social and behavioral science. We arranged complex institutions through which to teach what we know and to protect our domain.

Our history is characterized by persistent attempts to bring unity to a diverse field of social endeavor where rambunctious participants pushed first in one direction and then another. We have moved toward grand psychological theories and then to less ambitious ones. We have engaged in activities to control our profession and then moved toward greater openness in partnerships with others moving in our direction. Our practice settings, knowledge and practice wisdom, educational programs, and professional groups have pushed, pulled, and shoved each other.

The practicing social worker is influenced by each of these—educated in a particular way, expected to work in a context's demands and expectations, using whatever knowledge and experience are available while listening with part of an ear to exhortations from NASW. The worker's goal is to help people who hurt, who are in trouble, who aim to improve themselves, or who are locked out of full participation by injustice. Most social workers know there is not just one way to do what needs to be done. Most recognize that creativity, innovation, perseverance, and above all, testing to discover what is effective will be necessary. This is what makes our field or occupation or profession challenging and rewarding.

Chapter Three

CONCEPTUAL FRAMEWORK

What does the world look like through social workers' eyes? This chapter presents major concepts social workers use to describe, explain, and make predictions about their practice. These concepts help us build word pictures or models of our client systems and what we might do to assist them.

WHAT IS A CONCEPTUAL FRAMEWORK?

A conceptual framework is a set of ideas and relationships between and among them. Usually ideas are expressed as concepts which connote and denote a phenomenon. Relationships among concepts tie these ideas together in some pattern. All of us use such frameworks in everyday life to describe and explain our worlds. Although we may have common or similar frameworks for many things, not all our ways of seeing and describing our worlds are alike.

A conceptual framework provides the structure for organizing and making sense of our observations. When we term a society "patriarchal" or "matriarchal," we have used a set of concepts about how that society is organized, which describes who makes what kinds of decisions and how lineage is identified. When we talk about Third World countries, we use concepts about how far such countries have advanced in industrialization, urbanization, and forms of governance. When a social worker contrasts a disease model with an ecological model, she or he refers to concepts and their relationships based on different assumptions and different pictures of the practice world.

All social workers have one or more frameworks to use in practice. Sometimes it is difficult to identify a worker's framework because we do not see it in the same way we see the blueprint used by a building contractor. Social workers usually do not talk in formal terms about their conceptual frameworks. If we asked workers to tell us what organizing concepts they used, they might find it difficult to do so, not because they lack concepts, but they do not ordinarily make them explicit. Nevertheless, all social workers have a framework within which practice occurs. Frameworks contain three main elements or parts: explanations of client systems, explanations about change, and explanations about social worker action.

Client-System Concepts

First, social workers have an explanatory system to organize and understand observations of client systems. For example, we use concepts to help us understand troubled teenagers, unemployed parents, differently challenged employees, and groups of persons who experience discrimination when we are responsible to assist them. Concepts about client systems such as these help us talk about what they are like: their characteristics, relationships among members of systems, and how they are related to other systems. The function of such explanations is to "apprehend the dynamics of the client system" (Chin, 1969; 297). Social workers do not just do something to help people; they first describe and explain what it is they are trying to help. The term "client system" means something and that meaning gives directions for taking action.

Change Concepts

Second, social workers have concepts about change and how it occurs. Since our purpose is not only to describe and explain something, we also have ways of explaining how change comes about and what may be done to promote it. For example, we describe and explain how troubled teenagers' feelings and behavior may change and how the force of law may reduce discrimination against a group. Concepts of change are based on assumptions about influence and causality in human behavior and events. They help us narrow and focus our actions to reverse negative change directions, ameliorate dysfunctional outcomes of change, and/or prevent change which has dysfunctional outcomes.

Behavioral Constellations

Third, social workers' frameworks contain concepts that identify social worker actions. These concepts are organized into constellations or categories of social worker behaviors, each of which is assumed to match the needs of and purposes for change with client systems. Social workers often describe their actions as methods or techniques or strategies. These labels are used to convey the idea that social workers' actions have been grouped into categories or constellations which can be distinguished from each other. For example, we may use clinical strategies to help troubled teenagers, advocacy strategies to reduce discrimination, and educator strategies to improve the level of social functioning of differently challenged employees. Although some behaviors in a constellation are similar to those in another, constellations of worker actions are distinguished from each other by the combinations of behaviors grouped together to achieve specific purposes or outcomes.

FRAMEWORK CONCEPTS

This section presents major concepts social workers use to construct theoretical frameworks for practice. Social workers do not pick and choose concepts randomly. Our choices are a function of assumptions we make about human conditions and the way concepts fit our profession's goals and purposes. Because social work focuses on human issues, problems and opportunities that are social rather than medical or ethical, we seek concepts that describe and explain people and problems in a social context. We assume it is important to talk about human beings and what we are like, about the social context of human society, about what causes human problems, and about how problems can be ameliorated and prevented (cf. Catton and Dunlap, 1980).

Social work's tradition always has placed simultaneous importance on the individual *and* larger social systems in which individuals live. We used any concept that appeared to assist us to better understand, describe, and predict how human conditions could be improved for the individual, group, and society. Our search took us to sociology, psychology, education, political science, history, medicine, and economics among others. Out of these fields, social work distilled those concepts that seemed to fit our concerns and gave us ways to talk about human growth and behavior, dynamics of human groups, and reciprocal relationships among individuals, groups, and society. We drew in more limited ways from disciplines that characterize our physical world, such as geography and engineering. But some concepts from these fields helped us to describe society and its influences on the people who comprise it.

Because social work chose concepts from such a wide array of fields and disciplines, it has not been easy to organize them into a comprehensive whole. Nevertheless, certain concepts are commonly accepted by most social workers as representing their preferences for conceptual framework elements.

Concepts for Client Systems

Several propositions establish the general structure of concepts social work uses to describe and explain client systems. First, social work always concerns itself with one or more social systems. This means individuals are systems and members of systems. We do *not* focus on individuals bereft of social, cultural, and biological contexts and content (Falck, 1984). A social worker does not talk about individuals, groups, or organizations as clients but about client systems whose characteristics vary. We always work with groups and understand these groups to be social systems.

Second, social work's more specific concern is the dynamics of social systems. System dynamics are the relationships among system parts and their characteristic patterns. These patterns describe how systems function and especially the nature, quality, and outcome of reciprocal influence within systems. For example, we examine a family's communication pattern and how it affects family members. We want to know how systems develop, what makes them stable, and how they adapt to internal and external pressures. Although the dynamics we examine include patterns of human development and behavior, they also account for intergroup and institutional variables and relationships.

Third, social workers identify and explain specific cultural, physical/material, political, and institutional environments of social systems. These environments provide resources, structures, norms, values, traditions, and regulations that support and constrain systems. We recognize, for example, that material resources are necessary to support basic life necessities. The absence of or limitations on resources may adversely affect or threaten a system. Similarly, social norms may constrain or support decisions system members make. The physical environment in which a family lives influences health, member behavior, and the structure of opportunities available to it.

Fourth, social workers recognize the complex interplay of all internal and external system variables in explaining causality. We seldom see one variable or event as *the* cause of system problems and opportunities. Social workers view causes and effects as multidimensional, complex, and reciprocal. A simple cause and effect statement or hypothesis is insufficient to capture the combination of factors or circumstances that interact to promote positive and negative system outcomes.

Some complex relationships among events may be amenable to reversal while others are not. When social workers help a client system where one member has been adjudicated delinquent, we look for influences that caused delinquent behavior in many different places, inside and outside the family system and in the total relationship structure of all relevant systems. We do not say simply that delinquency resulted from a poor environment or resulted from low intelligence or was caused by parental indifference. We assume many factors may have interacted to influence this system member and led to this outcome.

Fifth, social workers recognized that change is constant. No social system is static or unchanging. Therefore, our concepts must account for change, choice, and conflict. Since we assume change is ever present, we use concepts that describe how it occurs, conditions that support and inhibit it, how choices are made about its directions and where and under what circumstances system conflict is associated with change. Our particular concern is to support change toward positive system outcomes and to prevent, where possible, negative system outcomes.

Social workers assume all change may have both intended and unintended consequences, which may be detrimental to social systems. Although our knowledge of change processes is limited, such processes are not helter-skelter, random events without pattern. Although social workers view relatively few change processes as irreversible, we attempt to be realistic and recognize that certain laws of change exist. Our generally optimistic view of human possibilities is tempered with an understanding that finite limits exist beyond which change efforts can not go.

These propositions provide social workers with a general outline of framework concepts for client systems. This outline gives us the following picture: Our clients are ever changing, dynamic systems whose intrasystem and intersystem relationships are constrained or supported by a wide range of material and nonmaterial resources. Causes and effects of system possibilities and problems are complex, multidimensional, and reciprocal. While some problems can be reversed, others yield only to amelioration, and others cannot be reversed. Social workers use three sets of concepts to elaborate this picture of client systems: concepts about wholes, parts, and relationships; concepts about dynamics of change; and concepts about similarities and differences.

Wholes, Parts, and Relationships One hallmark of social work is our insistence upon recognizing wholes, parts, and relationships. A person hospitalized for medical care is not simply a patient but a person with a family, employment, and other social, neighborhood, and community ties. Because of this, progress of a medical regime may be affected by factors outside the specific disease. A mental hospital day treatment group is not simply an aggregation of individuals or a single group, but part of the ward, the hospital, and the total service delivery community. A social service agency is a system comprised of individual units and is part of still larger systems in the community. Social workers have selected concepts from two perspectives to describe what we mean by wholes, parts, and relationships—general system theory and ecology.

General system theory was outlined first by von Bertalanffy (1968) and introduced to social work by Gordon Hearn in 1958 (Hearn, 1969). Von Bertalanffy, a biologist, began work on these concepts in 1937 and published his ideas after World War II (von Bertalanffy, 1968). His original purpose was to solve problems he perceived in the field of biology.

General systems theory identified and responded to emergent trends in many disciplines and today forms the basis for most theoretical frameworks in science. Social work has used themes from general systems theory, which were adapted by sociologists for social phenomena. Structural-functional analysis in sociology defines society as ''a system of interrelated parts in which no part can be understood in isolation from the whole'' (Theodorson and Theodorson, 1969; 167). This emphasis on social structures and the functional relationships among parts of a structure is consistent with social work's focus and provides us one way to account for wholes, parts, and relationships. A system is defined as: ''An organization of interrelated and interdependent parts that form a unity'' (Theodorson and Theodorson, 1969; 431).

The term *system* has wide acceptance and use in social work and is referred to as system *theory*. A more accurate term is system *concepts*, some of which are useful in explaining a social worker's observations. Because we use system terms somewhat loosely and as a shorthand way to talk about wholes, parts, and relationships, it is important to be clear about major system concepts and assumptions.

First, all systems are assumed to have *boundaries*, which make it possible to distinguish them from each other. To establish these boundaries, we must identify and describe a specific set of units in interaction and distinguish them from others which are said to lie outside these boundaries and comprise the system's *environment*. The units of a political system, for example, are defined as ''political actions'' and the boundary is identified ''by all binding decisions for a society'' (Easton, 1957; 383). Everything outside this definition is part of that system's environment.

Identifying a specific system is neither easy nor self-evident. A political system might be the legislature or a city council. A social welfare system might be all public and private units whose actions provide individual, group, and community support for life necessities. A social welfare system might be one agency, such as a community kitchen, which provides one such service. A family system might be those persons who bind themselves together for the purpose of emotional and financial support. The specific units comprising the family system, its boundaries, and its environment will differ from one family to another.

The units or parts of a system and the boundary separating these from their environment are determined by identifying the function of related units. As the function changes, units in a system and its boundaries also change. A community's economic system is comprised of specific industries; one or more of these industries also may be part of other systems. While flexibility of system definitions is useful as we move from one set of units and function to another, system concepts cast a wide net into which we mistakenly might include almost anything and everything and explain very little.

Second, system boundaries are assumed to possess some degree of *permeability* and can be characterized as being more or less open or closed to exchanges to and from the environment. These exchanges usually are termed inputs and outputs. Since all living systems need various resources for survival that require regular renewal, input to a system from its environment is critical. It is assumed that actions taken in a system exit the system as outputs that affect other systems in the environment. Social workers use this as a way of recognizing, for example, that families are influenced by other systems outside their boundaries and in turn influence them. Similarly, we recognize the criminal justice system is influenced by, as well as influences, other social systems.

Social work has not developed any conceptual scheme for classifying types of input or output for client systems. We usually describe reciprocal system influences on a continuum of positive to negative pressures and describe intensity of influences. But we do not have a comprehensive theoretical model for intersystem exchanges across instances of practice from which we can make predictions about intervention.

In another context, Dye (1981) has shown how environmental influences, such as special interest groups, citizens' educational level, and unemployment level can be identified for state political systems and related to laws they enact. His scheme shows how to focus on specific system and environmental properties, make predictions about their relationships, and test the accuracy of these predictions. For a planner or organizer, critical change variables can be identified. Social work, in part because our field is so broad, may need more than one conceptual scheme for understanding system-environment exchanges.

Third, system concepts include the idea of *differentiation* within systems. System units perform somewhat different functions or a division of labor occurs. A degree of *integration* is needed so that cooperation toward the system's goals can occur. Where it does not occur, the system may tend toward disintegration and/or may disintegrate. For example, most social agencies are structured according to traditional hierarchies with division of labor. If these efforts cannot be or are not coordinated to the extent needed for timely service provision, the quality of system outputs in the form of client programs cannot occur.

When social workers use system concepts, we should be cautious about several issues. First, system concepts emphasize equilibrium while social workers also need to explain conflict and change (Leighninger, 1977). We assume some type of change can be initiated for three purposes: preventing system problems from occurring; assisting systems to maintain given levels of equilibria; and helping systems achieve different types of equilibria. As we assess systems, select goals, and determine interventions, we need additional concepts to recognize potentially disruptive consequences of change and conflict within and between systems.

Second, system concepts take us only so far in describing the nature of relationships between system parts and between systems. They can be used to tell us relationships exist, that we should look for them, and that we need to characterize them. System concepts, however, do not tell us *how* to characterize intra- and intersystem relationships except in the most general way. Social workers usually add the idea of positive and negative influences in relationships. For example, parents who physically abuse their children or employers who discriminate against minority group persons in promotions have negative influences in relationships. Teachers who give praise and encouragement in classrooms are positive influences.

Finally, social workers use system concepts to describe and explain social units of different sizes and types. System concepts alone do not discriminate sufficiently to provide all the data we need to predict what actions to take. If the client system is a small group organized for the purpose of learning independent living skills in a community mental health center, we need to use additional concepts about how people learn to supplement the picture. When we analyze the behavior of two family members in conflict, we need to use an explanation of individual behavior to supplement system concepts. Where the social worker's purpose is to understand and subsequently modify an organization's resource allocation procedures, we must use concepts about organizations.

When these precautions are observed, social workers can use system concepts to say: *Our client systems are groups of persons bound together by common functions in dynamic interaction such that parts of the whole affect each other. These systems can be distinguished from each other by identifiable boundaries characterized by forms of exchange between systems and their environments. Systems usually work out internal arrangements for achieving their purposes; as a system changes, its parts also change and adapt so that equilibrium is achieved.*

A second set of concepts about wholes, parts and relationships has been adapted from the field of ecology. William E. Gordon, by training a quantitative ecologist, began work in the 1950s on a framework for practice. Much of his early work focused on developing generalizations about practice. He used samples of activities in medical social work (Gordon and Bartlett, 1959; Gordon, 1959), and observations as a member of the NASW Commission on Practice (National Association of Social Workers, 1964). Later Gordon summarized the major constructs in a practice framework that appeared in Hearn's (1969) symposium report on general systems theory. Although some of Gordon's concepts are related to general systems theory, the basic ideas resemble specialized concepts and principles from ecology.

Ecology is the study of "complex relationships between plants and animals and their surroundings, how they interact with one another, and how their numbers are limited by the resources of the world" (Owen, 1974; v). Its historical antecedents are in the work of naturalists who observed, counted, described, and preserved samples of plant and animal life. Although observations and descriptions continue to be integral to an ecologist's work, the field has become increasingly analytic and develops and tests models of complex interactions within and between living systems. The use and application of ecological concepts and research findings, frequently called environmental sciences, now includes such diverse areas as agriculture, meteorology, fish/marine production, transportation, and public health (Calder, 1973).

When ecologists write about their concerns without reference to specific organisms or problems, their language and foci are much like those of social work. This similarity of concern is part of social work's special attraction to ecology. Our interest in people and their environments and interactions between wholes and parts matches the broad focus of ecology. There are, however, special foci, concepts, and assumptions in ecology that cannot be adopted without change to the needs of social work.

The central concern of ecology is to understand the processes needed for the reproductive success of living organisms (Owen, 1974). While social work shares this concern with other fields, our more immediate focus is upon groups of persons who experience a social problem or are at risk with respect to a problem. Social workers are concerned about nuclear disaster or famine in Third World countries which threaten human reproductive success. But our immediate concerns are more mundane and less directly related to actual survival of significant numbers of human beings. We are concerned about qualitative aspects of survival such as enhancing the quality of human life, achievement, and opportunity.

The unit of analysis in ecology is an *ecosystem,* defined as "an area with a distinct community of plants and animals and takes into account the interrelations among the living organisms and between them and the non-living environment" (Calder, 1973; 20). Usually the idea of an ecosystem includes the assumption that each system is independent of "external sources of matter and energy other than light from the sun" (Owen, 1974; 109). Thus, such an ecosystem, while not a closed system, nevertheless, is open to and dependent upon environmental exchanges in a different way than human systems with which we deal.

Some human systems, such as utopian and certain ethnic and religious communities, severely restricted the types and quality of exchanges with their environments but failed because they could not renew themselves sufficiently for long-term survival. A study of two small Jewish communities near Tunisia points out some of these ecological/system problems (Geertz, 1985). Since our concern is with more open systems, we need different concepts for the term "ecosystem" if the idea is to reflect what we want to explain in practice and to generate practice principles.

The definition of ecosystem contains a second concept from ecology which social work uses—*environment.* As noted above, environment is everything outside the ecosystem's boundary and usually is non-living in character. One use of the term in social work defines human environments as comprised of social and physical (natural and built) parts or elements (Germain, 1979). Balgopal and Vassil (1983) used the term "habitat" for the total environment and its physical and social elements including family, social networks, organizations, and communities.

Some scientists urge caution in studying and developing generalizations about environments. In meteorology, for example, Smith (Calder, 1973) proposed that since all environments are different and ever changing, only the most careful research and analysis gives us sensible generalizations about relationships between environments and systems. Watt (Calder, 1973) has shown how extraordinarily complex human environments are. His models of environments include concepts about population, land use, transportation, economics, capital allocation, energy, and other natural resources, and pollution. Although his attempt to understand society and make predictions about policy issues are complex, they provide ways to consider larger system problems about which social work is concerned.

When social workers use concepts from ecology to describe our client systems, we can say: *Our clients are human systems which exist in and have patterned exchanges with their complex physical, social, and cultural environments. While equilibrium may exist in these ecosystems and their environmental exchanges, survival of the ecosystem requires adaptation and constant renewal of resources. Because ecosystems and environments vary, they change each other in ways that are not highly predictable but may be estimated and modified to protect both systems and environments.*

System and ecological concepts, the predominant elements in contemporary frameworks, are *perspectives* for practice. They are general and abstract ways of thinking about client systems. They represent the best way social work has found to describe wholes, parts, and relationships. These concepts need further development to be more precise explanations of social work's client system domain. They hold promise of providing ways to more precisely and powerfully explain our focus.

Dynamics of Change Although social workers describe wholes, parts, and relationships, our ultimate purpose is to understand how system change occurs so that we can influence its directions and outcomes. Our particular arena for change is understanding and explaining exchanges between systems and their environments. This arena is the *interface* between persons and environments where social workers are concerned about reciprocal exchanges or *transactions* between the two (Gordon, 1969; 7). Social work's interest in this arena is two-fold: First we are interested in coping behaviors and patterns of systems in response to environmental demands. Second, we wish to examine the qualities of environments that impinge on systems (Gordon, 1969; 8).

Germain (1979), drawing in part from Gordon, identified human *adaptation* as the central concept in change. Adaptation is the assumed tendency of persons to strive to match their environments' requirements and change them for successful survival, development, and achievement. Adaptation implies a reciprocal process between environments and persons in which each changes and is changed by the other. Whether the idea is transaction or adaptation, it locates the arena for change and social worker influence to preserve our historical interest in individual adjustment/behavior and social reform. It does not limit us to practice for the purpose of individual adjustment or provision of resources or social change but connotes a broad arena where social workers may assist.

Little work has been done to conceptualize relationships between systems and environments. Coulton (1979) measured person-environment fit of hospitalized adults in such domains as economics, work, family, and need for information, order, control, and personal achievement. Her work suggests some concepts useful in future conceptual frameworks.

Gitterman and Germain (1976) suggested the change arena consists of problems of living experienced in reciprocal relationships with environments. These problems develop in transitions to different roles, the ways people use and influence environments, and in interpersonal relationships. This way of describing the change arena appears to focus primarily on social psychological variables. If so, the concepts are not sufficiently broad to help explain change dynamics in organizations, institutions, and societies that do not depend only on such phenomena.

Social workers can use the distinction Hamburg and others made between adaptation and coping (Coelho and others, 1974; 412, 414). Adaptation consists of processes used by any species to secure reproductive success. Coping consists of patterned behaviors humans use in responding to change. Individual system coping occurs in the context of developmental stages and includes the person's capabilities, his or her motivation to respond to the environment, and behaviors used to maintain stability. Although these concepts also focus primarily on individual systems, some of them have been used to characterize coping patterns in larger systems such as small groups and organizations.

Social work's concern with change includes locating the arena where it occurs and characterizing its qualities. We frequently refer to system-environment exchange as out of balance or as lacking some essential feature. One way to characterize this exchange is in terms of equilibrium. Social workers accept the principle of homeostasis at all system levels, which posits that systems strive for a relatively stable state of equilibrium.

Our special concern is causes and effects of equilibrium disruptions. We recognize that some (so far) unknown factor(s) internal to a person diagnosed as having Alzheimer's disease upsets her or his functioning and equilibrium. The dynamic state previously achieved between person and environment is disrupted by the onset and progress of the disease. As the number of persons diagnosed as having the disease increases, it influences and, in some instances modifies, the equilibrium established within the health care system serving the elderly.

Social workers attempt to identify, understand, and make predictions about dynamics of system changes on a continuum from maintaining established equilibrium, to assisting systems to achieve different forms of equilibria, and preventing negative disequilibrium. System-environment equilibrium is characterized by the balance needed for continued survival, role performance, group continuity, organizational survival, and productivity.

Social workers examine three sets of factors in determining the nature of system-environment equilibrium: system characteristics with emphasis on the nature and quality of system resources; environment characteristics with emphasis on the nature and quality of its supports and limits; and the nature and quality of exchanges between these two. For example, if we described a family in conflict, we would emphasize its internal resources such as members' commitments to each other and its environmental supports such as extended family and we would show how these influence each other.

It is imperative that we use concepts appropriate to the system level of concern. System concepts that fail to go beyond social-psychological variables will not account adequately for critical features of large systems, their environments, and their system-environment exchanges (Hasenfeld, 1980).

When social workers use the concepts transaction, adaptation, coping, and system-environment exchange to refer to change dynamics, we can say: *Since reciprocal relationships exist between systems and environments, the character and quality of these exchanges locate where change is needed to prevent system dysfunction and promote positive system functioning. All systems develop patterned ways of coping with their environments, which can be observed or inferred from observations. The complex nature of system environment exchanges needs extensive further study and elaboration as framework concepts for social work.*

Similarity and Difference A third hallmark of social work is our concern not only for commonalities but also for differences across systems. Frequently termed diversity, the idea is that we expect to find differences in the ways systems are organized and respond to their environments. We draw concepts about similarities and differences from many sources including anthropology, regional, ethnic, and women's studies, and practice experience. Social workers use these concepts to correct traditional white male middle-class explanations of client systems, which are inadequate for effective practice and also discriminatory.

We expect to find similarities and differences within and across systems primarily as a function of culture and ethnicity. Kroeber and Kluckhohn defined culture as explicit and implicit patterns of and for behavior "transmitted by symbols, constituting the distinctive achievements of human groups" (Theodorson and Theodorson, 1969; 95). This concept helps us recognize that subgroups in a society may differ in significant ways. Differences develop and persist primarily as a function of "the ecological circumstances under which the cultures operate" (Coelho and others, 1974; 411).

In order to fully understand groups and organizations in the Appalachian region, for example, we must refer to that region's history, culture, and ecological patterns. While not everything in Appalachian culture differs from other cultures, behavior of persons who migrate to large Northern industrial cities reflects special features of their culture of reference. Similarly, the structure of Latino families is different from that of most white families. The social worker not only expects to observe such differences, but appreciates them and understands they will influence actions he or she takes.

Similarities and differences that derive from ethnicity are represented in a "process of perceiving, understanding, and comparing simultaneously the values, attitudes, and behavior of the larger societal system with those of the [client system's] immediate family and community system" (Norton, and others, 1978; 3). This requires the social worker to examine client systems' cultures and styles of interaction and behaviors in a sociocultural context and to recognize how her or his own attitudes, values, and styles also have been developed in such contexts.

Social workers sensitize themselves to similarities and differences in many ways. Examining demographic data helps us discover one type of difference. Census reports, surveys of regional characteristics, and reports prepared for a state's economic development activities are examples of data sources for identifying statistical similarities and differences among subgroups. Historical analyses of people, institutions, events, and regions are important sources of information about attitudes and values. Oral history, such as slave narratives, helps us gain a more realistic sense of events, problems, and strengths of ethnic groups.

Literature and the arts are significant products of social groups and reveal much about how we frame important values and attitudes. Exploring fiction, drama, poetry, and music written and composed by women gives social workers a different view of the world than that produced by men. Our purpose is to respond differentially to client systems and to prevent and redress discrimination client systems experience because of differences.

When social workers use concepts of cultural and ethnic differences, we can say: *Although human systems have many similarities, there are important differences among them which derive from their cultures and ethnic origins. These differences are reflected in values, norms, attitudes, and behavior; in the products of subgroups in society; and in the ways they engage in helping processes. Differences must be recognized, appreciated, and accommodated to prevent discrimination, preserve ethnic and cultural values, and promote cultural and ethnic identity.*

Summary Social workers use many concepts to elaborate conceptual framework elements to explain client systems. Most concepts from general system theory and ecology provide perspectives on client systems. Because additional work must be done before these concepts help us predict as well as describe, they represent a transitional stage in social work knowledge development. Usually we adapt concepts by applying them to selected instances of practice. A limited amount of work has been done and more is needed to adequately build practice concepts that suggest practice principles and generate hypotheses about practice.

Concepts for Change

A second major part of practice frameworks consists of explanations about how change comes about. Social workers do not act simply on the basis of an understanding of client systems. We take an intermediate step between what client systems are like and what to do, which reflects our assumptions about how change occurs. These assumptions focus on general themes in influence processes.

In general, social workers make assumptions that are optimistic about the possibility of change and the sources and nature of influences they can use. Since we use complex sets of related variables to explain client systems, we expect change to be governed by similarly complex phenomena. We assume change can be initiated both in systems and in their environments although our emphasis in a given situation may be on one or the other and not both. We make assumptions about change depending upon the goal of change, strategies to be used, and relationships these strategies require.

Social workers seldom talk about the sources and nature of their influence on client systems. Instead most speak simply of methods and techniques. Every set of actions a social worker takes is based on an assessment of what needs to be done and an assumption about the type of influence needed to bring change about. Change processes differ in the nature and quality of influence. One way to distinguish them from each other is Chin and Benne's typology (1969). This general scheme groups professional change processes into three categories depending upon the type of influence used.

Rational/empirical processes imply the issues prompting change can be understood and acted upon rationally. Social workers often assume change will occur when client systems are provided with and use new information. We use many educational, research, and knowledge dissemination activities and assume client systems will change by making rational choices. If the client system is a company group organized to plan for retirement and the social worker chooses to present information about resources, the assumption is that group members will act on the basis of this information and change in the desired direction will result. The social worker's source of influence is the information she/he has and the way it is organized and made available to group members.

Normative/re-educative processes are based on the assumption people can learn how to modify their behavior and change their environments. Social work's concern with helping people improve problem-solving and coping skills fits this general category. Most if not all of our counseling, socialization, and resocialization efforts are based on such an assumption about client systems. When the client system is a group home for teenagers whose behavior does not meet society's expectations, the social worker might choose a set of actions designed to influence the group and its members to change by confronting them with behavioral consequences. Another example is a social worker's actions of reflecting, listening, and suggesting as family members adjust to the death of a member. The worker's influence originates in her or his construction and use of a helping environment in which certain issues are discussed, members' ideas and emotional reactions are recognized and accepted, and system members' energies are directed to problems confronting them.

Explanations of human conditions which give rise to *power/coercive* processes generally focus upon entrenched patterns of social interaction which change only when strong political and/or economic power is exerted. Our profession has been involved in many activities such as the civil rights movement and negotiating and bargaining on behalf of client systems that use such explanatory concepts. When the social worker threatens public disclosure of discriminatory housing practices, she or he has assumed change will come about only through the use of a powerful sanction.

When social workers use such concepts of change dynamics, we can say: *All social work action is based on one or more assumptions about the nature and quality of influence needed to initiate and sustain change. Social workers' general sources of influence are information, construction of helping environments in which the impetus for change can be manipulated, and varying degrees of sanction, or a combination of these. While social workers are optimistic about influencing change, we recognize change in positive directions is not always possible. Although most of the profession's change efforts are based on the assumption that change will occur on the basis of rational choices, re-education, and conforming to social norms, social workers also assume some change will occur only with strong influence of legal and moral sanctions.*

Concepts for Social Worker Action

The third set of concepts in a social worker's conceptual framework refers to categories of action he or she takes. This framework part serves several functions. First, it organizes general categories of social workers' action. Social workers have ways of grouping change activities, not just a mental list of all the things they can do. These action categories are comprised of general procedures that fit together around a common theme to form a logically consistent whole. Usually we categorize and label action sets by the purpose or function they are designed to achieve. When we say that a social worker is lobbying for increased mental health funds, we refer to a set of actions we think fit together for the purpose of persuasion under particular circumstances.

Social workers use and our literature records many different action category names and labels. Some are case work, group work, community organization, counseling, behavior modification, social action, and advocacy. These labels mean different things to different social workers and do not refer to actions at the same level of abstraction and generality. The term "counseling" usually refers to all the things a person called "counselor" does. Behavior modification refers to a category of specific procedures derived from certain theories. Advocacy is used to denote an action category for the purpose of protecting entitlements. Group work refers to a broad category of actions taken by a social worker with a particular size client system. At this time social work does not have a generally accepted scheme for organizing and labeling action categories.

The classification system used in this book highlights the second function of change typologies in conceptual frameworks. All categories of social worker action are directed to a purpose and should be selected *after* we understand the client system. Thus, change typologies organize actions we take that match the needs of client systems, proposed directions of change, and assumptions about how to influence change. This book organizes categories of change actions by using the following concepts: client system goal, social worker role set, and strategies.

We assume that broad categories of social work action or role sets are comprised of: (1) a goal toward which the client system and social worker will engage for change and (2) a logically coherent set of social worker actions that are (3) arranged into strategies appropriate for the goal. The role sets are broker, advocate, social reformer, educator, clinician, and mediator. Each is directed to a different general purpose of change and each is comprised of one or more strategies to achieve the goal, depending upon characteristics observed in client systems and their environments. This way of elaborating categories of change actions reflects the profession's major historical concerns and its dual focus on individuals and larger social issues.

When social workers use these concepts to describe their actions, we can say: *Social worker activities consist of action categories or role sets directed to the goal(s) of client system change as a function of client system characteristics and needs and assumptions about change.*

SUMMARY

All social workers have a conceptual framework, which organizes the major concepts and assumptions in their practice. These concepts and assumptions contain general information about client systems, change, and social worker action. Social workers usually emphasize wholes, parts, and relationships and reciprocal relationships between systems and environments as the arena for change. They construct categories of actions to match client system needs and goals, which recognize a range of sources for social worker influence.

Chapter Four

PROBLEM SOLVING IN SOCIAL WORKER ROLE SETS

Social work practice involves a general approach to problem solving directed to four purposes: (1) to discover the system's status, needs, and opportunities; (2) to establish how client system and social worker will work together; (3) to engage in goal-directed change; and (4) to evaluate whether or not change objectives were achieved. The steps in problem solving are problem identification and analysis/assessment, planning and contracting with the client system, engaging in change, and evaluating change efforts.

A general problem-solving approach is not meant to convey the special or particular knowledge and activities required of social workers. Problem solving is not all of social work practice, but one part of the foundation for all practice. It is modified and supplemented by particular knowledge needed in different situations. Social workers teaching high school students about drugs need specific information on that topic, knowledge of the age group, and techniques appropriate for this age group. A social worker consulting about agency program development needs knowledge of the community, organizational dynamics, and program development and clarity about a consultant's role. Nevertheless, the underlying activities of discovery, analysis, change, and evaluation are similar.

PROBLEM-SOLVING CONTEXT

Problem-solving activities occur in and are influenced by a context and are carried out through exchanges between the social worker and client system members.

The context is comprised of three main elements: (1) the structures that support and constrain the social worker and client system; (2) the worker's characteristics; and (3) the client-system characteristics.

Structural Context

All practice occurs in a place. This place usually is termed an "agency" but also is called a "private practice," a "setting," an "organization" or a "field." Locations are systems that function to achieve one or more social policy objectives. Systems are designed to respond to a social need or problem by offering one or more programs to prevent or ameliorate such problems. A food stamp program is a set of activities and resources organized to alleviate hunger. A probation program is a set of activities and resources organized in another system to protect society and rehabilitate offenders. An employee assistance program is comprised of activities and resources offered by some companies to help employees solve personal or family problems and to increase company profits by reducing absenteeism rates, increasing productivity, and reducing staff turnover.

Agencies establish a structure of rules, procedures, and resources to carry out a program. Social workers and client systems meet in programs, and problem solving is influenced by the program's structure and the agency's environment. Features of this environment include, but are not limited to, the agency's mission/sanction, design, climate, programs, resources, rules and procedures, connections to other community systems, and the characteristics of the community in which it is located. Some of these are discussed below to illustrate how they may influence problem solving. These are the relationships between what social workers do and (1) agency function, (2) agency climate, and (3) community environment.

Agency Function An agency's function is the composite of purposes that underly its reason for existence and reflect the nature and source of its sanction to operate in the public interest. This function is made operational in programs agencies offer and the structures used to carry them out. Responsibility for basic life necessities, for example, is assigned to certain agencies that are sanctioned to provide them consistent with a social policy about care of needy persons. A community mental health agency is sanctioned to provide programs that implement a social policy statement on mental health.

These social functions and the policy guidelines under which they are implemented serve as a framework for what social workers do in problem solving. This framework establishes general client-system goals, rules, and procedures workers must follow, and resources workers use. Each of these may influence one or more of the following: client-system population served, client-system problems workers identify, problems they are permitted to assist with, goals they are expected to achieve, how they are permitted to assist, resources available for helping, and their discretion in making decisions.

The relationship between agency function and social worker activities has been analyzed in two ways. First, agency functions have been classified as *people changing, people processing,* or a *combination* of these two (Hasenfeld, 1974). People-processing functions have the purpose of conferring public status on persons who use a program. People-changing functions have the purpose of changing behavior of persons who use a program. Some agencies or programs exist for both functions. An agency's or program's function tells us much about the way it is designed, from which some characteristics of a worker's practice environment can be inferred. This environment supports and constrains the worker's problem-solving activities.

People-processing agencies or programs change and confer statuses through classifying program recipients. A food stamp office is designed to determine applicants' eligibility and classify them as recipients or reject them as recipients. When the status of recipient is conferred, an important service is provided but no attempt is made to change recipients' behavior significantly. Agencies or programs that function to change behavior, such as family counseling agencies, do not classify persons and confer a status. Their workers make assessments of needed behavior changes and use methods thought to be effective in bringing these changes about.

The structures of people-processing and people-changing organizations and programs differ in terms of agency design, environment, methods used, and rules and procedures. People-processing agencies and programs require designs that emphasize routine and systematic procedures based on clearly identified rules carried out in a consistent way by all workers. Thus, workers who classify and confer status are subject to rules and procedures that usually allow relatively little discretion. A worker in people-changing programs and agencies usually has more discretion about assessing and engaging in change.

Agency and program structural constraints have been characterized further in terms of task uniformity (Litwak, 1978). This is the extent to which workers' actions are standardized, and major sources of uncertainty about worker actions are reduced. Task uniformity is a function of the extent to which an agency's or program's product is standardized across all client systems and the amount of repetition required of workers to achieve standardization.

When both standardization and repetition are high, practice is characterized by high task uniformity. Financial assistance programs are structured to achieve high standardization with program workers performing tasks repetitively and uniformly. A half-way house program for status offenders is less standardized, fewer tasks are performed repetitively, and workers' activities are less uniform.

The agency's or program's function sets in motion program design decisions about the structure needed to carry out the intent of a policy. Depending upon the function and how a structure is designed, a worker's problem solving may be more or less constrained by rules about who can be served for what problems and how. Depending upon the extent of standardization required to meet program purposes, problem solving is constrained by many or few uniform tasks performed repetitively. Later in this chapter several principles are discussed that assist workers to practice in a professional way in response to system constraints.

Climate Agency and program climate also influence workers' problem solving. Workers use climate to mean those things which make for comfortable and supportive working conditions. Climate may refer to office space, support personnel, communications, size of workload, and quality of supervision. Whether these factors directly influence problem solving in a predictable way is unclear. But social workers often assume they influence motivation, confidence and security and, ultimately, client-system services. Workers speak of preferring to work in small agencies with little bureaucratic control where they feel supported and appreciated.

Olmstead and Christenson (1973) studied how some climate variables are related to employee satisfaction, agency performance, and worker absenteeism and turnover rates. Several climate factors were associated with these dependent variables. The most important factors were clear and realistic goals, clear agency policies, worker perceptions of effective communication patterns, and able and supportive leaders and supervisors. Extent of worker autonomy, agency stability, and agency size were related but less important. Climate appears to be a complex phenomenon and no one dimension, such as size, accounts for workers' experiences.

Some of these factors might be related to problem solving. Where agency goals are not clear, workers' may be confused in deciding how to identify client-system problems or select change strategies. If agency policies are not realistic, workers may need to rely on their own judgments in selecting goals and objectives. Workers seem to prefer, and to some extent be influenced by, knowledgeable supervisors who provide them with support. Since problem solving is monitored by supervisors, workers may attempt to anticipate supervisors' reactions and evaluations. The more closely, directly, and authoritatively supervision is provided, the greater the worker's reliance on direction in problem solving.

Although more research is needed about climate variables as part of problem-solving contexts, workers should use available findings in social work and related fields to better understand this aspect of their practice.

System-Environments All agencies operate in community environments comprised of complex sets of social systems. These systems include other agencies and those which carry out a community's economic, governmental, religious, judicial, and educational functions. The interdependence of an agency system and this environment serves as a major source of constraint on and support to an agency and its workers. The agency's mandate and its resources originate in this environment. The community has expectations about what an agency will do and how it will do it. Agencies develop reputations about their performance. Workers establish networks of personal and organizational ties in the community. Sometimes these are informal networks; at other times, formal ties exist among agencies offering different services to the same client population.

All units in the social service network may influence a worker's problem solving. Although how these lines of influence operate is not known precisely, some relationships between problem solving and external system environments exist. Briar (1963) found different patterns of worker resource utilization in child welfare agencies. Some agencies were more likely to use foster care and others were more likely to use institutional placements. The important variable in worker's placement choice was more likely to be the agency's resource utilization pattern than needs of a client system.

A community's demographic composition may influence worker problem solving. Wolock (1982) found staff members with difficult caseloads in agencies in socially and economically deprived communities rated child abuse and neglect cases as less serious than did workers in less disadvantaged communities. Wolock suggested community environments produce typical client systems, which become referents for workers' judgments about specific client systems. If this explanation is valid, agency environments may influence problem identification, goal setting, and choices of change strategies. Workers might misjudge problem severity, adjust expectations about possible improvements and/or attempt more or less dramatic changes whether or not these are appropriate.

Social work needs to know more about how an agency's external environment influences what workers do. Some important factors appear to be resources, interagency networks, and demographic characteristics.

Summary Agency and community context variables appear to influence problem solving. Workers should recognize what they do is not only a function of client systems they serve. Other variables also interact to influence their actions in significant ways. Although these influences are important, social workers also are expected to act on the basis of professional commitments and values, including commitments to justice, equality, and fairness. Workers should examine how these are acted on in specific situations and are influenced by agency context and community environment.

Worker Characteristics

Social workers bring their personal characteristics to problem-solving exchanges with client systems. Every worker can be characterized in terms of age, race, sex, marital status, attitudes, values, intelligence, competence, education, and experience. The significance of these or any other factors lies in how they are part of the worker's perception, judgment, and action. The worker perceives, decides, and acts on the basis of personal characteristics as well as agency structure and environment. Much research is available about relationships between worker variables and practice. The following discussion illustrates some of these.

Gender and Sex Roles Perceptions of client-system members may be influenced by a worker's gender and sex-role identity. Although there are contradictory findings in social work research, most findings in situations similar to our practice suggest men and women helpers differ in perceptions of client systems, in expectations for the direction of change, and in change strategy choices. Female workers have been found to stereotype client systems as needing more self-reliance and emotional expression than male workers (Dailey, 1980). Others have not found consistent differences in workers' judgments based on gender (Gingerich and Kirk, 1981). Dailey (1983) found androgynous workers were more likely than feminine workers to encourage emotional expression. Findings in related fields suggest helpers' gender biases influence how client systems are perceived (Broverman and others, 1970; Nowaki and Poe, 1973; Teri, 1982; Behling and others, 1982).

Most studies have been done either in people-changing settings or in psychology and business (Kanter, 1977 and Brown, 1979). Thus, we do not know how important gender and sex-role identity may be in social work. Is gender more influential in judgments of mental hospital patients than of boards and committees in community groups? Does gender have a significant and predictably consistent effect on perceptions, judgments, and actions irrespective of client system and task? While most studies suggest gender is an important bias in judgments, social workers should be cautious about concluding that the effect is similar in all situations.

Race A second important characteristic is worker race. How we perceive others who are different from us is framed by attitudes, values, and expectations formed in our own socialization. This issue is critical, particularly for white social workers, in their perceptions of minority client systems and communities.

Racism may be unintentional and/or disguised and not part of a majority group worker's conscious understanding about his or her biases (Morales, 1971). Workers must examine sources of misunderstanding and misperception in all problem-solving activities. When a worker and client systems do not construct a problem or solution in the same way, the worker should examine whether these differences are due to an inappropriate worker bias arising from her or his race and acculturation. Garcia (1971), for example, suggested areas of unique difference between cultural backgrounds of Chicano families and majority whites. Problem solving may be skewed when workers do not recognize, appreciate, and accept the meaning of these differences.

Worker's failures to account for racial differences may have serious consequences for client systems. For example, Olsen (1982a) found a much longer period of foster care for black children five years and younger than for either white or Hispanic children of the same age. While this may reflect lack of resources, it also might be a function of systematic discrimination. Majority group social workers often do not understand the structure of black families and other support networks and fail to use the full range of placement opportunities.

Olsen (1982b) found that race is a relatively weak predicator of length of foster home placements with white children spending a longer period in their first placements prior to permanent custody than minority children. However, parental rights of minority children were terminated more quickly than those of white children. Thereafter minority children spent more time than white children in permanent custody before adoptive placements. These findings suggest that social workers may give greater benefit of doubt to white parents than minority parents as they engage in assessing and planning change.

Finally, Franklin (1985) found that black and white social workers differed in theoretical orientations and perceptions of their effectiveness with clients from working- and middle-class backgrounds. If workers' theoretical orientations are significant guides to problem solving, client systems may have different experiences depending upon workers' race.

Cognitive Style A third illustration of personal characteristic variables in relation to problem solving concerns workers' cognitive styles. This refers to the ways workers perceive, process, and construct meaning from information. Most data in psychology about this general set of variables have not been tested in social work.

Practice involves collecting and making sense out of client-system observations, work context, and relationships with many persons and events. We use concepts that are more or less explicit as a framework for collecting information and to give it meaning. These concepts are part of our cognitive structures, and the ways we use them are influenced by more or less consistent patterns of thinking and acting.

Orcutt (1964) found that concepts workers used to anchor assessments can distort conclusions. When workers used a dichotomy such as sick-well, they lost client system information that would have been useful in making distinctions about system members, problems, capacities, and opportunities. Rosen and Connaway (1969) found persons differ in the ways they classify information. Some use many categories and name them with high reliance on specific, concrete data characteristics. Others use few and name them more abstractly and generally.

Such findings might have several implications for problem solving. All workers are not expected to use exactly the same concepts in precisely the same ways. Neither do we wish to lose information that might make a significant difference in helping client systems. One step workers can take is to identify concepts they use and avoid converting them into dichotomies such as sick/well. These terms bias the search for information and require thinking in either/or terms. A more sensitive approach might be to use continua that permit gradations along a dimension of more to less of a quality or characteristic. For example, rather than thinking "socialized/unsocialized" about a teenager in a court setting, we might think about the more or less "socialized" behaviors we observe.

Workers might examine how they move from collecting information to assessing what it means. We can discover the concepts we use, how they guide us, and what information is lost when we analyze the meaning of data. Concepts need empirical referents so we can identify events, actions, and characteristics in a consistent and reliable way. We can examine information from several perspectives and more than one preferred meaning. Workers can make explicit their classification schemes and how these affect assessing and data analysis.

Client System Characteristics

Client system characteristics comprise a third set of variables in the problem-solving context. They are examined routinely for all client systems to build a picture of system status, needs, and opportunities.

System Composition The worker discovers system composition by asking who the members are, noting membership size, and learning the purpose of system membership. Answers to these questions help establish a system's boundaries and distinguish its environment. The system may be called a family, an informal group, a task group, a formal group, an organization, or a community. But in all instances it is important to understand how members define membership purpose.

System Demographic Characteristics Members are characterized in terms of factors such as age, sex, race, ethnic identity, and social status. These permit us to describe the system, anticipate the ways it shares characteristics in common with other systems, and ascertain its unique features.

System Culture All systems have histories, traditions, norms, rituals, and values. These are reflected in what members do and what they consider important in the system's present and future functioning. Some aspects of culture are related to age, sex, and race. It is important, however, not to assume all systems with similar characteristics have similar cultures.

Culture influences how systems function through patterns of organization, problem solving, decision making, leadership styles, and distribution of power. These factors describe how systems function, the constraints systems place on themselves, and what members define as important.

System Resource Characteristics Workers examine a system's strengths and weaknessess by identifying its resources. Some characteristics members possess, which comprise system resources are: intelligence, social skills, verbal ability, self-respect, confidence, experience, flexibility, stability, emotional health, and physical health. Others are personal functioning or coping styles in intimate relationships, work, and leisure. Systems have tangible resources such as financial assets and physical structures in their environments. Finally, systems may use resources from support networks.

Society (unfortunately) often defines systems in terms of appeal characteristics. Because of social norms, some systems are more accepted and appealing than others. Systems with high appeal are those that experience difficulties through accident or through no fault of their members. Those with lower appeal are thought to have caused their difficulties through negligence, insufficient effort, or rejection of accepted social norms.

System Vulnerability Vulnerability is the extent to which the system and its members are at risk with respect to environmental assaults and internal disorder, which threaten functioning. Highly vulnerable systems experience assaults that threaten life, health, and system continuation. Those with low vulnerability experience less serious threats.

System vulnerability results from lack of match between system resources and the impact of environmental stresses. Where a system's composition, culture, and resources combine to provide a strong barrier that matches or exceeds stress impact, environmental assaults need to be greater to result in high vulnerability. If the system's features provide a weak barrier and few resources to respond to stress, minor assaults may result in high vulnerability.

Commitment to Change Client systems vary in the extent to which they are committed to change. These variations are a function of several related factors. System members may or may not share clear perceptions of what change is needed, how feasible it is, effects of change on the system, and how to bring change about. The term commitment to change is used rather than motivation for change, since the latter implies emotional states of system members, which are difficult to measure.

Some systems request assistance. Others may be required to use worker services. Commitment to change is not necessarily correlated with the voluntary nature of worker-client system contacts. A so-called involuntary system may have high commitment to change while some voluntary systems do not.

Summary

The problem-solving context is fluid and interactive. Some context variables change over time, are potentially subject to influence, and are possible influences on client-system outcomes. This means regular reassessment of agency, worker, and client characteristics is required in problem solving.

PROBLEM IDENTIFICATION, ANALYSIS, AND ASSESSMENT

Discovery and Analysis

Problem discovery and analysis are based on three practice principles. *First,* the worker should identify, locate, and characterize the problem and its impact throughout the client and related systems. The worker traces the impact of the problem by answering such question as: (1) What is the network of impact? (2) Who and what is influenced by the problem? (3) Who or what maintains the problem? (4) What other problems, if any, seem to result from the first problem? As the worker engages in this discovery, he or she develops a picture of the client and related systems which is filled in later with more detail and significant nuances of meaning.

Second, the worker should assume responsibility to identify, locate, and characterize problems not identified previously. A worker is responsible to help remedy immediate problems and to anticipate other problems. A family might request medical assistance for an unemployed father. If the worker notes that an extended family member requires care, he or she explores how this system member might need future assistance even when the family does not identify an immediate problem. It is not assumed this member *is* a problem, but *may be* or *may become* part of a problem in the future.

When a worker conducts a community needs assessment, she or he focuses on problems residents identify. The worker also thinks about what any neighborhood requires, explores and observes the neighborhood, and contributes this thinking and these observations to the assessment. This professional judgment and discovery process extends problem definition *and* contributes to prevention of future problems.

Third, workers always should consider policy implications of the present problem. Workers assume the client system is only one instance of a problem and represents a larger number of systems with similar problems. The issues, barriers, and difficulties discovered for one system may be similar for others with the same problem. The worker asks questions about this larger population group: (1) How large is it? (2) Where are its members located? (3) Are they being served and if not, why not? (4) How can they be reached and what resources are needed to reach them? (5) What new or revised policies may be needed to serve them? Answers to such questions are used in agency and community meetings to plan service improvements.

Problem identification forms the basis for analysis and assessment. The result is a descriptive statement about the problem, its location, its impact and influence networks, contributing and maintaining factors, and any other data the worker thinks relevant. The worker makes sense out of this description in problem analysis by relating facts to each other, making judgments about factors that contribute to or maintain problems, determining where strengths and weaknesses exist in the system and its environment, and identifying critical starting points for change.

Assessment

An assessment is the formal statement of conclusions reached in problem analysis. Usually it is a one or two paragraph analytic summary, which specifies relationships among facts, identifies information needed to extend the picture of the client system, and makes predictions about what needs to be done to resolve the problem(s). It contains one or more general client-system goals.

Each goal is the general purpose for social work assistance in terms of role sets. If the assessment shows that a family needs resources, the goal is to match resources with needs. If conflicts exist between two community groups, the goal is to reduce or resolve them. If a group of employees is discriminated against and prevented from obtaining entitlements, the goal is to secure entitlements. Where an assessment shows a group of retarded persons need new skills, the goal is to provide educational opportunities.

Although a major portion of problem identification, analysis, and assessment occurs early in client-system–worker contacts, it is subject to constant revision. The worker regularly checks the validity of assessment predictions and incorporates new data, which either confirm or modify predictions. In addition, some change efforts may occur immediately based on goals selected in the first or early contacts. In other instances goals are not selected until later in worker–client-system contacts. Problem identification, analysis, the assessment are first steps in problem solving. However, they recur throughout worker-system contacts.

ENGAGING, PLANNING, AND CONTRACTING

The second stage of problem solving is engaging, planning, and contracting between the worker and client system. These activities are based on the assessment and general goals of change. The purpose is to establish what will be done by whom and how.

Social Worker–Client-System Exchange

Interpersonal communication is the vehicle for problem solving. The worker's purpose is to discover the system's difficulty and begin to engage system members in change. It is important to develop the type and quality of communication needed for continuing joint problem solving. When there is a tentative conclusion about the problem and goal, the worker's emphasis moves to using communication for problem resolution.

Social work literature emphasizes the importance of this communication system or relationship. The purpose of this relationship is to achieve client-system goals. Relationship is defined as the totality of exchanges between workers and client systems. These exchanges are comprised of verbal and nonverbal information, which has structure and content. In early exchanges, participants share little or no information in common. As their contacts increase, they share more explicit and implicit communication content. In professional relationships, the worker does not seek or share information that is not needed for problem solving. The worker does not use these exchanges for other purposes, including those which are unethical. These latter include, but are not limited to, imposition of personal power by sexual harassment of any type.

Most research suggests worker–client-system exchanges can be made more effective when workers explicitly recognize system-member statements. Worker responses are congruent when they contain content that reflects some portion of a system member's statement (Rosen, 1972). If a system members says, "My problem is that I am unemployed," a congruent response contains content about the problem of unemployment. A congruent response is, "Tell me about where you have worked in the past." An incongruent response is, "Tell me about your family." While the person may respond by describing his or her family, the opportunity has not been afforded to talk further about relevant content. As a result, system members may gain the impression that the worker is unconcerned about their problem. Congruence in communication may be examined in each information exchange or across one contact or the total problem-solving process.

The structure and content of communication is important for system continuance and effective problem solving (Rosen, 1972). Voluntary continuation in helping relationships initially depends upon being satisfied that problems are attended to (Rosen, Connaway and Duehn, 1972). While continuance is not sufficient for problem resolution, it is an instrumental or facilitative objective in worker–client-system relationships.

Workers also have expectations for exchanges. These should be introduced in ways that do not disconfirm interest and potential helpfulness. Worker responses that enlarge the scope of interaction are orienting responses (Duehn, 1970). The worker introduces these to meet position requirements and professional expectations.

Worker–client-system relationships are influenced by worker and system characteristics and by the relationship's context. The worker is responsible to adjust to differences across systems and discover the forms or types of exchange that facilitate the client system's engaging in problem solving.

Planning and Contracting

An outcome of engaging the client system in problem solving is a shared agenda, which is translated into a plan for change and formalized in a contract to guide subsequent activities. A worker–client-system contract is a statement of goals, objectives, and procedures for engaging in change that specifies all participants' responsibilities.

Contracting is not a static activity that is fixed and not subject to change or renegotiation (Seabury, 1976). Because this implies active system-member engagement, special variations of contracts may be needed in some situations. Care should be taken to avoid imposing contracts when client systems have few choices or when severely disturbed persons, small children, the aged and infirm, or persons with certain disabilities are involved. Contracts may be developed with system representatives such as family members, guardians, or allies (Seabury,

1976). Some contracts must be agreed to by a legal entity such as an agency board or state official.

Two aspects of planning in addition to client-system participation are critical. First, the worker is responsible to match the goal and objectives with an appropriate change strategy. Failure to match the goal and strategy may result in significant misapplication of strategies (Rosen and Connaway, 1968). Some workers select and use strategies they personally prefer rather than those that correspond to the goal. The practice principle in matching goals and strategies is called purpose-method correspondence. It requires workers to consider carefully the fit between the goal and a strategy to achieve it.

Second, from among strategies that correspond to the goal, the worker selects those that are effective in achieving the system's objectives. Workers often find it difficult to locate and evaluate research findings to meet this second criterion. Some barriers to using research include inadequate statistical knowledge (Witkin and others, 1980), the need to act more quickly than time permits to search for answers (Rosen, 1983), and difficulty in setting aside personal preferences (Kirk and Fischer, 1976). Nevertheless, it is imperative that workers actively seek and use research in planning change.

This may be done in several ways. Computer searches are available in many libraries. Workers can examine periodic summaries of research in social work and related fields. Workers may use journals such as *Social Service Review, Journal of Social Service Research,* and *Social Work Research & Abstracts* for outcome studies. Where it is feasible, agencies should install computer connections to nation-wide data bases for information about the populations or problems they serve. Finally, a practical five-step method for organizing and using research findings is available (Mullen, 1978).

Selecting Goals and Objectives

Goals and objectives are key elements in worker–client-system contracts. Clearly stated goals and objectives are important to guide subsequent action and to evaluate practice effectiveness. A practice *goal* is the overall purpose of the social worker and client system's work. It is a broad, general statement of outcomes to be achieved. Practice *objectives* are specific, operational statements of outcomes. Objectives are *not* statements of worker activities.

Three types of objectives are used here. *Outcome objectives* are specific system achievements, activities, actions, or products that comprise the practice goal. *Instrumental objectives* are steps to achieving outcome objectives. *Facilitative objectives* are preconditions client systems must meet to achieve outcome and instrumental objectives (cf. Nelson, 1984).

The goal and objectives for an adolescent with poor academic achievement might be: **Goal:** Mike's stress will be reduced and his academic performance will be improved. **Outcome Objectives:** (1) Mike will read at the tenth grade level by the end of the term; (2) Mike will comprehend concepts taught in American Government and English Literature classes by the end of the term. **Instrumental Objectives:** (1) Mike will attend and participate in classes and complete homework assignments each week; (2) Mike will discuss his feelings about school achievement in relation to his parent's expectations. **Facilitative Objectives:** (1) Mike will stay in school; (2) Mike will participate in counseling; and (3) Mike's parents will support his school and counseling attendance.

Engaging, planning, and contracting result in a work plan that contains client system goal, specific outcome objectives, instrumental and facilitative objectives (as appropriate), and the responsibilities of all persons including worker. The workers' purpose is to establish a communication exchange that promotes client system participation and continuance. The worker must be flexible, creative, and sensitive to client-system characteristics and how these affect system members' participation in problem solving.

ENGAGING IN CHANGE

Social work generalists deal with a broad range of client-system goals and change strategies using one or more role sets. Role sets are constellations of worker behaviors designed to achieve a general client-system goal (cf. Thomas and others, 1967). Roles are enacted in the context of an organizational position, its expectations, and the worker's professional role conceptions.

Positions

Positions are locations in organizational structures that recognize and name occupants' functions and activities. Positions exist independently of the persons who occupy them. Positions may be named in different ways and defined so as to specify, for example, the functions and activities of an intake worker, social worker, or case manager. Position holders are expected to carry out position activities.

Role Expectations

Positions prescribe duties, responsibilities, and authority of position holders. These are termed *role expectations* or *role demands.* Expectations derive from a written position description, its location within the organization's structure, and the meaning ascribed to it by others. These expectations or demands are one source of external influence on position occupants.

Role Conceptions

In addition to the formal and informal expectations of position holders' behavior, individuals have *role conceptions.* These are a position occupant's personal expectations about rights, responsibilities, and activities. Conceptual frameworks for practice are one important source of role conceptions. Expanded role conceptions are important in generalist practice. The principle is that, to the maximum extent possible, social workers extend a position's role expectations. The worker accepts position expectations *and* brings a strong, clear conception of what needs to be done in role enactment on behalf of a broad range of client systems. Five characteristics of expanded role conceptions influence traditional role enactment.

First, the worker defines her or his work with initiative and autonomy. Workers define their tasks and do not rely only on others' role expectations. Workers need to develop a sure sense of self, be reasonably comfortable in using the power that exists in a position and his or her expert knowledge, and assume responsibility for her or his actions.

Second, the worker's assessment is multifaceted and not limited to the position's or agency's problem definition. This implies flexibility in being able to see client systems in their own terms and not primarily in terms the agency or position prescribes.

Third, although workers occupy organizational positions, they also are members of professional and community groups. As such they think about role enactment in terms broader than the focus of their agencies and positions. These memberships provide additional perspectives on problems and other sources of assistance to client systems.

Fourth, the worker constantly inquires about effectiveness of solutions to client-system problems, including those the agency prefers to use. Finally, workers bring a dual focus to their role conceptions. While engaging in change efforts with a particular system, the worker's concern extends to that larger group of potential client systems with similar problems. This focus may lead the worker to examine how organizations and positions need to be changed to provide more adequate and effective service.

Role Sets

Six social worker role sets are presented in subsequent chapters. These are broker, advocate, reformer, educator, clinician, and mediator. Each is a set of worker activities designed to achieve one general client-system goal. Role sets are carried out in positions and require expanded role conceptions to reflect the five principles discussed above.

Roles are constellations of worker activities designed to: link client systems to needed resources (broker); secure or protect an existing right or entitlement for one or more client systems (advocate); establish a new entitlement for client systems or potential client systems (reformer); provide opportunities to learn skills and/or information for effective role performance (educator); modify sources and effects of internalized stress (clinician); and resolve or reduce inter- or intrasystem conflict (mediator).

The worker chooses one or more roles based on the assessment and general goals to be achieved. If an assessment identifies a goal and role that the worker is prevented from carrying out for any reason, she or he is responsible for referring the client system to a resource where the need can be met.

EVALUATING OUTCOMES

A final step is to evaluate the impact of change efforts by discovering whether or not and how problems identified in the assessment have been modified. Evaluating occurs during and after each contact with client systems and other systems in their environments. The purpose is to determine progress in meeting the objectives set forth in the contract. Because objectives have different priorities, those that are critical to a system's immediate welfare and those that facilitate achieving instrumental and outcome objectives should be evaluated most quickly.

This step also identifies barriers to goal achievement and provides information to confirm or disconfirm assessment predictions. Barriers may be located in the system, in its environment, and in the agency and/or worker. When these are noted, the contract may be modified to reflect either new objectives or different participant responsibilities. When predictions are confirmed, contract changes are not needed. However, confirmation provides greater certainty about the assessment and directions for change. If predictions are disconfirmed, the assessment is modified, one or more new hypotheses are formulated, and the contract is modified. Reassessment may identify new problems for which the problem-solving process is repeated and the contract changed to reflect additional goals, objectives, and activities.

Evaluation is critical to maintain direction and clarity in change efforts. It provides information used in knowledge development in the profession. The social worker is responsible for moving beyond evaluating specific client-system outcomes to evaluating outcomes for groups of similar systems. This can be carried out in two ways.

Systematic Comparisons

Workers systematically compare client systems and practice outcomes in their work loads. For example, a worker who assists neighborhoods to secure grant funds might examine characteristics and processes of different neighborhoods and how these are related to goal achievement. Similarities and differences might be noted in demographic characteristics, power structures, leadership patterns, geographic location, and racial and ethnic composition, and funding outcomes.

The worker uses this information in several ways. It is shared with other workers and administrators in staff meetings to plan service changes. It is shared with a broader professional community in examining trends in the incidence and prevalence of problems for community planning. It is shared with other social workers through writing and publishing.

Workers also systematically examine their caseloads to determine whether or not certain change strategies are effective. In the example given above, the worker examines whether or not a given strategy was effective across work with a range of different neighborhoods. Whether it was or not, information from this appraisal is shared with colleagues in and outside the agency to improve the quality of service.

Formal Evaluations

Formal evaluations of change-strategy effectiveness may be conducted in two ways. First, workers participate in agency studies of a program's impact. These studies examine whether program objectives were achieved and, if so, note the magnitude of change in the target population. The worker provides information to the evaluator and shares in planning the research project. If the program is effective and the need for it continues, the worker is expected to continue using the change strategies outlined in the program. If it is not effective and the need for it continues, the worker shares responsibility to revise the program to increase its effectiveness.

Second, workers use single-system designs to evaluate their own practice effectiveness with specific client systems and groups of similar client systems where the same change strategy was used. A single-system design is one procedure to identify objectives, strategies, and outcomes with one client system. It requires precise statements of outcome objectives, worker actions, the relationship expected between these actions and outcomes, and systematic data collection and appraisal.

SUMMARY

Problem solving is the systematic collection and analysis of data about client-system characteristics and problems, which lead to change. It occurs in a context and is influenced by organizational structure, worker characteristics, and client-system characteristics. Workers extend position expectations to account for professional role conceptions that broaden the view of practice responsibilities and opportunities. Much remains to be discovered about the interplay of context variables and problem solving. The complex relationships between these two can be used to client-system advantage if we are careful to avoid mystifying problem-solving processes.

Chapter Five

BROKER ROLE

Social worker activities designed to link client systems to needed resources.

The broker role recognizes that some client systems' needs can be met most effectively by resources located in social service agencies, other institutions, and other environmental opportunities. These resources may assist persons more successfully to accomplish life tasks or alleviate current distress (Curriculum Policy, 1982). The importance of these professional activities was noted by NASW; one of four practice goals was identified as "interventions to link people with systems that provide them with resources, services and opportunities" (NASW, 1981; 7).

Early Practice of the Broker Role

The broker role has been important throughout social work's history. Lowry's (1939) collected essays described and analyzed broker activities in case work practice from 1920 to 1938. Hamilton's essay on basic concepts recognized the diversity of human needs as the basis for this practice:

> People require material things and to the social conscience of the Western world subsistence needs have at last taken on the character of elementary justice or social obligation. People need also experiences that bring satisfactions, and when they cannot manage these experiences or arrange their activities in a way to bring them such satisfactions . . . they may be the concern of social workers (Hamilton, 1939; 155).

Hollis' essay presented a case example of a young couple, which she analyzed for the worker's use of investigation, budgeting, work relief, and hospital care. Contemporary workers will be interested to note that the couple was given $3.50 for rent and $3.00 for food each week from agency funds (Hollis, 1939a)!

Much early discussion about the broker role dealt with the function and place of material relief in practice. Glenn (1939) chaired the Section on Social Case Work of the International Conference of Social Work and presented a paper on this topic in Paris in 1928. She described the prevailing view of material relief: It "has come to be recognized as not in itself an evil if it be used as a resource in treatment, a tool which can be handled creatively if the user has a sure touch" (Glenn, 1939; 74). She also posed strategy questions about the relationship between material relief and treatment.

A second early theme shows how much effort charity institutions expended in trying to avoid duplication in relief giving and conservation of resources. The New York Charity Organization Society led the movement to design confidential exchanges to provide information about users of resources. They published charity directories and promoted cooperative work. Their development of information and referral centers in both the private and public sectors is well documented (Long, 1973).

Although social work has a long history of connecting persons in need with resources, relatively little attention has been given to the knowledge base for this practice. Hollis (1939b) listed several areas about which the social worker should be knowledgeable, including budgeting, establishing eligibility, and understanding the meaning of relief. Contemporary social workers are concerned about adequate client system assessments, which make it possible for them to provide needed resources. At different historical periods, workers have emphasized doing for client systems or refusing ever to do anything for them. Hollis (1939b) recommended continuing assessments over time to determine appropriate worker behavior and Hamilton (1951) disapproved of either too much or too little social worker help in securing resources.

The environment in which resources are located has become more complex in recent years. Wilensky and Lebeaux remarked that client systems need "guides through a civilized jungle" (Wilensky and LeBeaux, 1965; 14). Recent federal actions, which altered the quantity and quality of resources and eligibility regulations, suggest the broker role is needed still and is more complex to carry out.

To be effective, workers must be knowledgeable about the variety of services and resources in their communities, be able to assess needs accurately, and possess knowledge of organizations for planning and implementing appropriate matches of needs with resources.

PROBLEM IDENTIFICATION AND ASSESSMENT

Need for the broker role may exist at any time in worker-client system contacts. It may be the sole purpose of their contacts; it may be one of two or more goals of their joint work. Often the need for broker activities does not become apparent until other goals have been achieved. Using this role is not limited to workers who hold intake positions but is used any time when the goal is to match a resource with a client-system need.

Nature and Location of the Problem

Analysis of problems should determine if material and/or nonmaterial needs exist. Basic survival needs are matched to material resources such as food, housing, clothes, and money. Although survival needs commonly are the basis for the broker role, nonmaterial needs are not infrequent. Such needs reflect problems in interpersonal functioning, system conflict, lack of information, and insufficient opportunity for system development. Job training and placement, stress reduction services to abusive parents, and opportunities to learn social skills are examples of nonmaterial resources often needed by client systems.

During problem identification, the social worker establishes the system's composition. The system might be a community seeking additional police protection. The system might be a family without food and shelter. The system might be a task group seeking expert advice to resolve internal conflict. Systems usually are represented by one or more members in their contacts with the worker. Representatives might be a neighborhood leader, one or both parents, or the task group leader. No matter who contacts the worker and represents the system, the worker asks questions about who else is involved so that a picture of the system can be formed.

ASSESSMENT OF THE CLIENT SYSTEM

The focus for assessing is guided by an initial determination that the client-system problems can be alleviated by connecting resources to needs. Information the social worker obtains should relate to two major client-system characteristics, namely, vulnerability and resources.

Vulnerability of the Client System

One assessment focus is on how system characteristics combine to provide it with resources to resist environmental assaults and stresses. The assessment focus is to determine if the system is at risk without the provision of additional resources. Client systems may be more or less vulnerable by reason of age, health, and living situations, for example. Street persons are at high risk and vulnerable in frigid, windy weather and must be provided with shelter quickly. In different weather conditions these persons may be at less risk although their life situations may be viewed as deviant by local standards. Small children without adequate supervision and parenting are highly vulnerable. Task groups with extensive resources to achieve most of their work are not highly vulnerable.

Demographics, Culture, and Resources

A second focus should be on specific system characteristics, which will influence planning and obtaining resources. System demographic characteristics, culture, and resources influence the worker's judgment about the extent to which system members can participate in obtaining resources, the resource agency to be used if alternatives are available, and any special preparation needed by client system members for contact with the resource agency. Some important characteristics are examined below.

Verbal Ability The worker should assess client-system members' ability to describe their needs clearly and completely. The assessment includes a judgment about whether or not they are able to report the kinds of information necessary to determine eligibility for some resources.

System members may have difficulty in presenting their needs. Some lack experience in discussing private matters with strangers. If this is so, the worker assesses the extent to which coaching may be needed so that system members can present their needs to others. Physical impairments such as speech and hearing problems may limit ability to communicate as fully as needed to obtain a resource. Some persons may have difficulty presenting their needs due to limited command of English.

Appearance Clients' personal appearance often affects others and may influence the extent to which resources are provided and how the system is treated.

Stability An assessment includes attention to whether or not at least one system member is able to present needs to others in stressful situations. Members may have learned interactive styles that do not serve them well in achieving their current goals. The system's current distress may be sufficiently overpowering that members are unable to maintain cognitive control to negotiate the steps required to achieve help.

Self-Respect Experience in asking for and receiving help combined with current stress may affect the self-respect of system members. Their skills in participating with the worker in problem solving may be affected by the amount of confidence and worth they feel. The worker's estimate of system members' self-respect may be helpful in preparing for a resource agency and/or in selecting a resource agency from among alternatives.

Intelligence Two aspects of intelligence are assessed. The first is the extent to which the system is aware of and/or knowledgeable about the social world. The second is the social skills system members possess for negotiating that world. The first area often is considered most important. It is useful to know the extent to which system members understand the complexity of social resources, can analyze their situations, and have cognitive skills to engage in problem solving. It also is important to assess members' skills in interacting with different kinds of persons to gain cooperation in obtaining help. These two aspects of intelligence, which may not match, are important in developing an effective plan.

Appeal Characteristics Social norms usually support provision of resources to persons whose needs can be attributed to something other than their actions and choices. These persons have higher appeal characteristics than those viewed by society as having caused or contributed to their own problems. Client systems are more likely to gain sympathy and receive resources in a timely and nondemeaning manner when their appeal characteristics are high.

Commitment to Change The assessment includes an estimate of a client system's commitment to obtaining the needed resource. Commitments to change may vary with the type of resource needed and the activities required to obtain it. It may be easier for some systems to make commitments to change involving a material resource to which systems perceive they are entitled than those that appear to be gifts. Some systems have difficulty requesting resources that involve nonmaterial resources, such as counseling for family problems, which reveal personal and system weakness. The degree of commitment to a goal may influence the extent to which members carry out tasks needed in planning and engaging in change.

ASSESSMENT OF THE RESOURCE AGENCY

A careful assessment of each resource agency is made prior to planning for change. This agency may be the worker's own agency as well as other community agencies. Resource agencies may be assessed along many different dimensions. Those described below are considered the most essential in effective broker-role performance.

People Processing or People Changing

An early determination is made as to whether or not the resource agency is organized primarily for a people-processing or a people-changing function or some combination of the two (Hasenfeld, 1974). Client systems will be treated differently and expectations of their behavior also will vary as a function of the purpose and structure of the resource agency. People-processing agencies will require more extensive information for eligibility determinations than most people-changing agencies.

Discretion of Staff

Even in people-processing agencies and programs there may be some worker discretion about the quantity or type of resources. The worker may plan for a client to be seen by a particular staff member who by reputation may be willing to exercise maximum discretion in instances where eligibility for services is not clear.

Shared Goals of Agency and Staff

In agencies of considerable size and complexity, information about the extent to which staff share goals with higher level administrators may be useful in selecting an agency and in predicting successful outcomes in meeting client-system needs. Administrators may be under social or political pressure to reduce caseloads and show less need for resources while staff are oriented to meeting fully the needs of client systems in their community (Lipsky, 1980). Assessing this characteristic guides the worker's choice of resource agency and in preparing client system members to seek assistance.

Availability of Resources

An assessment is made whether or not resources are available only on a seasonal or intermittent basis and the relative scarcity of resources. Some resources are available to all who qualify throughout the year. Others are seasonal and/or available in limited supply on a first-come, first-served basis. Financial assistance for heating costs often is available seasonally to a limited number of systems that apply first. Resources for socialization, growth enhancement, and opportunities to improve social functioning may be available periodically. For example, new parent education groups may start every two months. Workers should be aware of the extent of demand for services and resources in their communities, whether or not early application is advised, the presence or absence of waiting lists, and any other factor related to availability.

Staff Resources to Serve Client Demand

Whether or not an agency is staffed adequately is assessed in preparing client systems to use a resource. Waiting lines for service and large caseloads, which limit time given to client systems, result when staff resources in an agency are inadequate.

Accessibility

This dimension refers to physical location, physical accessibility of resources to persons with mobility and general health problems, and to hours and days of the week services are provided. Resource agency access is examined in relation to the client-system's physical characteristics and what can be done to overcome limitations they pose. The location of the resource agency in relation to transportation also is assessed.

Agencies vary in the extent to which they provide twenty-four hour, seven day a week service. Spouse abuse shelters and emergency services at community mental health centers and hospitals are available continuously. Many others are open during fixed daytime hours, five days a week. Short-term, emergency resource provision may be needed as a result of access restrictions.

Behavior Norms for Client Roles

Expectations for client-system members' behavior vary among agencies. Some differences include the expectation that members show evidence of gratitude and compliance, especially if the need is met by a material resource. Other agencies expect system members to participate fully in the service process and show independence of thought and judgment. The worker should be aware of such behavioral standards in general and consider them in relation to a specific client-system's characteristics.

Costs of Services

An assessment is made of the amount and type of direct and indirect costs the client will incur in obtaining a resource. At least three costs can be identified—money, time, and psychological effort. Money costs include fees for services and loss of income that would have been earned during the process of obtaining services. Alternative child care and care of ill or older persons may be client-system costs. The cost of time includes time away from work and loss of wages as well as personal time taken from accomplishing other tasks. Some client systems have little free time to engage in lengthy eligibility determinations. Client-system members may be able to attend parent education groups for a period of six weeks but not groups that extend over three months. Psychological costs, particularly those incurred in applying for and receiving material resources, are assessed as well as costs to self-worth when the process is known to be demeaning.

Resource Agency Management

The social worker should make a general assessment of how well the agency is run. This information usually is available by reputation. If records are misplaced, client appointments routinely not kept, information about resources not well known to staff, or posted service hours not kept, it is obvious the client system will not receive good service in a timely fashion.

Characteristics of resource agencies described above suggest workers should maintain personal and public information about resources in their communities. Most communities have some type of social agency directory that lists services, hours, and general rules and requirements. When this is not so, the task of compiling information often is undertaken by workers with volunteer help. Public information may be available through an organization similar to the older information and referral exchanges. Governmental units may have citizen advocates who provide information about services they provide.

Information is provided in human service guides prominently located in some telephone directories. Public information is essential but not sufficient for adequate planning with system members to obtain a good fit between their needs and agency resources. A worker also should have personal knowledge about how agencies function and what their staff do to provide help. This argues for workers to be involved in their communities and in professional meetings that bring staff from different agencies together. It also suggests workers should be involved personally in the social fabric of their communities to increase their informal, personal handbook of information about resource agencies.

Data obtained in problem identification and assessing client system and resource agency result either in a plan for action or a decision to withdraw from the process. Withdrawal may occur when systems discover ways to resolve problems without further help from the worker.

PLANNING

Planning consists of projecting and devising a method for taking action. Its purpose is to identify outcome objectives and steps to achieve them. Generally it is assumed client systems will participate fully in planning except where assessment of their characteristics indicate otherwise. The principle of client self-determination is upheld as a first practice principle unless shown to be impossible. Even so, there are degrees of participation and self-determining behavior; the worker's obligation is to maximize them.

Planning includes the formulation of a contract between client system and worker. Worker behaviors should be a function of the assessment of the client system and the resource agency. The worker may actively engage in change (matching resources to needs) or prepare the client system to act on its own behalf. The worker's approach is determined by the assessment and takes the form thought to be most effective in matching resources to needs in a timely manner.

Contracting includes establishing a priority of needs for which resources are sought. Outcome objectives should be stated in terms of the client system. The client system and worker should be clear about what is expected to the client system. Information, documents, and specific procedures system members will need to use should be identified. Client-system members should be coached (as needed) about how to proceed.

Some plans may specify that the worker contacts resource agency staff to determine the availability of resources and eligibility requirements or make an appointment for system members. When such a plan is made, the worker and system members should discuss the extent and type of client-system information that will be shared by the worker with the resource agency. Confidentiality between the worker and the client system is discussed and understood within the framework of potential benefits to be gained by the client system.

If all needed resources are located in one agency, the system has little choice about alternative sources for assistance. Thus, system members may experience the psychological effects of being treated as and feeling like a nonvoluntary client. Furthermore, if there is a low commitment to change, particularly in securing nonmaterial resources, the client system may withdraw from the process by failure to keep appointments and use services.

When the client system is comprised of a large number of persons related only by a common task or purpose, contracting involves additional worker behaviors. Formulating goals and objectives for such a group probably will take longer than with an individual client system. Time must be spent encouraging and permitting members to state their perceptions of needs to determine whether or not the same resources match all members' needs. The worker's skills in helping group members communicate with each other and the worker are critical. Agreements about the division of labor will require time. However, it is likely that more skills and information will be available to a larger group because all its members bring life experiences and resources to problem solving. Discovering and utilizing these resources require the worker's skilled assistance.

The norms for group members' behavior may influence actions the system chooses and how it plans to carry them out. Whether or not the group reaches a decision formally or agrees informally about its directions for change represent different group decision-making processes, each of which influences the way contracts are accepted. Some groups permit designated leaders to act for them while others do not and it is important to know which way a system operates when contracts are developed. Contracting and establishing goals are similar activities irrespective of client-system size. However, workers need additional knowledge and skills in working with larger client systems. Some areas for special attention in systems include the decision-making processes, communication processes, group norms, leadership arrangements, resources, and the possibility of diverse needs in large systems.

ENGAGING IN CHANGE

Four strategies are identified to achieve the goal of the broker role. These are referring, distributing resources, creating resources, and coordinating resources. The choice of one or some combination of strategies depends upon conclusions reached in assessing and upon outcome objectives.

Referring

Referring is the process of connecting client systems to resource systems either within or outside the worker's agency. It involves selecting appropriate resources that match client-system needs in the order of priority established in the contract. Second, it involves providing information to the client system about the resource agency. This includes information that assists the client system to present itself in such a way as to increase the probability of receiving resources: what documentation to take, what questions need to be answered, and how members should present themselves. This information should be presented to system members consistent with their ability to understand and use it. If the information is complex and easily misunderstood, it should be described in simple, uncomplicated fashion. If members are not familiar with the community, more specific information needs to be provided. Information should be consistent with what the worker knows about the resource agency as it applies to the client. Eligibility standards, religious sponsorship (if any), procedures used, and details about location and service hours are provided consistent with specific system characteristics.

Third, the worker should arrange transportation to the resource if it is appropriate and needed. Transportation may be provided by the worker, other staff, or volunteers. The client system may be able to identify neighbors, friends, or relatives who can assist. Fourth, the worker may "pave the way" for the client system by telephoning another agency staff member with system members' knowledge and agreement.

Distributing Resources

Distributing resources is the strategy chosen when the worker can act to provide a resource and does not need to refer the client system to a different agency or elsewhere within the worker's agency. There are several variations in this strategy. For example, the worker may provide some resources and refer the client system to other agencies for different resources. The worker must estimate whether or not the available resources fit the needs of the client system. If so, client-system eligibility must be established within policies, rules, and restrictions. In using this strategy the worker must be aware of and respond to feelings client-system members have about receiving help. All possible effort must be made to preserve the client system's dignity.

Creating Resources

Communities often do not have resources of sufficient quantity and variety to meet a range of needs. Creating resources out of informal resources is a strategy required of many social workers. It draws upon the worker's and client system's imagination, personal skills, and creativity. Such resources may provide temporary assistance or may meet fully the client system's need. Creating resources requires locating informal support networks, promoting the interest of groups such as service clubs and churches and synagogues in helping certain groups of client systems, and recruiting businesses and industries to provide resources.

Whenever the worker identifies repeated gaps in resources, steps should be taken to rectify this situation. It is a professional obligation to call attention to lack of resources, meet with other professionals sharing similar concerns, involve groups of concerned citizens, assist in formulating plans, and take actions to provide resources the community's citizens need. These activities extend beyond the broker role, but are professional responses to identification of lack of resources in performing the role.

Coordinating Resource Distribution

Resources client systems need may be located in several different agencies. Because service delivery systems are complex, many client systems experience difficulty in negotiating them. Thus, they do not receive resources in a timely manner. When several different agencies provide resources to a vulnerable client system with little capacity to participate in the change process, workers are responsible to see that needed resources are arranged for, that they match identified needs, and that they actually are provided in a timely way. This combination of characteristics often requires social workers to engage in coordinating resources. The activities involved in this strategy closely approximate some aspects of case managing (Weissman and Savage, 1983).

EVALUATING OUTCOMES

Evaluating determines the extent to which client system outcomes were achieved. Successful evaluations depend, in part, on clearly identified goals and objectives. Achieving goals depends upon availability of resources and the worker's skill in using one or more broker role strategies.

Although much social work practice experience and literature identify "follow-up" as a worker activity, insufficient emphasis has been placed upon whether or not client systems received resources to meet their needs. The term follow-up usually refers only to keeping appointments made as part of a referral strategy rather than actual delivery of needed resources. The worker also must determine if resources were provided.

The broker role often is time consuming and workers may find it difficult to evaluate the outcomes of their work. Time devoted to this step is essential to test techniques and strategies with particular client systems and to increase the probability of success.

Miller and others (1979) reported attempts to increase the efficiency of referrals. Referral activities were categorized into those designed to achieve therapeutic outcomes and those designed to acquire material resources. They examined the number of worker contacts with client systems and with collaterals in relation to how frequently client systems kept appointments. They found that the complexity of client-system characteristics was an important factor in predicting whether or not systems kept appointments. In particular, the race of system members and the number and ages of their children appeared to be moderating variables. Differences in keeping appointments were noted as a function of referral type. Keeping appointments was associated with successful referrals for material resources but not for therapeutic resources.

When evaluation of client-system outcomes is undertaken, variation in results should be expected. At least two explanations for failures to achieve outcomes can be identified. First, insufficient or no resources may exist to meet client system needs. Social workers who fail to secure resources for this reason should extend their practice activities to identifying problems in the service delivery system and to changing community conditions.

Second, failures occur when client-system rights are violated by agencies that do not provide resources systems are entitled to. If this occurs, the worker is obligated to engage in case advocacy activities with the client system or, if sufficient numbers of client systems have been denied similar resources, class advocacy is required. Case and class advocacy strategies are discussed in Chapter 6.

Evaluating outcomes is a professional obligation as part of problem solving. Results may show that goals were achieved, and resources that matched client need were obtained. Results also may indicate the need for additional resources or for the advocate role, both of which are professional social work expectations.

The Broker Role and Public Emergencies

The everyday practice of most social workers requires using the broker role strategies. Social workers increasingly are recognizing the special contribution of this role in responding to public emergencies. Such emergencies include floods, airplane crashes, tornadoes, and chemical spills. All social workers are expected to assist as needed in such emergencies (The NASW Code of Ethics, 187). Although such assistance is not limited to the broker role, a major set of activities in response to public emergencies requires connecting persons with needed resources. The remainder of this chapter examines the broker role in public emergencies.

In recent years we have witnessed many events that left people in great need. Floods in Northern California, the eruption of volcanoes in Washington State and throughout the world, airplane crashes and hijackings, hurricanes in the Gulf of Mexico, and nuclear and chemical plant failures have resulted in loss of life. They also disrupted seriously the lives of hundreds of survivors, families, and communities.

Some events were caused by natural forces; others were caused by human error or intentional acts. They all have common features and may be classified as disasters. These features are: (1) the presence of a destructive force; (2) little or no warning of their occurrence and probable effects; and (3) a widely disruptive impact on normal human functioning. Disasters are physical, social, and psychological phenomena about which we should be informed to provide assistance based upon knowledge and skill. The following section summarizes what we know about disasters derived from several different fields of study.

Knowledge About Disasters

Research about disasters has investigated four areas: (1) psychology of individual responses to disasters; (2) consequences of mass behavior in disasters; (3) behavior of formal organizations in disasters; and (4) recovery of communities following disasters. We know something about how people are affected psychologically by disasters from studies of survivors of the Buffalo Creek flood (Gleser and others, 1981), and persons affected by the Mount St. Helens eruption (Shore and others, 1986). Sociologists have studied convergence, evacuation, and looting as mass behavioral events. The American Red Cross has been studied as an example of a voluntary organization designed to provide emergency assistance (Adams, 1970). Communities in South America have been studied by sociologists and political scientists to identify factors that contribute to community recovery (Wright and others, 1979).

In addition to studies of particular disasters, attempts have been made to generate guides for understanding and engaging in action. Shader and Schwartz (1966) cited a model of disasters, which consists of seven phases. These are: the **warning phase** when there is awareness that danger potentially exists; the **threat phase** when danger becomes imminent; the **inventory phase** during which the extent of loss is assessed; the **rescue phase** when persons in danger are located and assisted; the **remedy phase** in which rebuilding and mourning begin; and the **recovery phase** during which persons work to achieve or approximate the level of functioning enjoyed prior to the event. This model is useful as a guide for planning and engaging in change through a disaster cycle.

A second model focuses on variations in disasters. Berren and others (1980) identified five dimensions for classifying disasters, which are important to consider in assessing psychological reactions to disasters. They are: (1) type of disaster; (2) duration of disaster; (3) degree of personal impact; (4) potential for occurrence; (5) control over future impact.

A third way to classify disasters has been suggested from the perspective of survivors (Michael and others, 1985). When established social systems are affected, the event is called a **centripetal** disaster. Two examples are the Buffalo Creek flood and the flood created by the collapse of the Grand Teton Dam. In these, persons affected were members of a defined, functioning social system and geographic location. In contrast, a **centrifugal** event is one that affects persons who happen to be together at the time of impact and scatter following the event. Persons who died in as well as survived the Beverly Hills Supper Club fire were from many different communities in Ohio and Kentucky. Survivors and families of persons on the Delta Air Lines Lockheed L1011, which crashed at Dallas, did not share a common geographic and social locality.

These models and concepts provide ways to generate hypotheses useful in the broker role. For example, if the duration of the warning phase is long and is communicated to potential victims, then the need for material resources may be lessened. If the event is centripetal, service provision locations can be in place for use over some period of time close to the affected area.

PROBLEM IDENTIFICATION AND ANALYSIS

Information derived from disaster models and characteristics guide problem identification. Some examples indicate how they are applied. Most data suggest that when disasters are not thought to have been induced by the survivors, the general public will be sympathetic and resources can be obtained easily. In contrast, most citizens viewed the urban riots of the late 1960s and their resulting social misery as caused by or the fault of rioters and the general public was less willing to provide assistance.

Floods can be caused by sudden and unexpected dam breaks (as in the Grand Teton and Buffalo Creek disasters) or by several days of rain during which rising creeks and rivers provide warning of impending danger. The presence or absence of a warning phase influences the amount of preparation time potential victims have for storage of personal belongings and evacuation. This may reduce loss of life and loss of household and business furnishings.

The length of impact phase is important to identify. Flood waters may remain high for days and prolong dislocation, increase uncertainty, and delay the remedy phase. In contrast, a tornado, plane crash, or explosion may last only seconds or minutes. The size and boundaries of the impact area should be located. Destruction of a total farming valley or mountain hollow have very different effects than the destruction of a few city blocks by an isolated tornado. Erickson (1976) described the psychic and collective trauma that resulted from the extraordinary damage of the Buffalo Creek flood in which a total settlement of people and the geography of their mountain hollow were altered forcibly. These examples suggest variables workers should consider in identifying the problem and its impact.

ASSESSING

Client System Characteristics

Wholes, Parts, and Relationships The extent to which victims and survivors comprised functioning social systems prior to the disaster is assessed. It is important to examine whether the disaster was centripetal or centrifugal in character. When the impact area is a community or some subunit of it, boundaries of that system should be located tentatively. General demographic information about people in the area should be obtained. Broker role tasks will differ when the impact area was settled by farmers with access to personal resources or was settled by tenant or migrant farmers. Low income persons living in poorly constructed homes built on a flood plain can be expected to have great material as well as nonmaterial needs.

System Composition Sex and age factors in system composition are assessed. Some findings indicate that stress scores for adults and children and for males and females differ in the sample of persons who experienced the Buffalo Creek disaster (Green and Gleser, 1978). Higher stress scores of the children and women might be attributed to their relative inactivity following impact when they remained in communal shelters while their husbands and fathers engaged in rescue and recovery operations.

Friedsam (1961) found persons age sixty and over were more likely to react to disaster experiences with a higher sense of deprivation than younger persons. This suggests older persons may be less able to start over again than younger persons. Older persons' definitions of themselves may be associated with personal effects such as pictures, dishes, furnishings, and clothes which had high symbolic meaning. However, Huerta and Horton (1978) replicated Friedsam's work and found no support for his main finding. Similarly, Bell (1978) found that: (1) younger and not older victims scored higher on scales measuring emotionality; (2) younger and older victims did not differ in the expression of anxiety; (3) younger victims reported more stress than aged victims. This research also reported that older victims described their relationships with family, friends, and neighbors as much better following disasters while younger victims reported no change.

These conflicting findings might be explained several ways. First, Huerta and Horton as well as Bell studied groups ranked above the national standard on education and income. Second, published reports of disasters have not examined fatalities as an indicator of special risk. It is possible that studying only survivors ignored fatalities of older persons who could not have been part of the sample interviewed during the recovery phase. Third, findings from retrospective reports of victims up to six months after the event may not be reliable. Finally, the concept of socialization to disaster events was not considered by the researchers. Some areas are more prone to certain types of disasters than others. Older persons in these areas may have survived such events many times while young persons or persons new to an area may have experienced their first disaster.

Some findings from of the 1980 Mount St. Helens eruption were based on a sophisticated research design which included an exposed and control community and reliable and valid measures of mental health consequences (Shore and others, 1986). They found symptoms persisted longer when persons were exposed to the greatest degree of disaster stress. And a relatively higher risk was found for older females with prior health problems who also were concerned about finances. It may not be possible to derive definitive practice principles from this research.

But, workers should be alert that some categories of persons may be more at risk than others.

When an established geographic area has been affected, persons who are usually in decision-making positions need to be located and included in planning for distribution of resources. Although the system's functioning will have been disrupted, the major functions of that system should be supported. However, the creation of new structures on an ad-hoc basis may be needed until equilibrium is regained.

Characteristics of Resource Agencies

Federal and state governmental disaster units are in place to activate resources for rescue operations and provide resources. The American Red Cross sends personnel with authority to provide material resources and to meet immediate food needs of victims and rescue workers. Trained rescue teams are prepared to function in coal mine disasters, plane disasters, explosions, and fires. Citizen groups also respond to disasters according to established plans. These may include such groups as ham radio operators and clubs of four-wheel drive vehicle owners.

When an event is designated officially as a disaster, resources to victims become available for distribution. Resource agencies are primarily of the people-processing type and function to provide basic survival necessities. Some resources are granted only if persons meet certain eligibility requirements; other resources are available uniformly to all victims.

Food and clothing often are transported from outlying areas and collected by religious groups and voluntary agencies. Businesses and industries provide equipment for rescue and reconstruction or provide their unique services modified to meet special needs. For example, milk companies have bottled and transported safe drinking water to affected areas. State social service workers are available for immediate counseling services.

To prepare for providing services, workers should become informed about agency services and resources that can be used following a disaster. The local NASW unit could sponsor a workshop to provide this information or the city or county governmental disaster unit could conduct workshops to prepare us for service.

PLANNING

This step necessarily is compressed in time. Victims and survivors are at risk; the need for resources is critical. Immediate survival needs must be met as quickly as possible, including both material and nonmaterial resources. It is important for persons to talk immediately about their disaster experiences and reactions to them. The planning phase as we generally understand it can be undertaken at a later time when goal setting and contracting can occur for less pressing needs. We should encourage victims to participate actively in these processes.

Descriptions of resource provision after disasters alert us to several special problems. The first is the prevalence of separate application forms from each of the different agencies providing resources. When this occurs, victims have to repeat information at each agency location. One application form, which includes common information needed by all agencies and unique items needed by particular agencies, can be developed. Computers can be used at disaster sites to facilitate collecting and sharing data and decreasing the number of times victims must repeat the same information. When electricity is not available in an area, generators can be used to provide power.

A second problem is long waiting lines for assistance. This is tiring to those who already have suffered much and is damaging to persons who are weakened by preexisting illnesses, disabilities or the frailties of advanced age. It is not difficult to plan a different system. Assigning numbers to families as they enter, and placing chairs for people to sit, visit, and rest are not difficult services to organize.

A third problem is the physical arrangement of a disaster service center. Physical facilities should be designed to ensure victim and helper privacy. Workers should influence the planning and delivery process at all points to try to preserve the dignity of the persons served. Provision for confidentiality of information is one way to uphold this value.

We should find ways to involve ourselves in disaster planning activities to prevent these problems from occurring. In the next section, examples of how social workers have organized themselves to participate in planning and in responding to public emergencies are presented.

ENGAGING IN CHANGE

Broker role strategies identified previously also are applicable to disaster situations. We should be alert to the social network of the community and attempt to maintain its support systems. Usual methods of distributing resources according to how people happen to be in lines may serve to disrupt these networks. For example, in Eastern Kentucky mobile homes were distributed by order of requests and, thus, separated family and kinship systems accustomed to close proximity. The result was destruction of an important source of mutual help and violation of important cultural values and traditions.

In order for us to provide most effectively appropriate services in times of public emergencies, we may need to organize ourselves for this purpose and make known our availability to disaster preparation groups. Several examples suggest how this can be achieved. The work of the Dallas NASW Unit, which responded to the plane crash at the Dallas-Fort Worth International Airport, is described in the NASW *News* (Dallas Disaster Aid, 1985). The article describes how the unit was organized, prepared, and related to the American Red Cross. Its activation plan and services to survivors and families of the victims and to airline officials, nurses, doctors, and clergy are presented. The Kentucky NASW Chapter offered services to families of the Army 101st Airborne Division victims in the Newfoundland plane crash (Milanof, 1986). Rapid response mutual aid groups developed by social workers in New York provide a different example (Michael and others, 1985). This program responds rapidly to stressful events by a specially trained cadre of social workers prepared to meet with groups for crisis counseling.

EVALUATING OUTCOMES

It may not be possible to evaluate results of disaster efforts on a case by case basis. We should participate, however, with others in evaluations that examine the total response effort. Results of these evaluations will influence future planning and preparing for responses to disasters.

Chapter
Six

ADVOCACY ROLE

Social worker activities designed to secure or protect an existing right or entitlement for one or more client systems.

Throughout our history social workers have been outraged at injustice and violations of human dignity. We have acted alone and in concert with others to reverse negative effects of social structures and norms that discriminate against people or devalue them. We have been concerned especially about minority groups, the mentally ill, women, children, and older adults (Khinduka and Coughlin, 1975; Kutchins and Kutchins, 1978; Thursz, 1977). Two roles may be used by social workers to redress social problems and help create a more just society in which the dignity of all members is preserved.

Porter Lee identified two different tasks or functions for social workers on which these roles are based—participating in causes and working to assure that changes resulting from causes are implemented. He observed:

> It seems to be true that once the elimination of evil is accomplished, once the new positive good is established, interest in it is likely to slacken. . . . At the moment of its success, the cause tends to transfer its interest and its responsibility to an administrative unit whose responsibility becomes a function of a well-organized community life (Lee, 1930; 4).

Social causes develop when a significant number of persons, including social workers, identify an urgent social problem and seek to change the conditions that maintain it (Kotler, 1971). Social workers participate in causes to achieve such social reforms by using the social action role. We participate in protecting or implementing social reforms by using the advocate role.

Even though new rights or entitlements often are created when social institutions and norms are changed in response to a cause, much effort is needed to protect and secure these entitlements for the persons for whom they were intended. Implementing changes in social structures and institutions requires adherence to new norms. The purpose of social work advocacy is to insure that new rights and entitlements are protected and secured by requiring social institutions to adhere to these norm changes. Case advocacy is used to secure and protect entitlements of a client system. Class advocacy is used to secure and protect entitlements for a group of client systems that share a common status and problems.

BACKGROUND

A right is a person's power or privilege given in law or nature, which conforms to standards of justice and duty in harmony with moral standards (McKechnie, 1970). To entitle means to give a right or claim. In the 1960s and 1970s cause-oriented social action activities changed social norms and established new legal rights. Discrimination in public accommodations, voting, and housing were declared illegal and new rights were established. Regulations, procedures, and institutions were created to protect these rights for all citizens. Some ways rights are protected include hearings, grievance procedures, appeals, and regulations about distributing federal funds. Institutions charged with responsibility to protect rights include federal and state human rights commissions and equal opportunity offices in government, businesses, and industries. Social workers serve as advocates to help secure these and other rights so that they are granted fairly and equitably. Therefore, advocacy emphasizes that individuals and organizations must adhere to certain social norms. They must play by the rules.

Social work's concern with protecting rights and entitlements was renewed and extended during and after the civil rights movement and War on Poverty. We recognized that access to entitlements was not assured when norms were changed and new rights established. Each time a new entitlement theoretically was available, effort was required to assure it actually was obtained. This concern was legitimated by NASW in its statement on advocacy and in the Code of Ethics (Ad Hoc Committee, 1969).

Concurrently, many citizens' rights movements developed in society. Consumers' rights were protected in some states by law; hospital patients' bills of rights were formalized to specify expectations about medical and mental health care; rights of children were identified in the 1970 White House Conference on Children. When each was established, advocates were needed to make them into realities. Social workers, lawyers, patients' representatives, teachers, psychologists, physicians, and other activists adopted the term "advocacy" to describe how rights were secured and protected. Certain rights also exist for persons who use some social systems: clients of public social services, children in public school, students in higher education, clients in mental health systems, and prisoners in the criminal justice system (see, for example, Annas, 1975; Ennis, 1973; National Senior Citizen's Law Center, 1984).

The term advocacy became very popular. It was used so widely and in so many different ways, it came to mean almost anything one did to assist and/or speak for another. Some used it to mean social reform as well as protecting existing rights. Others meant any activity where social workers were not neutral about client systems but took a system's side. Still others used it to distinguish what was done for a group of client systems from what was done for one client system. The term advocacy is used in this book to identify a set of social worker activities designed to achieve the goal of securing and protecting *existing* rights and entitlements. Social action to establish *new* rights and entitlements is discussed in Chapter 7.

The protection of rights continues to be an important professional activity, which permits social workers to express concern for relationships between individuals and social institutions (Curriculum Policy, 1982). Since newly changed norms are not accepted universally and efforts to modify or withdraw rights are constant threats, social workers must be knowledgeable, committed, and alert to the need for advocacy.

Case Advocacy Practice

Case advocacy is selected when the worker's assessment shows that a client system's entitlement or right needs to be secured or protected. Client systems are entitled to life necessities, protection, and opportunities for growth and development. Entitlements are established in three ways. First, some rights are established in *law*. Second, some are established in an organization's *policies*. Third, rights are established in an *interpretation* of an organization's policies. Rights differ in the extent to which they affect all persons in a given jurisdiction. Legal rights are universal for a jurisdiction while policies and interpretations are less universal and entitle only those persons who receive service from those organizations.

PROBLEM IDENTIFICATION AND ASSESSMENT

This problem-solving step requires making a determination of the nature and source of the problem including client-system and adversary characteristics.

Nature and Location of Problem

The Entitlement The worker determines specifically what the client system is entitled to and where the problem in securing it is located. The worker determines whether the entitlement is a legal right, a right under agency policy, or a right in an interpretation of policy. The worker answers the question, where in the system is failure to provide and protect the entitlement located?

Public Law 94-142 includes specific rights of parents of exceptional children. In working with a client system that includes such a child, the worker determines which of these rights has not been made available. If he or she learns the parents do not know about the child's educational program, the worker asks whether or not the parents were invited (as the law requires) to attend an educational planning meeting. While parents are not required to attend such meetings, they have the right to do so and the school system must notify them of the meeting set at a convenient time and place. The worker may discover that the means of notification was ineffective or worded in such a way as to appear threatening.

If the parents were not notified, the worker determines the source of this failure. Most agencies are structured so that activities can be monitored and accountability established. The worker explores how the school system is structured and who has responsibility for notification. In some instances failure to notify parents may be inadvertent. In others, it results from an ineffective administrative structure. In still others, it may be a deliberate failure to follow the law. The worker's assessment of the nature and location of the problem identifies what the entitlement is and where the failure to provide it originates.

Assessing the nature and location of the entitlement problem is similar in situations where the right exists as an agency policy. Where an administrative policy provides for a hearing about a system's complaint, procedures exist for hearings. The worker assesses whether the client system knows about the right and knows how to request a hearing.

Failure to know about a right may result when an agency fails to inform all clients about a policy and procedure. It may result from a client system's inability to understand information provided it either because information was presented in a way or at a time when it could not be understood or because of limits on comprehension (Hagen, 1983). Even though policies and procedures for hearings exist, agency personnel may have been instructed not to provide this information. This occurs when agencies are understaffed and underfunded or when administrators do not want complaints registered about services.

The worker determines who controls the entitlement. To do so, the worker needs to know the organization's structure, lines of authority, and how work is divided, assigned, and monitored. Often the immediate work supervisor monitors and controls a staff member's work. But where supervisors have little discretion over work assignments and are accountable for limited portions of the work of their subordinates, authority for an entitlement may be elsewhere in the organization. The worker needs to be familiar personally with staff who provide services and knowledgeable about the structure of these agencies: how they operate, what procedures are used, how staff groups are organized, the authority in supervision and management, and who ultimately controls controversial decisions.

This assessment should state: (1) the specific entitlement, (2) the source of the entitlement in law, policy, or procedure, (3) where failure to provide or protect the right originates, (4) why the entitlement has not been provided, and (5) who controls the entitlement.

Nature of Adversary

The worker makes an assessment of the adversary to assist in change strategy selection. This assessment describes the adversary's characteristics and those of the system in which she or he works. The adversary is a specific person or group of persons who control decisions about the entitlement within the organization. Several factors are examined to determine an adversary's strengths and the supports and constraints of his or her organization.

Problem Vulnerability The worker assesses how vulnerable the adversary is with respect to the entitlement. If failure to provide it is an illegal act, the adversary may be highly vulnerable to public disclosure and/or legal sanction. Vulnerability results when the agency and adversary fail to provide an entitlement established in law. Agencies that accept Title XX funds are required to comply with a 1974 amendment to the Social Security Act for appeals and hearings on complaints from clients who have been denied service because of race. If the assessment shows a reasonable likelihood that such discrimination occurred, the adversary may be highly vulnerable to public disclosure or to disclosure to the Department of Health and Human Services, which provides Title XX funds. If the entitlement problem cannot be determined precisely or can only be inferred as an interpretation of policies, the adversary is much less vulnerable to advocacy actions.

This part of the assessment estimates the extent of risk to the adversary from advocacy activities. Risks may be personal and organizational, but the worker should not emphasize personal risks and underestimate organizational risks. The worker does not focus only on personal risk to adversaries in disclosing illegal or improper actions to supervisors. Simply getting an adversary in trouble with a supervisor may not result in the desired outcome. An assessment of risks to the organization as a whole may provide more firm bases for worker action.

Power and Authority The worker assesses the amount and source of an adversary's power and authority. Some questions to consider are: (1) What is the adversary's status? (2) Where does his or her power and authority originate? Does it come from organizational position, community position, and/or overlapping and related positions? (3) How much weight is given to an adversary's statements and decisions within the organization, in the community, and in related organizations? (4) What is the adversary's capacity to influence important others? Even when an adversary has high status, power, and authority, it should not be assumed that difficulties in the advocacy process will be increased. Such persons may not be threatened by complaints or conflicts but work to resolve them quickly.

Usual Response to Conflict The worker examines how an adversary usually responds to complaints, conflicts, and adversarial actions. Some adversaries see any complaint in conflict terms. Others distinguish among complaints based on their sources. Conflicts that originate from peers rather than client systems may be easier for some adversaries to confront; the reverse may be true for others. How an adversary responded to previous conflicts and experiences other client systems have had with the adversary may be useful information. While such information does not always predict future responses to conflict, it assists in estimating the adversary's probable reaction to the current issue.

What Convinces the Adversary? Adversaries are convinced in different ways. Two considerations are the types of documentation that can convince and the types of presentations that convince. Some adversaries respond to a telephone call on the client system's behalf. Others respond to specific written documentation. The worker determines what alternative types of documentation will be acceptable if the usual types are not available. The worker needs to be creative, particularly when client systems do not fit traditional patterns or where the documentation process is complicated.

A second consideration is how to present documentation. Some studies (Hagen, 1983; Briar, 1966; Handler, 1969) show that where client systems are accompanied by a representative, they have a greater chance of effective presentations and successful outcomes than when they are unaccompanied. The worker explores the process to be used, the agency's record with this process, and what is known about client system self-representation versus outside representation. Hagen (1983) showed that procedural safeguards in welfare hearings have serious limitations when client systems represent themselves.

Attitudes Toward Clients Often it is possible to anticipate attitudes the agency staff will display toward and expect of client systems. Such attitudes may affect how a client system will be stereotyped when entitlements are discussed. Problematic attitudes are those that stereotype unmarried parents, alcoholic persons, the mentally ill, and retarded persons, for example. Some staff members may view certain client systems as trouble makers who are unmotivated and unwilling to be helped.

Shared Goals and Objectives The worker estimates the extent to which an adversary shares client-system's goals and objectives. Where goals are shared, it may be easier to assist the system to obtain an entitlement. If goals are not shared, resolving the problem may be more difficult. Adversaries may state similar goals but privately not share them. They may be constrained by their organizations about procedures or processes to use in solving complaints even when they share similar goals.

Assessing the adversary and his or her organization provides information about possible supports to and constraints on advocacy strategies. The assessment tells us what the adversary is like, how she or he usually responds to conflict and this type of client system in particular, how he or she is supported and constrained in the agency, and the power and authority she or he has to use on the client system's behalf.

Client-System Characteristics

Vulnerability The worker needs to assess how vulnerable the client system is in terms of its characteristics and in respect to the immediate entitlement problem. We act quickly and take more responsibility to solve problems where high vulnerability exists. If any combination of system characteristics shows the system needs immediate protection or is likely to be at risk if an entitlement is delayed, the worker acts immediately. Abandoned, neglected, and abused persons; the very young and infirm aged; and persons with serious health or mental health impairments are among those at most immediate risk and highly vulnerable. Some minority group members are at special risk because of lack of services, employment, and other entitlements.

Client-system vulnerability is related to the nature of the entitlement. Those that deal with basic life necessities or protection make the client system more vulnerable even if other risks do not exist in the system. Rights to growth and development opportunities may not result in immediate vulnerability but may result in higher vulnerability later.

Client-System Resources The worker assesses resources the client system can use in securing entitlements. Knowledge of such resources helps us select strategies and decide how actively we involve ourselves in change processes. Several factors usually are examined.

The worker determines the extent to which system members can present the entitlement case clearly and articulately. Many, but not all system members, have limited verbal skills or limited experience in identifying problems, wishes, and choices. Some are retarded persons; others have speech difficulties; others are children and impaired elderly persons.

We are concerned about how system members' appearance may affect an adversary. Not all adversaries share our tolerance for differences and it is useful to estimate what impression the system will make on an intolerant or inexperienced adversary who does not accept deviations from accepted norms or who is repelled by certain physical appearances. This evaluation assists the worker to select a strategy and estimate the extent to which system members confront the adversary.

Since advocacy requires adversarial activities, the worker assesses how system members may react in stressful situations. Is it likely that system members can present themselves in a coherent, systematic manner? If not, strategy selection will need to take this factor into account.

Client systems' members vary in the degree to which previous experiences have confirmed self-respect and confidence in their own problem-solving skills.

Some system members have low levels of self-respect and little confidence in their ability to act in their own interest. Others have high levels of self-respect and confidence in their ability to resolve difficult problems. This variable is assessed separately from educational level, verbal skills, and stability since it is not necessarily correlated with these. Where self-respect and confidence are low, system members may be intimidated easily, and workers will need to be more actively involved.

Two factors are considered in assessing system members' intelligence—basic ability to comprehend what is happening and level of social skill. Some highly intelligent persons may not have social skills that facilitate interaction in problem solving. Others with limited basic ability have moderately high social comprehension and skill that facilitate interaction and problem solving. Both types of intelligence may affect the relationship between client system and adversary. Where both are low, the worker's involvement will be more direct and intense.

Client systems vary with respect to their commitment to change in pursuing entitlements. Since adversarial processes may involve risks to client systems, the worker pays particular attention to whether and how risk taking has been evaluated by the system when it selects goals and objectives.

When the social worker has evaluated all these factors, an assessment of client system is made. This statement presents facts, relationships among facts, and the worker's estimate of system vulnerability and resources to participate in an adversarial process.

PLANNING AND ENGAGING IN CHANGE

Advocacy literature provides few typologies of change strategies for case advocacy. Sosin and Caulum (1983) suggest a two-step planning process based on assessment of the adversarial context and the strategy that fits this context. Strategies are characterized, following Gamson (1975), as coercive, utilitarian, and normative. However, these concepts do not account for the specific entitlement problem, client-system vulnerability, or the advocate's power and resources.

Davidson and Rappaport (1978) classify strategies as positive, neutral, and negative based on an advocate's probable effect on the adversary. Laue's (1978) typology characterizes roles and practice orientations but omits attention to strategy. Chin and Benne's (1969) power-coercive strategies are associated with social reform, but may be adapted to case advocacy.

Advocacy strategies are conceptualized here on a conflict continuum based on two related variables: the amount of change sought, and the degree to which advocates and client systems share similar goals with their adversaries. These variables assist social workers to identify five important aspects of advocacy: (1) practice outcomes; (2) relationships expected between client system and adversary; (3) amounts or degrees of conflict; (4) types of power needed by advocates; and (5) types of risks advocate and client systems may experience.

Two types of change can be identified. First, a minimal change or outcome is one that seeks to obtain an existing right to which the system clearly is eligible, using well-established procedures. For example, welfare fair hearings are existing rights for certain groups of welfare recipients. Second, a fundamental change is one that seeks to establish new and different interpretations, policies, or procedures or to extend these to members of a particular client group not covered previously.

Two types of goal sharing can be identified. First, advocacy occurs in situations where adversaries and client systems share similar objectives. Second, advocacy occurs where adversaries share no objectives with client systems. Between these extremes is some sharing or agreement about outcome objectives but disagreement about instrumental and facilitative objectives.

A schema combining these two variables and the strategies they yield is shown below:

Nature of Change Sought by Advocate

	MINIMAL	FUNDAMENTAL
Shared Goals	Problem solving Educating Persuading	Negotiating Bargaining
Goals not Shared	Negotiating Bargaining	Pressure tactics

Shared Goals and Minimal Change Outcome Strategies

Three strategies are appropriate where changes are minimal and goals are shared. Each assumes that relatively little conflict will exist in these situations. It is expected advocates will need little or moderate amounts of power since the strategies are based on the use of information in personal relations with adversaries.

Problem Solving This traditional social work strategy involves sorting out a problem, making an assessment, and changing something. Adversaries participate in and support this process. Little or no confrontation between advocate and adversary occurs since they agree about goals and the adversary is not required to make any significant change in policies or procedures or their interpretations.

Problem solving is appropriate where failure to provide an entitlement resulted from a misunderstanding or inadvertant adversary action. It is not sufficiently powerful where adversaries and client systems share ultimate goals but disagree on instrumental objectives. Where an adversary and system share the goal of providing disaster relief, for example, but disagree about appropriate and sufficient claims documentation, a different strategy is needed.

Educating This strategy is used when most goals are shared but differences exist about the means to achieve them or about policy interpretations and procedures. While conflict is expected, the advocate has determined that the adversary is likely to respond favorably to new information or alternative interpretations of the client system or the entitlement. This strategy relies on the power of ideas and information as the source for change and the advocate either knows more than the adversary or uses information differently.

Persuading A strategy involving more conflict and greater pressure on the adversary is needed as fewer goals are shared or greater disagreement exists about instrumental objectives or policy interpretations. The advocate uses new or different information combined with some degree of personal pressure on the adversary. Such pressure might involve the threat of more highly conflictual strategies or of contacts with supervisors to have the adversaries' actions reversed.

Shared Goals and Fundamental Change Outcome Strategies

Two strategies are appropriate where advocates and adversaries share goals but the outcome sought requires fundamental change on the adversary's part or in his or her organization. The adversary protects existing procedures, policies, or interpretations and is expected to resist the advocate's change efforts. The level of conflict is high and risks may be involved for the client system and advocate. The advocate attempts to preserve shared goals while obtaining a fundamental change. She or he recognizes conflict but attempts to limit it to the outcome arena while continually affirming the value of whatever part of the process is shared. Thus, the advocate does not choose the most conflictual strategy.

Negotiating The advocate identifies and presents potential agreements to the adversary which may not be all the client system sought. The advocate needs considerable power derived from position and status or from the nature of the entitlement itself. Although conflict is inherent in this strategy, it is assumed that some type of compromise is possible. Elements of negotiation for the mediator role are described more fully in Chapter 10.

Bargaining This strategy assumes the advocate will have to give up or exchange something in order to gain something else for the client system. The threat is stronger in bargaining than in negotiating. The advocate needs something to exchange that is potent enough to induce the adversary to change and achieve the outcome sought.

Goals not Shared and Minimal Change Outcome Strategies

Negotiating and bargaining strategies also are appropriate when goals are not shared but the outcomes require little or no change on the part of the adversary. The advocate emphasizes that since minimal change is required, goals can be negotiated and bargained about.

Both strategies as used in this advocacy condition require advocates to have something to negotiate about or to bargain with. The advocate must determine whether or not such flexibility exists for the client system and, if so, what system members choose to use in bargaining or negotiating. To the extent system members can make such choices, the advocate must respect their decisions since each strategy may involve giving something away or exchanging one outcome for another. Occasionally the exchange involves the advocate and not the client system so that the advocate gives up something.

Goals not Shared and Fundamental Change Outcome Strategies

This adversarial situation involves the highest level of conflict and risk taking for the client system and advocate. Since there may be little or nothing about which advocates and adversaries agree, the advocate must use the most powerful strategy available and be prepared for the adversary to act in similar ways. Conflict is escalated and advocates often commit or use resources they may need in subsequent advocacy situations. Thus, advocates should examine how and when to expend their capital. These strategies often are referred to as pressure tactics and involve threats to exert pressure on the adversary and actual use of the pressure involved in threats.

Threat of Disclosure The advocate threatens to disclose the entitlement problem to the general public, to an affiliated agency, and/or to an administrative level within the organization. The advocate must be prepared to follow the threat with actual disclosure if the threat is not sufficient to achieve the outcome. An empty threat may be worse than no threat at all! The advocate must estimate what disclosure and to whom constitutes sufficient coercion to bring change about.

Disclosure The advocate makes a public disclosure of the entitlement problem. Disclosure might be to the media or to an affiliated agency which can bring pressure to bear on the adversary or his or her agency. The means of disclosure highlights the client system's plight and maximizes the impact of public response and sympathy. Since disclosure often makes the system's name and problem public information, system members must not only agree to this strategy (as to any other), but must be informed carefully about the notoriety that may result. A range of risks the system may incur should be reviewed thoroughly and examined carefully before a decision is made to use this strategy.

Administrative Hearings The advocate pressures adversaries for favorable decisions by securing administrative hearings. Hearings may be held in the agency where the entitlement problem exists or in other agencies that have some control over the first agency's actions or funding. The advocate must understand what policies and procedures to use, how to prepare for the hearing, and what data will be needed to support the client system. It is important to discover whether legal representation is permissible, whether the system wishes legal representation if permissible, and how legal representation usually affects outcomes. Recent literature suggests alternatives to adversarial proceedings with less emphasis on conflict strategies (Hagen, 1983; Sunley, 1983). These alternatives are provided for in less conflictual strategies outlined above. Some systems will not obtain entitlements without conflict and some targets must be recognized as adversaries.

Legal Action A strategy of final resort is legal action. While this strategy is not chosen often in routine social work advocacy, recent advances in the patients' rights movement indicates legal action may be required to obtain and protect some entitlements. Most legal action is on behalf of one or more specific systems as representatives of a class in class advocacy. However, legal action also may be used as a strategy in case advocacy.

Class Advocacy Practice

Most case advocacy practice is related closely to class advocacy. It is the unusual case situation which does not highlight problems in other cases as well. It is a short step from the issues in one entitlement to examining whether or not other systems have similar problems. Barozzi and others (1982) noted the close connection between case and class advocacy and suggested workers need to keep records that make it possible to plan class advocacy. It is inefficient to continue a series of case advocacy interventions when records show that additional similar cases probably will occur in the future.

The need for class advocacy may become known in at least two ways. First, agency records may document violations of entitlements in a number of cases. Second, the need for class advocacy may develop when the social worker recognizes that the particular characteristics of one system may be unique in one agency but could not possibly apply only to one client system. When a worker in a medical hospital, for example, cannot locate a suitable facility that will accept a severely chronically mentally ill patient who requires skilled nursing care for a medical problem, this is not likely to be a singular event even though there is only one such case in the hospital. The rights of all these persons to appropriate care is denied. Class advocacy is a set of social worker activities required to protect rights of a group or class of persons most of whom are not known personally to the worker.

Our Code of Ethics (The NASW Code of Ethics, 1980) requires us to act to prevent practices that are inhumane or discriminatory against any person or group of persons and not to engage in any action that violates or diminishes the civil or legal rights of clients. It is clear that social workers have a professional responsibility to engage in class advocacy.

Although much social work class advocacy is on behalf of identifiable client groups, where the goal is to protect and obtain entitlements, we also work to protect existing entitlements in a more general sense. Recent events show that federal voting rights and affirmative action entitlements may be abrogated by administrative regulations or by administrative and legal interpretations. Social workers often participate in political, professional, and community groups to advocate for maintaining and protecting significant existing entitlements.

PROBLEM IDENTIFICATION AND ASSESSMENT

Problem identification and assessment in class and case advocacy differ little. Case advocacy activities in assessing the nature and location of the problem apply in class advocacy. An additional class advocacy task is to identify the extent of the problem.

Where class advocacy is on behalf of agency client systems, agency records are used to determine the extent of need. Agencies should have record keeping systems that provide reliable and uniform information, including nature of entitlement issues, adversaries' agencies, client system characteristics, case advocacy activities and outcomes (if any), and the number of client systems that have entitlement problems. With such an information system, advocacy activities can be recognized formally and resources made available to carry them out. This permits recognition of advocacy at the policy-making level within and outside the agency.

When the entitlement problem is not limited to client systems in one agency, different activities are required to estimate the problem's extent. A community or state task force may be needed to determine need. The extent of the problem also may be determined by an existing group whose goals are compatible with the rights and entitlement issue or by groups generally concerned about the particular client group. Some of these include the Human Rights Commissions, NAACP, Parents of Mentally Retarded Children, and Gray Panthers.

Although exceptions occur, most classes of clients who need social work advocates are those most vulnerable in society, who have a limited capacity to engage in activities on their own behalf. If any particular systems of the class are known, the worker assesses their vulnerability and capacity to insure their rights to self-determination, to participate in change, and to confidentiality.

Activities of workers in class advocacy require knowledge and skill in work with groups. This requirement begins in assessment and continues throughout problem solving. Content about practice with groups discussed in this section focuses on task groups. Additional content which may be relevant is presented in Chapter 7 on social action.

Knowledge and Activities for Assessing Task Groups

Groups of persons (who may or may not benefit directly from the results of their efforts) engage in activities to secure and protect entitlements. These groups are referred to by Pincus and Minahan (1973) as the action system. The action system's composition characteristics, the entitlement issue, and the social context within which they function may differ, but they are like all tasks groups in fundamental ways. The most essential characteristics are discussed below.

Group Purpose A group's purpose is the reasons it exists. Statements of purposes and how these are understood by group members may be general and abstract or specific and concrete. The worker assesses purpose by reading a group's written materials (constitution or mission statement) and by listening to members describe their perceptions of purpose.

If a group is formed only for the purpose of a specific class advocacy activity, the worker assesses the extent to which members understand and accept this purpose. Where groups have purposes beyond a specific class advocacy task, the worker assesses the connection between the advocacy task and the group's general purpose. In both instances, the worker also assesses the extent of commitment to class advocacy issues.

Clarity about group purpose is essential for a group's subsequent functioning. Social workers clarify purposes to insure understanding of and acceptance and commitment to the action system's purposes. They also continually assess this area as members engage in their work.

Group Size and Resources The number of members in a group influences all other aspects of its functioning. The larger the group, the more rules and procedures are needed to ensure orderly participation and to reach decisions. In large groups, leadership positions usually are prescribed; persons who hold them are elected by members or appointed by some outside person or group. In smaller groups, leadership positions may or may not be fixed. Positions are formed when members identify needs or when members assume them as work proceeds.

Each member brings resources to the group such as knowledge, skill, community position, and money. Larger groups have more resources than smaller ones. Each member has expectations and demands—for time to speak, recognition, and the chance to contribute to the group's process and outcomes. Social workers assess the resources and demands of group members and try to ensure that they are utilized and met.

Decision-making Styles Established groups have adopted ways to reach decisions. Some groups decide by majority rule where conflict is governed by rules of order such as parliamentary procedures to ensure orderly communication and problem solving. Although this form is most suited to large groups, it also is utilized by small groups.

Other groups use a consensus process to identify the maximum area of common agreement. A consensus process results in decisions supported by all members as their best effort at a given time. This process has been used by large groups, but it is best suited to small groups because of the time it requires to ensure participation of all members. Although decisions by consensus philosophically is attractive to social workers, a worker should consider its value in relation to majority rule and examine the tasks best suited to each style (Gentry, 1982).

History, Tradition, Rituals, Norms Groups create their own history, habitual ways of working, stylized repetitive activities, and standards for member behavior. Each is assessed in any group not formed specifically for class advocacy. Past successes or failures at similar tasks influence members' expectations about new advocacy tasks. Each area is analyzed for its usefulness in advocacy, and consideration is given to altering traditions, rituals, and norms that are not useful. Analysis of past successes and failures may provide insight useful for the current task. Newly formed groups create their own traditions, rituals, and norms. Workers should be observant of these areas and assess their functional nature. The test of each is the extent to which a group's patterned behaviors support achieving its advocacy goal.

PLANNING AND ENGAGING IN CHANGE

Case advocacy strategies also are used in class advocacy. However, if an action system participates in change, further knowledge about groups is needed.

Knowledge about Groups at Work

Groups engage in problem solving in sequential patterns. These patterns occur in three phases—orientation, evaluation, and control. Early in problem solving, group members communicate to identify and understand the problem. Later communications are about evaluating the problem. Finally, communications are about controlling the problem—identifying and discussing strategies for solutions (Bales, 1950).

In assisting action systems to engage in advocacy, the worker assesses group stage and assists members to assess and discuss the problem fully, evaluate it carefully, and explore strategies to solve it. If the group has time constraints, it is helpful to structure each session to include all three phases. If time is not an issue, each session can be focused on a single phase or part of a phase.

A worker participates in sessions by asking questions, giving information, and assisting the group to evaluate its progress. Special attention is given to helping the group understand advocacy strategies and what each will require the group to do (Toseland and Rivas, 1984).

It is important for action systems to establish communication patterns in problem solving, which help maintain a dynamic equilibrium (Bales, 1950). Although instrumental activities predominate in task groups, socioemotional acts are necessary for effective group functioning. The worker assesses both and assists the group to achieve a balance between them which promotes the group's problem-solving purpose.

Group Participation in the Change Process Where it is important for an action system to participate in the change effort, the worker assists the group to implement the strategy it chooses. If threat of disclosure is chosen, the group decides specifically what threat will be made and how it will be made. Insufficient attention to detail at this crucial point often diminishes the group's effectiveness.

The group decides who its spokesperson will be. This person may or may not be an official leader, but one who holds a position of influence in the community or one least vulnerable to public scrutiny. An agreement should be reached about what information will be made public. All members should participate in deciding, to reduce the possibility of member defections and prevent confusing messages to the public. When specific client systems are known to (or are members or relatives of) group members, the group must consider how to protect confidentiality and assure anonymity.

As engaging in change proceeds, the group should continue to meet regularly to keep all members informed and to make decisions. A tendency to turn the work over to a few should be avoided. Regular meetings permit changing strategies in an orderly way and help avoid crises or emergencies.

The change process may be short or extend over months during which groups need to be sustained. The worker considers risks that action systems face in advocacy, including those that are socioeconomic, that either may heighten group cohesion or separate members from each other and threaten goal achievement. Some useful tactics are pep talks, social occasions, use of humor, and identifying small but essential achievements to assure members they are making progress. The "care and feeding" of action systems is a critical worker task in class advocacy.

EVALUATING OUTCOMES IN CASE AND CLASS ADVOCACY

The advocate evaluates the outcome with the client or action system. Specific outcome statements must be made in the planning stage, which identify system outcomes rather than worker methods or processes. An outcome might be: The client system will receive Social Security benefits; or damages will be paid to a class of persons for past hiring discrimination. Outcomes would *not* be: A hearing will be held for the client system's complaint or bargaining will be used on the system's behalf or system members will gain self-esteem. Specific outcome statements make it possible to determine whether or not the change effort was successful by comparing the outcome obtained with the outcome sought. This evaluation can be used to make tentative inferences about the utility of strategies in particular types of adversarial situations.

The worker monitors other factors in advocacy cases. These include unintended consequences, information about adversaries to use in future advocacy, and other problems with the service delivery system not known previously. The advocate may note how the client or action system participated in and learned from advocacy. Advocates may monitor a system's experiences and how these relate to what was known about it earlier. At no time, however, should the system's characteristics (such as self-esteem) be the main foci since the central issue is obtaining and/or protecting entitlements. System members often learn new skills and gain self-confidence from obtaining an entitlement. This unintended positive outcome is welcomed even though it is not the central outcome objective.

Where the actual outcome is not consistent with the outcome sought, advocates and the client or action system reconsider objectives and strategies. If the problem and assessment remain essentially unchanged except for failure of the strategy to achieve the goal, a more highly confrontational strategy may be selected after risks are re-examined.

GENERAL PRACTICE PRINCIPLES

Several practice principles are identified, which serve as guides in planning and engaging in advocacy. These derive from the profession's values as well as special characteristics of the advocate role. First, the client or action system's right to determine goals and methods should be respected and protected. Although advocates assist in selecting goals, they should not substitute personal interests for the client or action system's choices and best interests.

Self-determination issues are complex and not easily solved in advocacy. Schultz (1982) argued that informed consent in refusing psychiatric treatment is not based constitutionally in either the right to privacy or due process clauses but is established by courts and state legislatures to protect a social policy interest. Others interpret this right much more broadly. The advocate who wishes to protect this right for a case or class often must protect the community's rights as well as the rights of a specific system. Pearlman and Edwards (1982) suggested ways this can be done.

Second, risk taking is a critical problem in advocacy. Risks exist for clients, action systems, and advocates, which range from failure to achieve successful outcomes to increased resistance and negative reaction in the adversary system. The first priority is a successful outcome for the immediate system. However, advocates must anticipate unintended consequences such as future negative reactions to this and other client systems. The worker may face personal risks such as threats to employment or in finding jobs in the future (Freedman, 1971).

Worker risks are lessened if supports exist in her or his agency for vigorous pursuit of client rights in both internal and external advocacy. Risks are lessened when agency positions exist specifically for advocates. Targum and others (1982) show that establishing such positions has a significant positive effect on the use of psychiatric treatment in a private hospital. Barozzi and others (1982) indicate the need to legitimate advocacy activities and to integrate them into the structure of other agency services.

Advocates examine risks by asking: (1) Who is likely to experience risk—advocate or client system or both? (2) How much and what kinds of risks might occur? (3) What is the source of anticipated risks? (4) How much risk is too much? (5) What supports may act as countervailing forces to anticipated risks? (6) Are anticipated risks offset by anticipated gains? (7) How are risk and likelihood of success related to strategies chosen?

Third, advocates usually select the least confrontational strategy that fits the situation first and move to more conflictual strategies if needed. If client systems and adversaries share goals and minimal change is sought, there is no point choosing a bargaining strategy first. Using pressure tactics escalates the conflict and need not be used unless no other alternative has worked or seems likely to be effective.

Fourth, advocates must understand the sources and nature of their power. As an advocate's power increases, the need for highly confrontational strategies and personal risk decrease. Sources of power are personal, reputational, and situational. Personal power originates in knowledge, persuasive capacity, and precise assessments of adversarial situations. Reputational power derives from an advocate's record of honesty, integrity, concern for client systems over self-interest, and past achievements. Situational power comes from the advocate's position and status and agency supports for advocacy including the power of an action system in class advocacy. While we are comforted by the rightness of the cause, adversaries do not change for this reason.

SUMMARY

Case and class advocacy are needed to protect and secure entitlements for many systems in contemporary society. Although this role's popularity ebbs and flows depending upon prevailing social conditions and supports, all social workers should be prepared to use appropriate advocacy strategies whenever and wherever the need occurs.

Chapter
Seven

SOCIAL ACTION ROLE

Social worker activities designed to establish new entitlements for client systems or potential client systems.

Social work's Code of Ethics specifically requires us to prevent and eliminate discrimination, ensure that all persons have access to needed resources, services, and opportunities; encourage respect for diversity of cultures in our society; work for changes in policies and laws to improve social conditions and promote social justice (The NASW Code of Ethics). These are awesome tasks! Our foremothers' and forefathers' legacy to contemporary practice is not limited to concern only for personal or interpersonal problems. Social work's vision of a more just society includes glimpses of successive utopias in which society supports each person and the good of all persons (Mannheim, 1936). We seek to redress inequities and injustices and to join and lead crusades through social action as persons with strong ideological positions and a desire to reform society itself (Klein, 1968).

Social workers do not own social action but we have been an important part of it and have helped shape it. Some workers hold full-time positions with responsibility for altering social conditions. Others engage in social action as a part of direct service or administrative work. We influence legislation at the national and state levels through NASW.

WHAT IS SOCIAL ACTION?

Social action is defined as a set of social worker activities that aims to establish *new* rights and entitlements as distinguished from advocacy that protects and secures *existing* rights. Two concepts—social problem and cause—identify the basis for social action. A social problem is a specific condition in society which is viewed apprehensively or distastefully by some of its members and which is thought to be susceptible to mitigation or elimination through collective effort (Kotler, 1971). Potential beneficiaries of and/or their representatives identify the conditions as problematic. A majority of society's members need not agree that certain conditions constitute a problem nor does the problem need to be widespread in society in order to take action to bring about change. A *social* problem, however, always suggests that collective action is needed for change. Although there are occasional success stories of single-handed persistence and determination, which achieve social goals, these are few in number. Most social problems require collective action to achieve change.

The term collective action may sound dispassionate—an idea without the fervor, zeal, emotionalism, and ideals usually associated with social action. Nevertheless, social workers are concerned about resource distribution, power allocation, human dignity, and protecting the most vulnerable. We have translated these concerns into collective actions that helped establish new rights: rape victims' rights to judicial procedures with dignity; children's and older adults' rights to be free from abuse; women's rights to make decisions about their own bodies; citizens' rights to be protected from drunk drivers; mountain people's rights to protect their land from strip mining; industrial workers' rights to breathe unpolluted air.

Obtaining these rights promoted human dignity and transformed a part of our social order. None was obtained without struggle and tremendous resources and commitment by some groups to achieve them. These rights are now laws, regulations, and policies. They are imbedded in programs and services administered by various social institutions whose performance we monitor as advocates. But we know that other rights still must be established to achieve a just society. We still have causes.

Types of Causes

Our social objectives may be classified as revolutionary, protest, and helping causes (Kotler, 1971). Revolutionary causes seek to eliminate institutions that contribute to or maintain a social problem. Causes of this type require fundamental alteration of societal values. The goals of the women's movement are revolutionary—altering accepted traditions and norms about the roles of women and men in society. The civil rights movement of the 1960s was revolutionary. The goals of gay and lesbian movements are revolutionary. Such causes are value-oriented movements that challenge society's fundamental philosophy, assumptions, and goals (Smelser, 1962).

A second category is the protest cause, which aims to discipline institutions that contribute to social problems. Industries and factories that pollute the air are targets for change in protest causes. The criminal justice and legislative systems are targets for removing drunk drivers from the roads. The Nuclear Regulatory

Agency is a target for protest when failed nuclear power plants are restarted. The Environmental Protection Agency is the target for protest to protect water and remove dangerous wastes. Each of these social institutions is perceived as contributing to a social problem and is the object of protests.

Social workers probably are most familiar with helping causes. These seek to assist victims of social problems by offering programs and services to assist actual or potential victims. Spouse abuse shelters and rape crisis centers are programs which resulted from helping causes. Such programs establish new entitlements for social victims and are outcomes of collective social action.

PROBLEM IDENTIFICATION AND ASSESSMENT

Nature and Location of the Problem

The purpose of problem identification and assessment is to discover how big a social problem is, whom it affects, and where it originates. Because our social objectives and causes potentially include any problem that diminishes human survival and dignity, social work is concerned about many different entitlements. A first step is to discover the ways a group of persons share common characteristics and conditions that are dysfunctional. We ask what these conditions are and how they affect a specific group of people.

Systematic fact finding using one or more needs assessment techniques assists us to define and locate the problem. These techniques include asking key informants, organizing community forums, determining rates under treatment in other communities, identifying existing standardized data, and engaging in formal surveys (Rossi and Freeman, 1985). The technique chosen should meet two criteria. First, it should assist us to involve others in recognizing the problem. Second, it should provide data that are reliable and valid.

Careful documentation of the problem's effects should be made. In some instances, this may be relatively easy to estimate. Economic effects such as loss of wages and medical costs can be estimated. Other effects may be more difficult to locate. These include, for example, personal, social, and health effects of inequities in wage payments to women as compared to men. Expert help often is sought in this documentation.

Assessing should include an examination of the social-historical context of the social problem. How and when did it develop? Who benefits by its existence and in what ways? What maintains it as a social problem—taxes, laws, regulations, economic profits? This helps to locate change targets—those persons and/or institutions who must change to mitigate or resolve the problem. It also provides clues for the focus of intervention and choice of change strategy.

At this stage in problem solving, access to knowledge about a problem and skill in analyzing it is crucial to the change effort. A social worker may possess this knowledge and skill or recruit persons with such resources to the action system.

Problem identification and assessment are keystones to the change effort in social action as in any other practice role. Unfortunately, emotional fervor about a cause may sweep a group into action before a problem is understood sufficiently. The social worker's major contribution is to assist the group to direct and involve their energies in this first critical step.

An outcome of this step is a statement about those persons, organizations, and institutions that must change to achieve the social objective. The statement identifies system boundaries and shows the multiple system memberships of persons who are critical to problem resolution. Slum landlords may be neighbors in the community or corporations in a different state and, thus, belong to more than one system. Locating violators in environmental causes often is difficult, given diversification of major companies with subsidiaries throughout the world. Persons who can read and understand stockholder reports and know what is available in public records and how to gain access and understand these data are examples of resources needed to locate and analyze social problems.

Assessing the Target System

At least four aspects of systems that must change should be assessed. Pincus and Minahan (1973) termed these systems "target systems."

Power The target system's sources of power should be assessed. Some specific sources of power may be money, votes, access to and control over information, expertise in the field, organization size, loyalty of followers, reputation, connections to and/or control over media, connections to and influence over political leaders, and charm and charisma of leadership and political acumen (Khinduka and Coughlin, 1975).

Shared Values, Goals, and Objectives The extent to which the target and action systems share or are in conflict about significant social values is examined. Values are statements of preferred social, interpersonal, or personal ends or the means to achieve them. Values may be shared at one level and not at others. There may be agreement about ends but no agreement on the means to achieve them. Data for this assessment are of a different sort than data from financial reports, for example, and more difficult to locate; therefore, they will have to be treated with greater tentativeness. Social action usually is required when there is disagreement about values.

Consequences of Change An estimate is made of the possible consequences of change on the target system. What effects might there be and for whom? Will these consequences be viewed positively or negatively by the target system? This assessment helps predict the type and amount of conflict that may occur. It assists in locating barriers to the change effort and may provide clues about the direction for change.

General Organizational Characteristics The assessment includes attention to whether or not the organization, business, or industry is public or private and its major stockholders and connections of board members to other social systems such as businesses and political institutions. Organizational characteristics identified in earlier chapters also should be assessed.

Action Systems

Most collective action takes place in an action system. Some examples of action systems are: a small neighborhood or community group seeking change that affects only its residents; a regional or state-wide group whose beneficiaries are not localized; several related units located in a large geographic area; centralized national organizations; local units of state, national or world organizations; and separate units at any level organized as coalitions.

These action systems may already be in place to respond to developing social problems. Some are the American Association of Retired Persons (AARP), Young Women's Christian Association (YWCA), National Association for the Advancement of Colored People (NAACP), Anti-defamation League of B'Nai B'rith, and National Organization of Women (NOW). Action systems may be formed by concerned persons to respond to a particular social problem.

Social workers use knowledge about action systems from three areas for social action. These are social movements, coalitions, and community organizations.

Social Movements Social movements are one form of collective effort to control change or to alter its direction (Lauer, 1976). Some movements are composed of persons who experience the same problem, such as women, students, or minority persons. Other movements are groups composed of a cross-section of the population. Such composition differences usually are associated with how specific or general a group's social objectives are. Social movements have been described and analyzed extensively (Evans, 1973; Howard, 1974; Lauer, 1976). Historical records of social movements show the diversity of social reform efforts: Chinese Student Movement, Women's Christian Temperance Union, Black Panthers, Black Muslims, Hippies, Women's Movement, and Gay Liberation Movement. What qualifies these as movements and how did they come about?

A social movement brings groups together who share common goals and preferences. Social movements are sets of opinions and beliefs in a population, which represent preferences about changing some elements of the social structure and/or the reward distribution of a society (McCarthy and Zald, 1977). The goal of justice for black Americans in the 1950s and 1960s, for example, was shared by the Congress of Racial Equality (CORE), National Association for the Advancement of Colored People (NAACP), National Urban League, National Council of Negro Women (NCNW), Student Non-violent Coordinating Committee (SNCC), and Southern Christian Leadership Conference (SCLC). Together they formed the core of the civil rights movement.

Social movements have the following characteristics (Killian, 1973): (1) shared values, social goals, and objectives; (2) a sense of belonging and participation that distinguishes between those for and against certain social goals and objectives; (3) norms of behavior that prescribe how movement followers should act, and (4) structure that provides for division of labor and leadership.

Social movements may develop out of the relative deprivation of some group or groups when change occurs in another part of society that deprives or disadvantages them (Howard, 1974). When the affected groups perceive disparities between their legitimate expectations and what actually is obtainable, an initial condition is present for the formation of a social movement. A movement is likely to develop when deprivations are shared by a number of persons, when individuals acting alone cannot resolve the felt problem, and when leaders appear with commitment and innovative ways to take action. Members act out of perceptions of status disadvantage and a desire to redistribute power (Howard, 1974).

Several structural conditions are necessary for movements to develop from perceptions of relative deprivation (Morrison, 1971). First, a large number of persons must experience the deprivation. Second, these persons must be interacting and communicating with each other. Third, potential movement members must share similar social roles and statuses. Fourth, a society's stratification system has well-defined boundaries and power differences between strata. And, fifth, voluntary associations must be present in society, which enhance the belief that change can come about through voluntary, collective efforts.

Although a relative deprivation explanation applies to movements comprised of persons with similar problems and characteristics, it does not explain movements composed of population cross-sections whose objectives are not limited to a social category or class and where outcomes directly benefit society as a whole. For example, environmental movements, nuclear disarmament, and peace movements and movements to alter a foreign policy appear to operate less out of personal deprivation and more from a broad sense of social justice. Other explanations for social movements may be needed to encompass the variety we observe in practice. Nevertheless, since social work's special concern is rights and entitlements that decrease or eliminate disadvantage and deprivation, this explanation is useful in social action.

Coalitions Social workers often participate in action systems composed of groups with formal arrangements about working toward social action goals. These arrangements include the coalition's goal; its resources to pursue the goal; communications about the goal and how to attain it; and agreements about distribution of payoffs or rewards (if any) when the goal is obtained (Kelley, 1968). Practice with such groups has been termed intergroup work (Newstetter, 1948). Research about coalitions from other fields can be used in social work (Gentry, 1987).

Coalitions differ in important ways, which suggest directions for social action practice (Black, 1983). First, coalitions may focus on one narrowly defined issue or choose a more general content area that includes several specific issues. Single issue coalitions, such as those that focus on specific legislation, have become prevalent. Second, the membership composition of coalitions varies. Some include only the representatives of certain organizations; others have members who represent organizations as well as individual members. Third, coalitions vary in the extent to which they have formal structures. A coalition may be relatively permanent with a staff, other resources, and a written structure that governs operations and decision making. Some coalitions have informal arrangements about sharing information and developing strategies that maintain high autonomy of participating groups.

If the worker assists to form a coalition, he or she should help the participating parties make several decisions. First, what is the coalition's specific purpose and do all members agree to the purpose statement? Second, is the coalition time limited or ongoing? Third, what resources do members and representatives agree to share? Fourth, what structure is needed to facilitate its work? If the social worker participates in an already formed coalition, she or he needs to discover what the purpose is, who the members are, whom they represent, and what structure is used.

Community Organization Although historically this social work practice area has focused on many different purposes and methods, the community always has been its action arena. Rothman (1979) proposed three models of community organization practice, which identify the major goals in community work. These are ideal types (in the sociological tradition) and in actual practice one may identify some overlap between them. They are not necessarily distinguishable by worker strategies, techniques, or tactics, but by the main outcomes sought. They are locality development, the social planning approach, and the social action approach.

Locality development assumes community change can be pursued best through broad participation by citizens in identifying goals and selecting actions. This model usually is described in our literature as community development. Locality development often is useful in social action when local-level action systems are appropriate.

The social planning approach emphasizes using technical processes to solve substantive social problems by rational, deliberate, and controlled change efforts. This model helps social workers recognize the complexity of social change, the need to assess linkages, and to apply social systems concepts within the large social arena.

The social action approach is related most clearly to the social action role. It seeks to bring about basic changes in major institutions and/or community practices in order to increase resources or improve treatment of disadvantaged persons consistent with social justice and democracy. The model does not suggest particular types of interventions to achieve redistribution of power, resources, or decision making. Although it does not distinguish between the goals of advocacy and social action, it suggests how social workers develop action systems and understand social conflict as a mechanism for inducing social change.

Grassroots organizations often are used by social workers to achieve social action goals. These groups form out of people's daily life experiences, which impel them to work for a cause that has direct personal meaning. They also aim to raise awareness about the cause so that others may experience more control over their environments. The assumption is that joint action increases the power needed to bring about change. Some grassroots organizations developed specific organizing techniques that are helpful to social workers in practice with politically influential action systems. A well-known grassroots organization is The Woodlawn Organization of Chicago, organized by Saul Alinksy's group in 1959. A more recent, multistate example is ACORN, The Association of Community Organizations for Reform Now, established in 1970.

Grassroots organizations share several characteristics (Perlman, 1979). Usually they are independent, community-based membership organizations or coalitions composed of people acting on their own behalf. Their goals are derived from members' own concerns for social, economic, and physical welfare. Ordinarily they use one or more of the following strategies: They make demands at public and private social institutions that control selected goods and services, such as utility companies and grocery store chains. They attempt to take over institutions through election registration and voting campaigns or by becoming stockholders in corporations. They design alternative arrangements to cope with needs that institutions fail to meet, for example, by forming food cooperatives or rape crises centers.

Alinksy's (1946, 1971) work emphasized how to generate conflict as the basis for change. Kahn (1970, 1982), who spent five years working with the Amalgamated Clothing and Textile Workers Union in its struggles with the J. P. Stevens Company, emphasized the importance of helping members identify their cultural roots and using these gifts as a part of consciousness raising in community organizing. Two training centers help social workers and others acquire skills in participating with grassroots organizations as action systems. They are The Midwest Academy in Chicago and the Highlander Research and Education Center in Eastern Tennessee (formerly called the Highlander Folk Community).

Summary Information about social movements, coalitions, and community organization practice suggests that social action may occur in various kinds of action systems. Voluntary associations and grassroots organizations can be linked to form coalitions. Under certain circumstances they may develop into social movements.

PLANNING AND ENGAGING IN CHANGE

Social workers usually assist existing action systems—voluntary associations, grassroots organizations or coalitions—rather than developing new action systems. Workers may be action system members or advisors. In either position they use professional knowledge and skill within social work's values. They use participation skills such as asking questions, sharing information, pointing out potential consequences of suggested strategies, summarizing, and focusing. Specific techniques are chosen in the context of the action system's history, characteristics, and leadership. Questions of the system's self-determination, participation of all members in decision making, goal clarity, and division of labor among members are examined and choices implemented within this system. Planning occurs in the action system, guided by an understanding of task groups.

It is important to distinguish among the action system's outcome, instrumental, and facilitative objectives. The right of all persons to live in peaceful societies is an ideal state and an ultimate goal, which can be achieved only through intermediate steps. Whether the goal is peace or construction of a senior citizens' center, the worker assists action system members to choose actions consistent with it. Instrumental objectives should be connected logically to the outcome sought. Facilitative objectives are engaged in for the purpose of maintaining the system. These include recruiting new adherents and increasing financial resources.

The worker assists the system to meet socioemotional needs of members. Systems use symbols such as logos, communication devices, and planned social activities. Many systems design T-shirts, for example, to raise money and to signify causes. Music, especially songs related to the cause, binds system members together and is a means for identifying the cause. Newsletters help inform members in large or highly dispersed systems.

Strategy Selection

Most social action strategies are familiar to us from newspaper, radio, and television reports. These reports tell little about how strategies were chosen to achieve specific goals. Perry (1976) examined strategy preferences of black community organizations, strategies actually used, the relationship of age of the organization and strategies they chose, and leaders' perceptions of strategy effectiveness. She found that most leaders of older organizations preferred cooperative strategies while half the leaders of newer organizations preferred conflictual strategies. Although both older and newer organizations used conflictual strategies, these were not viewed as more effective than cooperative strategies.

Using Warren's classification, Khinduka and Coughlin (1975) suggest three types of strategies—collaborative, campaign, and contest. Collaborative (cooperative) strategies are thought to be appropriate when few differences exist about the issue and there is agreement about both social goals and means to achieve them. Collaborative techniques include education and persuasion, which emphasize rationality and working together to achieve common goals. Campaign and contest strategies assume at least some and possibly much disagreement about ends and/or means. Khinduka and Coughlin suggest that a worker's assessment, using information about the target system, provides information critical to strategy selection.

Kotler (1971) proposed guidelines for strategy selection on the basis of social movement life cycles or stages. Each stage—crusading, popular movement, managerial, and bureaucratic—involves a particular set of problems, organizational needs, and leadership styles. The worker determines the stage and assesses problems that need to be solved for a movement to continue and to achieve its goals. Strategies used to gain adherents are different from those used to escalate pressure on a target system. The social worker also should be alert to the action system's changing leadership needs and help it find skills and resources to meet these needs.

The action system's and social worker's value orientations also determine which strategies are chosen. An action system comprised of persons who conscientiously oppose participation in war in any form probably would not choose strategies that are violent or potentially violent. The Society of Friends (Quakers), The Mennonite Church, The Amish, and The Church of the Brethren are recognized legally as peace churches for conscientious objector status (U.S. Code, 1982 Ed.).

Some action systems probably would not choose civil disobedience strategies that violate just and unjust laws. Others might violate unjust laws to achieve a social objective. The civil rights movement involved violating unjust laws that enforced segregation. Laws that govern actions such as breaking and entering, theft, and burning draft cards are perceived to be just laws that provide necessary social control and protect personal privacy and property. Action systems may or may not be willing to violate just laws to achieve goals and they may distinguish between violations against property and against persons.

Recent international terrorism has violent intentions and results in injury, death, and property destruction for both targets and bystanders. Since these actions clearly violate the profession's values, social workers should not knowingly associate with action groups that choose violent actions. If an action system considers violent strategies, the worker's professional responsibility is to attempt to alter the decision-making process and, if that fails, to disassociate from the group with a clear understanding as to the reasons.

There is no one set of rules for strategy selection. However, the following principles can be used. First, the strategy should be connected logically with the goals. Second, strategies should reflect the worker's assessment of target system vulnerability, barriers to change, and negative and positive consequences of change. Third, the strategy should be consistent with the action system's size, power, resources, value orientation, and leadership. Fourth, the strategy should be consistent with the stage in the life cycle of the cause effort. Fifth, since social, political, and economic climates constantly change, strategies should be chosen on the basis of continuous assessments of the change arena.

STRATEGIES

Three types of strategies are used in social action: collaborative or cooperative, campaign, and conflict, pressure, or contest (Warren, 1971). Collaborative or cooperative strategies are used when considerable consensus exists about the cause and means to make changes. Techniques include education about the problem, persuasion, providing specific information, and lobbying. Campaign strategies are used when there is misinformation or apathy about a problem. Some techniques are persuasion, education, reeducation, publicity, letter writing, endorsements by important people, lobbying, and public relations. Contest, conflict, or pressure strategies are used when opposition exists. Techniques include demonstrations, noncooperation, and direct nonviolent interventions (Oppenheimer and Lakey, 1964).

Although social workers should develop skills for the first two types, the techniques are not unfamiliar to us. Techniques used in contest, conflict, or pressure strategies are less familiar even though we may have seen television reports of marches or participated in vigils or boycotts. The remainder of this section deals with these less familiar strategies. Some historical perspectives are included to show their relevance to social work concerns and their fit with our values.

Social workers may choose from and combine many different techniques or tactics to form contest strategies. One group of these, including marches, picketing, and guerrilla theater, is designed to call public attention to a problem. Such activities are more dramatic than letter writing, standard news releases, or endorsements because they can be designed to draw extensive media coverage and promote wide public discussion of issues. It is assumed that public discussion of issues will generate interest in and pressure for change. If it does not, stronger pressure will be needed for change to occur.

A second group of contest activities is based on an assumption that the target system's normal, routine activities must be disrupted in order to pressure it to change. This disruption involves tactics based on some form of refusal to cooperate with the target system. While tactics such as strikes and boycotts do not involve physical violence, they may result in economic and other losses to action system members as well as the target system. These tactics also promote public discussion of an issue but are used primarily to escalate pressure on the target system.

A third set of tactics further escalates pressure on targets by even greater disruption of their normal activities. These activities, including sit-ins, mill-ins, and obstructions, are designed to make it difficult, if not impossible, for targets to carry on business as usual. Tactics used to disrupt target systems are described below in terms of increasing levels of pressure.

Pressure Level 1

Action systems historically have used one or a combination of many tactics to call public attention to an issue. A. Phillip Randolph and the Brotherhood of Sleeping Car Porters, Jacob S. Coxey and his Army, the 1963 Civil Rights March on Washington, the Poor People's Campaign, Vietnam War protest groups, The International Ladies Garment Union, New Left groups, and students are some action systems that dramatized significant public issues using this level of pressure on targets.

Randolph's threat of a March on Washington in 1941 was a major source of pressure, which led President Franklin Roosevelt to issue Executive Order #8802 which established a Fair Employment Practices Commission and banned employment discrimination in the federal government and defense industries. Randolph's pilgrimage to the Lincoln Memorial in 1956 protested the slow implementation of school desegregation after the Supreme Court's 1954 ruling in the Brown decision (*Defender,* 1979; Garfinkel, 1959). Coxey's Army protested unemployment and called for public works programs. Groups of women have held Take Back the Night Marches in many communities to call public attention to risks women take in unsafe streets or neighborhoods.

The tactics used in this level of pressure—marches, vigils, parades, guerrilla theater, pickets—have some common characteristics. First, they use a group of persons sufficiently large for the community or area and the problem and issue to make a dramatic impression on observers including media representatives. The 1963 civil rights March on Washington involved thousands of participants. Television shots, radio descriptions, and newspaper reports repeatedly emphasized the number who seemed connected to the goal of desegregation. Although Coxey's Army was dispersed by the Cavalry, the numbers were sufficient to publicize the problem and be perceived by public officials as threatening. Take Back the Night Marches can be ignored if they involve ten or fifteen people wandering down a street. But if they involve several hundred protestors marching through a small neighborhood, it is much more difficult to miss them.

Second, most of these tactics involve one or more symbols to represent the nature of the protest. Marches on Washington, which end at the Lincoln Memorial, use that destination as a symbol of civil rights concerns. The Poor People's Campaign used horse- and mule-drawn transportation and tents to symbolize poverty. Vigils may be held outside jails when the action system protests criminal justice policies or the arrest of action system members. Pickets have been posted and vigils have been held at missile and other defense sites by peace groups protesting U.S. military involvement in Central America and spending on defense. During the Vietnam War, some veterans renounced honors by refusing to accept medals representing their military service and achievements. Some actors and actresses have refused awards or used award ceremonies as a symbolic way to call attention to issues they protested. Take Back the Night Marches use neighborhoods that symbolize threats to women's safety and dignity. A destination for a walk through a college campus is chosen for the way it symbolizes students' complaints. Women who created and tied the Peace Ribbon around the Pentagon used it to symbolize their hopes and dreams for world peace and fears about war.

Third, most tactics are designed to provide information and increase the cause's adherents. A parade's route, day, and time are chosen to take advantage of large numbers of observers and media coverage. Leaflets can be distributed by persons who picket or hold vigils. Honors are renounced at public ceremonies or on occasions when the cause can be emphasized by the honoree's remarks and refusal to accept. Guerrilla theater performances are scheduled in parks and other public facilities where passersby are likely to be attracted to the event and watch. For example, members of the Community for Creative Non-Violence dressed as "Reagan's 'fat-cat friends' " and jumped into an apple pie 17 feet wide being used at the Washington Monument to celebrate an administration tax cut program (*Mother Jones,* 1983). The International Ladies Garment Worker's Union review, "Pins and Needles" included its popular song, "Sing Me a Song of Social Significance," which caught the fancy of protesters and observers alike (Price, 1962; Loney, 1983).

Fourth, all tactics at this lowest level of contest contain some risk for action system members, which should be anticipated and insofar as possible prevented. Parades and marches often require permits; sponsors should check local ordinances in advance. With advance notice, police departments may assist with traffic control and help protect marchers and walkers from an occasional threatening observer. If pickets or vigils are on public property, arrest usually is not risked unless disorderly conduct, disruption of commerce, or public nuisance statutes or ordinances are invoked. If a haunting tactic (constantly following a public official or other person representing the target system) is used, statutes about harassment might be invoked. And charges of malicious mischief, disorderly conduct, and unlawful entry (into the pie!) might be used either to threaten or punish protestors. Leaflets and posters used with various tactics may risk charges against protesters if they are considered libelous. Private and most federal property is covered by trespass laws. Protestors who hold vigils on Army bases, for example, can be (and usually are) charged.

Risks such as these need to be considered in planning. Action system members should be familiar with all relevant ordinances and statutes so that risks can be reduced. In some instances marchers deliberately choose to take risks. If so, plans should be made for the effects of the risks. For example, funds to bail members out of jail, pay legal fees and court costs, and support families often are needed and should be arranged. In some instances fines can be avoided by a simple plan to clean up the line of march or parade. The social worker *must* assume responsibility to help the action system select tactics that seem appropriate and relevant to the cause, understand specifically how to carry them out, and assess, choose, and plan for potential risks.

Pressure Level II

Tactics that escalate the level of pressure on targets by disrupting their normal activities have been used by many groups including professional social work action systems. Normal, routine activities of businesses, industries, schools, public housing offices, and social agencies have been threatened with disruption by pressure tactics that target their economic base or service delivery system. The Montgomery, Alabama Bus Boycott, ignited by Mrs. Rosa Parks in 1955, withdrew so much patronage that the city's economy was disrupted. The boycott of Nestle products was an economic weapon used to protest the company's marketing of infant formula in Third World countries. Groups such as unions and church organizations selectively boycotted certain produce companies in support of grape pickers' demands for decent living and working conditions. Rent strikes against slum landlords and public housing corporations have exerted economic pressure to improve housing and change policies.

Groups of parents have withheld their children from school to protest segregation, desegregation, busing, and school conditions. Such actions, if sustained by a large number of parents over long periods, threaten a school district's income where an attendance formula is used for state support. Some groups call attention to a cause by protesting certain taxes, threatening to withhold payment, or actually withholding payment. Although such refusals may not actually threaten a governmental unit's tax income, they disrupt usual procedures and would be a threat if sufficient numbers participated. A massive general strike, a hartal, has been used in India, Hungary, and Israel to shut down entire economies for short periods of one or several days (*The Denver Post,* 1985).

In addition to the economic pressure on which these tactics are based, they have other common features. First, although most of them are considered legal protests, they may become prohibited actions if they last for long periods or if they are carried out in such a way as to violate one or more statutes. Boycotts and selective buying need never violate any law—consumers can choose to purchase or not purchase anything including grapes, lettuce, and Nestle's products. But if the boycott includes protesters inside a market attempting to prevent purchases, it is almost certain they would be arrested on one or more charges.

When public service workers call in and complain of the "Blue Flu" for one or several days, little or no punishment can be expected. Blue flue cannot last for weeks or months, however, and reprimands or dismissals are likely. Parents who withhold children from school for extended periods violate mandatory attendance requirements. Alternative schools without state approval are not legal alternatives. Unless rent strikers place rent payments into a common escrow account, they are in default and subject to eviction. Even when an escrow arrangement is used, they may be evicted, although that action is somewhat less likely. Some prolonged strikes of companies aimed at improving salaries, benefits, or working conditions may erupt into violent incidents if scabs cross picket lines. And refusal to pay taxes, such as those that go to defense purposes, is a clear law violation.

Second, tactics at this level require strong commitments to the cause and a high level of discipline among action system members. They are directed to one of the most sensitive parts of the target system—its economic function. Because of this, action systems should anticipate targets will use all their considerable resources and power to counter the tactic. These will be deployed in ways that attempt to discredit, demoralize, and/or punish action-system members. Action systems must be cohesive, goal oriented, disciplined, and able to continue over a long time period if necessary to achieve their objectives. The Montgomery

Boycott succeeded because an alternative transportation system was established and sustained over a long period of time and supported by the black community in many different ways. The Nestle products boycott took six years but succeeded, in part, because it was translated into an international cause, which could withstand advertising and marketing campaigns by the company. Successful rent strikes have required solidarity among the majority of renters and outside support. Tax refusals in protest of defense policies have not developed either the number of participants or the support systems needed to counter the legal weight and resources of the federal government.

Third, these tactics require careful planning before action systems use them and leaders (including social workers) who attend to the care and feeding of these systems during the change phase. A decision to hold a rent strike is not made on Monday and begun on Tuesday! An action system may need to meet several times before choosing such an action. Economic impact must be estimated, and an escrow account should be established and supervised by a reputable financial institution or other community group. The target system's reactions must be anticipated and planned for. Procedures for on-going negotiations or bargaining should be arranged. The starting date and formal announcement must be worked out. If a school boycott is planned, the action system needs to decide if its conclusion is fixed by certain concessions and what these are. It must also anticipate what to do if no concessions are made. If a general strike is used, weeks or months may be required to solicit and develop the coalition of participating groups. A general strike, boycott, or selective strike that fizzles shortly after it begins not only demoralizes participants, but signals the target and general public that the action group has little or no power.

Pressure Level III

A few nonviolent social action tactics remain, which escalate the pressure even further by almost completely disrupting the target system's normal functioning or threatening to do so. They may focus indirectly on a system's economic functions. Their main purpose is the total disruption of an office, work site, agency, large institution, or society. College students, civil rights groups, Vietnam War protestors, peace groups, members of religious organizations, social service clients, and conservationists have used and continue to use these tactics.

Sit-ins at lunch counters and other public facilities were used by civil rights groups to integrate services. The Berea Interfaith Task Force for Peace, Lexington Task Force on Latin America and The Watermelon (!) staged a sit-in at an office maintained by U.S. Congressman Larry Hopkins in his district to protest administration foreign policy (*The Courier-Journal,* 1985a & b). Work on nuclear plants has been obstructed by persons who lie down in the middle of a work project. Women supporting the ERA fasted during the drive for states' ratification and Mahatma Gandhi, the master of civil disobedience tactics, often used fasts during India's drive for independence. Members of religious groups and others have provided sanctuary for slaves fleeing the South before the Civil War and for Central Americans fleeing violence in the 1980s. Social service clients have been organized to flood agencies with requests for services in mill-ins to protest both service levels and policies. Young men have protested the draft by refusing to register, burning draft cards, and not reporting when called.

These tactics have common themes. First, action system members usually have concluded that certain target system actions and the premises on which they rest are unjust and must be contravened. The tactic is designed to call attention to an unjust law, policy, or procedure or to violate it in some way. Sanctuary movement workers are convinced that the U.S. immigration law is unjust, discriminates against certain groups, and flouts a higher moral principle on which society must be based. College student sit-ins at financial aid offices in protest of policies are based on judgments that these policies discriminate unfairly against certain groups. Members of civil rights groups disrupted religious services in the 1960s to protest failures to integrate these institutions because of their conviction that religious institutions, above all others, ought to recognize segregation's evils. Lunch counters were integrated, not so much to eat as to demonstrate the right to be served. A fast for the ERA demonstrates the protestors' commitment to and belief in the rightness of the cause. When agency clients and potential clients over-use services, they are saying policies and services must be adequate for basic necessities and fairly distributed.

Second, these tactics present almost certain risk of physical harm, legal arrest, or harassment of action-system members. Harboring and transporting illegal aliens is against the law and violaters have been jailed, tried and are subject to large fines and long prison sentences (*The Christian Science Monitor,* 1986). Persons who integrated lunch counters and theaters violated laws existing at that time. Mill-in participants might be charged with disorderly conduct or harassment. Persons who enter nuclear sites and disrupt construction by lying in front of bulldozers probably will be carried away and almost certainly jailed and/or charged with trespassing. Failing to register for the draft is illegal and violators will be punished either by legal measures or withholding certain other opportunities such as financial aid for education. Prolonged fasts result in danger to health and risk of forced feeding in some circumstances.

Third, these tactics require exceptionally high levels of commitment to goals, cohesion, and risk taking behavior on the part of action-system members. They should not be chosen unless members have such commitments and support systems can be devised to minimize potential risks or reduce the effects of risks taken. The consequences of civil disobedience, including how to respond to conflict and deal with sanctions, should be examined. Oppenheimer and Lakey (1964) identify some training techniques used in the civil rights movement, which can be used to prepare action system members for nonviolent civil disobedience.

While mill-ins usually do not involve legal violations, they require thorough planning and extensive coordination. For a mill-in to be effective, large numbers of persons must demand services continually over a period of time. They request services to which they are or may be entitled and which normally are provided without cost, such as employment referrals, food stamp applications, university transcripts, advising conferences for curriculum changes, and medical cards. Participants should be polite, orderly, and sincere in their requests. The purpose is to overload a service system so completely that it ceases to perform its primary functions.

Social workers, although committed to social reform, have been reluctant to embrace conflictual strategies. We have difficulty understanding and utilizing power and manipulative techniques. Epstein (1970) found that we have a fairly limited view of our role and prefer political campaigning, testifying, and lobbying over more public protest techniques. Goldberg and Elliott (1980) recognize the dilemma of many social workers and suggest unethical conditions and situations can be met with ethical and effective tactics. For example, they identify "The Door in the Face Maneuver," "Next Logical Step Phenomenon," and "The Notebook Number," among others. These and related tactics are based on research in social psychology.

EVALUATING

Evaluating the social action role focuses upon ultimate goals as well as instrumental and facilitative objectives. The relationship of these objectives to achieving a longer term goal should be evaluated regularly so that strategies do not become ends.

Social workers can make an important contribution to general knowledge about social action by carefully documenting our work and evaluating our results. Most current research describes the histories of social movements. We can add to this record by analyzing our practice. We need to know what strategies are effective in achieving social reforms under what conditions.

Chapter
Eight

EDUCATOR ROLE

Social worker activities designed to provide opportunities for learning specific social skills and to supply information for more effective role performance.

One purpose of practice is to assist client systems to function more effectively by learning new information or acquiring new social skills. Think about these examples: A fifteen-year-old mother asks how to feed her baby. An exdrug user practices asking how to make up homework assignments. An outline for resume preparation is discussed with a group of recently laid-off managers. Women report results of their attempts to stop office jokes and other put-downs on their jobs. The residents of a half-way house practice daily living skills. These examples are different in many ways but have a common theme—persons are learning or practicing something new that should assist them to perform their roles more effectively.

System members who use social worker assistance in the educator role meet their workers in a diverse array of practice settings. These include neighborhood centers, in- and outpatient health and mental health facilities, employee assistance programs, women's centers, private practice, community planning groups, family agencies, and foster homes. When the worker participates in a television or radio forum on a community problem, some beneficiaries are never seen.

The educator role may be the only role required to assist a system. Often, however, it is embedded in a worker's total practice and overlooked because other goals are to secure an entitlement or mediate a conflict or match a resource with a client-system need. Nevertheless, much practice is directed to helping system members learn more effective role performance. It is important to make this role explicit so that workers can identify relevant strategies and increase their competence in using them.

While the above examples illustrate contemporary instances of the educator role, this general practice goal reaches back into early social work. Social workers helped Asian and European wives of returning servicemen to learn how to shop, cook, and negotiate social institutions in their adopted country. We taught budgeting and food commodity preparation to financially struggling families. We taught members of youth clubs how to make decisions. We assisted immigrants to learn how a democratic society works. We helped unemployed persons practice filling out job applications. We designed learning opportunities for persons with specific developmental lags and disabilities to acquire skills to master environmental tasks.

Social workers engage in the educator role in two major contexts: with one person who is part of a larger system such as a family or social or task group and with groups of persons who comprise a system or represent other systems. Groups often are used as the context for achieving the goal of this role. These groups may be formed for the purpose of assisting members to move from one system and role to another. We form groups and use the educator role in preretirement, orientation, and predischarge groups. We also refer to these groups by their composition. Groups for divorced persons, recent widows, parents, and single parents are examples. If we accept that changes occur throughout life, the term "life education groups" includes these specific examples (Apgar and Coplon, 1985).

KNOWLEDGE BASE

Several developments in the knowledge base for practice undergird the educator role. First, explanations about human behavior include influences of social interactions on personal development. We draw on extensions of early learning theories developed in psychology to analyze how behavior is reinforced and maintained (Bandura, 1977). The work of Piaget (1965) and Kohlberg (1981) in cognitive and moral development are available. Social anthropology documents the role of socialization in transmitting culture and contributes to our understanding of diversity. We know about the influence of social structures on the development of behavior (Hartman, 1981).

Second, these explanations are directed to the total life span from infancy to older adult years and death. Social workers no longer are limited to explaining early childhood and adolescence, but have ways to understand important periods throughout life. Furthermore, we have been reminded that not all persons are white, male, and middle class (Lott, 1981). Descriptions of the unique cultures and experiences of black, Hispanic, Asian, and Native American persons appear in texts about human growth and development.

Third, social work recaptured its historic interest in prevention of social dysfunction as a major practice purpose (Bloom, 1981). By drawing upon epidemiological concepts from public health, we recognized that a complex chain of circumstances can lead to social dysfunction and our assistance can be given at critical points in life.

Fourth, social workers understand more clearly that demands change across lifetimes in our complex world. Work, intimate relationships, leisure time, and family life are not regulated by clear, simple, or fixed norms. These areas are characterized by constantly changing norms and almost unlimited choices. The larger social context in which we live is shifting to increasing global interdependencies which affect daily activities. Technical developments are driven by complex information systems. Different and often unclear demands are made on people throughout their lives. Meyer's (1976) definition of social work as assisting people to command their own lives in an increasingly isolating, technological, and complex world is an apt description.

Fifth, we are not expected to possess all information and skills needed to negotiate these demands successfully. No one assumes that children are endowed innately with parenting skills; that a high school or college education captures sufficient information for a lifetime; or that social systems are able to weather repeated assaults from change with relative ease.

The educator role is consistent with these developments and assumptions. It is that set of social worker behaviors directed to improving role performance through providing information about and opportunities to learn specific social skills. It addresses a normative and preventive social work purpose as well as a remedial function in modern society.

Role Concepts

Since more effective role performance is the client-system goal in this practice area, role concepts are an important part of a worker's knowledge. Sociologists use these concepts to analyze social statuses or positions in social systems. Social anthropologists use them to understand and test socialization theory. Major role concepts are position, expectations, and role performance (Feld and Radin, 1982).

A status or position is a category of persons who are similar in some respect. Examples are students, parents, employees, supervisors, social workers, and teachers. Position occupants are expected to carry out the rights and duties of their positions. These expectations come from several sources. Other persons in the system have expectations about occupants' behaviors. Position occupants also have role conceptions about behaviors appropriate to fulfill their rights and duties. For established and well-known positions, social norms are guidelines for occupants' behaviors. Parents are expected to provide care and nurture children in safe environments. Norms about parental expectations are sufficiently strong that laws govern parents' behavior and punish certain actions such as neglect and abuse. The terms "role performance" or "role enactment" refer to position holders' behaviors in fulfilling position expectations.

The term "role playing" is used to mean different things in everyday conversation. First, it has an entertainment purpose when used in a theatrical context. Second, it is used to imply deceptive behavior to fool others by acting contrary to real intentions, emotions, or motivations. During the students' rights movement, role playing meant that people played roles and did not behave authentically. Third, in sociology the term means patterns of behavior dictated by social norms. This is the context for understanding role concepts in the educator role. Fourth, role playing is a technique for teaching and learning in which persons act out situations to learn about themselves, improve skills, and to analyze and demonstrate a behavior. This technique is described later as a way to help system members learn new social skills and demonstrate information acquisition.

Social workers use role concepts in two distinct ways. First, we describe and analyze social positions or roles people occupy (such as employee, voter, and committee member) and how they perform in them. Second, we use role concepts to mean worker communication techniques such as the role of listener or facilitator. Perlman (1968) distinguished between these two by calling the first "vital roles," which are central to our lives. Vital roles require occupants to do something in relation to one or more significant others in the context of ideas, expectations, attitudes, and judgments about themselves and others that are charged emotionally. When we help client-system members enact roles more effectively, we are helping them in areas of life central to their well being. We are concerned about their behaviors, cognitions, and feelings in relation to important other persons in their lives—children, lovers, bosses, neighbors, parents, teachers, and siblings.

PROBLEM IDENTIFICATION AND ASSESSMENT

Nature and Location of the Problem

The educator role is chosen when a system or system member's role performance is assessed as problematic or potentially problematic to the member and/or system. The former condition exists when a person occupies a position; the latter may occur when a person anticipates assuming a new position. Problems with a colleague at work are an example of the first; anticipating biological, adoptive, or foster parenthood is an example of the second (Fritz, 1985).

Role concepts assist the worker to examine position expectations and role conceptions to answer two questions. First, are role expectations and role conceptions congruent? Second, does the occupant possess the information and social skills needed to enact the role? Difficulties may arise in either problem area. Five additional role concepts are used to assess these problems.

Role Ambiguity When the rights and duties of a position are unclear or expectations are not guided by social norms, role ambiguity occurs. It results in uncertainty, confusion, and lack of confirmation about appropriate behavior, which may create inconsistent role performance. Role ambiguity is evident when new social roles develop and few expectations or little social validation exist to guide occupants' behaviors. Two examples are the roles of househusband and women in nontraditional jobs. Persons in these positions may have few or unclear social signals about expected behavior. Role ambiguity may be a problem for gays and lesbians who publically reveal their lifestyles. Role ambiguity occurs in rapidly changing societies.

Role Strain This problem occurs when position occupants have difficulty in role performance. Difficulties occur when new behaviors have not been incorporated in behavioral repertoires. It also occurs when persons have not been able to fit new position expectations with previous knowledge. Persons in new positions report excessive tiredness, which may be attributed to role strain. Others experience role strain when they are not comfortable with behaviors required in a role. This occurs, for example, when a position requires conflict resolution skills, but the position occupant prefers to avoid conflict.

Role Discontinuity This problem occurs when a person occupies a new position which has very different expectations, rights, and duties from those required in a previous position. Role discontinuity may be used to describe problems retirees experience when they move from positions of prestige, power, and a sense of productivity to the position of retiree, which has none of these characteristics. Women may experience role discontinuity when they leave work to remain at home with babies or when they enter work following a period of childbearing and rearing.

Role Conflict This term refers to conflicting or opposing role expectations. When it occurs within one position, it is called intraposition conflict. It also may occur when a person occupies more than one position in different systems and the combination of expectations from all positions is not possible to meet. This is called interposition conflict.

Intraposition conflict occurs when a position occupant holds role conceptions that are different from position expectations or when a significant other person holds expectations of the occupant that are contradictory. Persons who expect a partner to be both a wage earner and consistently at home hold incongruent expectations for the partner, which are impossible to meet. Parents may be expected to be in two places at once—in an office sales meeting and at home with a sick child—and experience role conflict.

Faulty Role Conception Persons sometimes experience difficulty as a result of their role conceptions. Where role conceptions are faulty or unrealistic for the person, position, or social situation, persons may be dissatisfied when they fail to meet their own standards of performance or the position's expectations.

These role concepts suggest areas to explore, describe, and analyze in relation to presenting problems. System members' statements about relationships with significant others or their own achievements are important clues to possible problems in role expectations, conceptions, and performance. These lead us to examine role problems that exist or might exist in the future. The educator role is used when system members perceive a difficulty. We also anticipate a need for the role when system members move from one role to another. Workers provide learning opportunities for groups facing similar role issues—financial planning for retirement, parenting skills, or any other life task for which persons may not be prepared. A strength of our profession is that we provide opportunities to acquire information and skill to prevent as well as remedy role performance problems.

Client System Characteristics

The educator role is based on an assessment of all client system characteristics identified in Chapter 4. Characteristics that require special attention for this role are vulnerability, verbal ability, self-respect, and culture.

Vulnerability When the presenting problem is explored, the extent of risk to the client system is assessed from the perspective of role performance problems. The worker asks questions such as: Is there potential for job loss due to conflicting expectations at work? How close to terminating a relationship are partners in a living arrangement? How is the client system reacting to stress from ineffective role performance? What are the effects of poor role performance on important others and what is their vulnerability? For example, what risks might exist for a two-year-old child when the parent does not understand his or her progress in relation to normal child development? Answering such questions assists the worker to locate problems precisely, understand their effects on the system and related systems, and determine their urgency.

Verbal Ability The ease with which client-system members use language and have vocabularies to describe, elaborate, and discuss the problems is noted. Since English is a second language for many client systems, our assessment should include the ability to use their first language. This assessment includes system members' uses of abstractions to explain, explore, and question.

Information about verbal ability is used in choosing change strategies since these vary in the extent to which they depend upon language for learning. Strategies also vary in terms of abstraction/concreteness and generality/specificity. We could use abstract and general developmental theories in parent education classes with persons able to understand and apply them. But we need to use specific behavioral principles and concrete examples with persons who do not understand theories.

Self-Respect An estimate is made of system members' self-respect. Those with low self-respect might be assisted most effectively if their initial contacts are in the privacy of an office with only the worker present. Later they may profit from sharing experiences and concerns with others in a group. This information influences choice and timing of an individual and/or group context for helping and specific helping strategy.

System Culture A general assessment principle is to understand the system's social and cultural context since role conceptions and expectations originate in reference groups. Ethnic group characteristics must be understood for a careful assessment of role conceptions (Davis, 1984).

Information about system characteristics and members' role expectations, conceptions, and performance is synthesized into an assessment. This statement explains role performance problems and identifies the general change arena.

PLANNING AND ENGAGING IN CHANGE

Planning is influenced by two different client-system conditions. First, some systems anticipate role changes or possible role performance problems and wish to prepare for effective performance. In this condition there may be no prior worker-system contact in the usual sense. Although some may have been referred for services, others learn about educational opportunities from media announcements and appear at the first session without prior contact. Many have assessed their own needs and chosen a solution.

Second, some systems are experiencing performance difficulties or relationship problems which result in role performance issues and seek or are referred for help. In this condition, services are provided after more extensive exploration, data gathering, discussion, and analysis of problems. Radin (1985) elaborates these two conditions and provides specific guidance to workers, especially when a group is chosen as the context for learning. Planning activities are discussed for anticipated role change and problematic role performance in the following two sections.

Anticipation of Role Changes

We plan for change even when no specific client systems request help by anticipating and identifying social issues where role changes for significant numbers of persons exist, which may result in role performance problems. Information about emerging issues and social trends comes from professional meetings and workshops and professional literature and research. If the worker's agency is a unit of a national agency, information is provided and programs described, which respond to social issues. We are informed about local issues through our community activities, local news reports, and community studies. Institutions, such as public schools and businesses, and interested citizens often approach workers about programs focused on anticipated role changes.

Planning in response to emerging issues may be carried out in a specific service agency or in a community planning agency. It may be carried out by agency staff, a staff committee, or a committee of staff and community persons. Potential recipients may participate in the process in two ways. First, they may be consulted about evolving plans. Second, they may be organized as the planning and implementing committee with a staff member serving as a resource to them.

Some elements of program development are central to the educator role. First, program goals and objectives should state in measurable terms how client systems will be different or changed as a result of the program. Usually a general goal is identified and outcome, instrumental, and facilitative objectives are identified. Developing communication skills through assertion training programs probably is an instrumental objective in relation to some more general role performance goal. When the outcome is effective parenting, an instrumental objective might be learning about cognitive, moral, and motor development of young children.

Contracting occurs implicitly when persons in the community respond to program announcements. Material prepared for radio, television, and newspaper releases or flyers distributed to church groups, PTAs, and business clubs, should state anticipated outcomes specifically. A reaffirmation of the goals occurs in the first group session and is one of the first tasks for the worker as group leader.

Public announcements should state specifically what procedures or activities will be used to achieve the program goal. If learning is to occur primarily through verbal participation in a support group, this activity should be stated. If some content will be introduced by the worker and/or through audio and/or video tapes, movies, reading materials, and resource speakers, potential participants should be informed of these plans in program announcements.

Where decisions have been made by program planners about length, frequency, and number of sessions or any other requirements, such as fees, this information is included in program descriptions. If participants will make some or all of these decisions, this option is stated. People want to know what they are getting into, what will happen to them while they are there, and what benefits they should expect.

Certain agency supports are essential for group educational programs. These include allocation of adequate time and resources for workers to plan, lead, record, and evaluate each session. Other resources are equipment and funds for the program's procedures and content. Since leading groups for educational purposes is time consuming, procedures to monitor and account for this time should not omit planning time needed. It should not be assumed that group sessions of one hour are equivalent to an individual interview session.

Historically, educational groups have been organized for set time periods. This practice still is prevalent in most educational groups where members come to the first session and continue until the set period has ended. Recently practitioners and researchers have used groups meeting for relatively short time periods, including single sessions (Alissi and Casper, 1985). Some groups accept new members regularly and are called open membership groups. These require consistent leadership and on-going attention to group norms, culture, and timing of members' entry and exit. Galinsky and Schopler (1985) addressed these group leader tasks and report research about open membership groups. Both closed and open membership groups have certain advantages and disadvantages (Henry, 1981). The choice of one over the other should be made on the basis of purpose, group composition, and context characteristics.

Planning should reflect the special characteristics of the population groups to which educational programs are directed. Locations, times of day, and days of the week programs are scheduled should be consistent with what is known about the population. Programs should be offered where people have access and feel safe and comfortable and at times which promote attendance.

Problematic Role Performance

Social workers discover role performance problems by examining caseloads across workers in one or more agencies. We determine whether these might be addressed better in a group or individual helping context. To make this decision, workers consider two important system member characteristics. First, system members' vulnerability of risk to self and to others is assessed. Role performance problems need to be addressed immediately on an individual basis when abuse of others or self is at issue. A second characteristic is the system members' self-respect. Since this may need to be addressed initially in a confidential, safe, helping relationship, a group context may not be appropriate.

Social workers also discover role performance problems in routine intake procedures. When the initial assessment identifies role performance problems, plans are developed to include the educator role. A particular context for helping—individual, couple, family, group, or some combination of service units—is chosen.

If groups are formed, planning includes many of the areas identified in the previous section. Consideration also is given to characteristics or qualities of groups that are helpful to members. Anderson (1979) identified six: altruism, cohesiveness, universality, interpersonal learning, instillation of hope, and social learning. These factors mean that group members should have opportunities to respond to others' needs in a helpful way, to feel more connected and less isolated, to feel accepted in a social situation, to recognize the shared nature of their problem, to experience safe environments for trying out new skills and seeing results immediately, and to experience social reality as continuously changing. As the group leader and members work together to modify role expectations, conceptions, and performance, these qualities and characteristics are the group's facilitative objectives.

Groups may not be a helpful context for some client-system members either because of their own characteristics or the group's characteristics. Although a norm of confidentiality is stressed, members have no absolute assurance other members will adhere to this norm. This risk may be too great for some to be helped in a group. This may be a special concern in small towns, cohesive rural communities, or groups in the work place. Some client systems have been socialized to maintain the privacy of personal or family information and are too uncomfortable to share it in a group. Seeking social work help itself may be a violation of personal and family values and norms.

Change Strategy Selection

Although social workers have used educational techniques for many years, we do not have comprehensive classifications of role strategies. Earlier in our history, we often categorized client systems as "sick" or "well" and assumed the latter were candidates for the educator role. This approach was based on an assumption that "wellness" was sufficient to guide strategy choice. Practice experience has not supported this assumption.

First, persons who experience difficulties in role performance hurt. These hurts take many forms and may resemble behaviors of persons for whom the clinical role is helpful. Second, medical metaphors such as sick and well tend to limit our assessments and change choices. Such a dichotomy may ignore the great variety of system characteristics and needs that point to more effective role performance as the change arena (Epstein, 1982; Mauzerall, 1983; Steiner, 1984; Breton, 1984). Some young persons who abuse drugs have not had opportunities to be socialized into the adolescent straight-world's norms, culture, and skills and their need for education is great (FORUM, 1982). Similarly, the need for parenting information and skills is shared by school-age mothers and fathers, single-parent professional persons, parents in middle-class nuclear families, and gay and lesbian parents. Despite all the ways these parents are different, they share a common need for effective role performance as parents (Barth and others, 1984/1985). A single dichotomy does not provide for an in-depth assessment of client systems and does not contain sufficient guides for choosing strategies.

Educator role strategies sometimes are organized by the size of social unit—a person, couples, families, small groups, or communities. This approach assumes strategies differ when used to help different social units. However, this assumption is not necessarily valid. For example, social learning principles are the same when the system is comprised of a worker and one client-system member and when the system is a family or a group of members not related by family ties. Although specific techniques may be adapted to system size, this does not always significantly alter the strategy.

An alternative to choosing strategies by traditional dichotomies and arbitrary classifications is to select strategies using three general guides.

Information/Skill Needed The worker should be guided by the substantive characteristics of the information and/or skill needed for effective role performance. If the assessment concludes that role performance issues exist in parenting, for example, a strategy is chosen that specifically addresses this substantive content area. The strategy should focus not on parenting in general but the *particular* information and/or skills these specific parents need. If a performance problem is anticipated for direct line workers who move to supervisory positions, the strategy should focus specifically on substantive differences in expectations of these two positions and role conceptions and skills needed to carry out new responsibilities. Sending a new supervisor to a management workshop or teenage parents to a parent education class simply because these resources exist does not represent careful strategy selection.

Communication Fit The worker also chooses a strategy on the basis of communication fit to the client system. The worker attempts to match a strategy with system characteristics, such as its composition, demographics, and culture. To whom will system members listen? Are some methods of communicating likely to be more or less influential? If so, what seems most likely to be effective? If the objective is to reduce the incidence of high blood pressure and attendant medical problems in high risk groups, what means of communicating information is most likely to influence them to take certain actions? Despite traditional reliance on television and radio announcements and public forums to achieve educational goals, Kurtz (1982) found these educational devices need to be supplemented with specific teaching in small groups to increase parents' attention to their children's developmental lags. With respect to how to communicate effectively, the worker asks: Given *what* is to be learned and the characteristics of the client system, *how* can that information and those skills be learned?

Social Context The worker selects a learning context that increases the probability that the outcome objective will be achieved. As noted earlier, this context may be the relationship of a worker and one client-system member or a larger group of any size and composition. This choice also is based on client-system characteristics. What would it mean to the system member to be singled out for more private help from a worker if the system is cohesive or usually achieves tasks without highly directive assistance or functions to give a high degree of support to members as they learn and change? The system's culture is useful as an indicator in choice of context. If the ideal context is not available, the worker decides whether or not it can be developed and what less than ideal arrangements can be made.

Special Issues The worker should be alert to client-system vulnerability and such characteristics as intelligence, verbal ability, and self-respect in choosing strategies. The strategy should not increase vulnerability or place excessive stress on system members since these have the potential for increasing system members' role performance problems and reduce the probability of successful learning. For example, highly confrontational strategies may be too stressful. Strategies that depend on high levels of self-revelation are inappropriate for many role performance problems and persons. In general, the most effective strategies are those that partialize information and tasks into manageable units applied to real problems or tasks. Some system members who do not tolerate stress well can benefit from learning opportunities arranged in a clear, step-by-step manner to fit their needs.

Change Strategies

Social workers design strategies to fit role performance issues and client-system characteristics from an array of available techniques and procedures for social skills training and information presentation. Some of these are identified and described briefly in this section. The list is not exhaustive but these examples illustrate the range of choices available.

Behavior modification techniques, including behavioral rehearsal, imitation, modeling, and use of rewards as reinforcers, are tools for teaching social skills. These have been used widely in social work and other professions. They have been shown to be effective for many different purposes with a range of different client population groups (Bandura 1969, 1977). Role playing as developed in adult education is useful for trying out newly developed skills in a comfortable environment (Shaftel, 1967; van Ments, 1983). Satir (1967) drew upon communication theories for techniques to alter communication patterns. Dissonance reduction and assertion training techniques have been developed from cognitive theories. Preferential selection, compromise, avoidance, and taking in order are some techniques used in role conflict resolution (Thomas and others, 1967).

Information can be presented in various ways. Commercial films and video tapes and those created by client-systems members may be appropriate. Experts offer audio cassettes on specific topics. Special resource persons may meet with client-system members to present specialized information. Handouts, pamphlets, comic books, posters, and other written material may be used. Content may be introduced by the worker and/or by client-system members.

Board games that simulate some social reality introduce content in concrete ways. "Choices or Chances?" is an example of a board game presenting life options for teens (Los Angeles YWCA, 1981). These games are available commercially or they can be constructed by the social worker and/or client-system members (Gentry, 1972).

Social skills may be developed through the planned use of activities and programs that provide learning opportunities. Activities such as trips to try out skills in ordering food in a restaurant, riding a bus, filling out job application forms, grocery shopping, or speaking at community meetings do not sound complex or professional. But if they are planned to meet specific objectives and carried out with appropriate attention to system-member characteristics and needs, they are significant aids to improve role performance. General social skills training manuals are available. Others have been developed for groups of persons with specialized needs (Curran and Monti, 1981; Kelly, 1982; Priestley and others, 1984; Barth and others, 1984/85).

Programs or activities in a group context are methods for teaching and learning. We may create problem-solving situations by altering group structures and processes to create opportunities for learning new information and testing skills. Decision-making skills may be developed by youths who plan trips or by parents who act to support affordable day care in their community. Guides for analysis of group activities designed to achieve specific objectives have been developed (Gump and Sutton-Smith, 1955; Vinter, 1985). Using activities or programs to teach and to learn has a long history in social work and is well documented (Wilson and Ryland, 1949; Churchill, 1959; Middleman, 1968, 1980, 1983a; Gentry, 1984).

Information is available about structured groups that focus on particular role performance issues. This information offers content and techniques to alter group processes and structures. Special attention should be given to constructing strategies that are adapted to the needs of group members. For example, Braun and others (1984) prepared a parent education handbook that encourages individualized application of content and techniques to fit client-system needs and characteristics.

Social workers are bombarded with workshops, books, films, and techniques, which purport to be the latest and most effective way to solve some problem. We are responsible to evaluate these claims against several criteria before we adopt them for our client systems. First, what evidence exists to support claims of effectiveness, and is this evidence sufficient? Second, is there a match or fit between the systems portrayed in these materials and the characteristics of our client systems? If not, how must the techniques and content be modified to fit? Third, do the proposed procedures fit our values? Just because something is popular does not mean we should use it!

Strategies are developed by selecting and combining techniques and content that fit our assessments using the guidelines identified earlier. Techniques can be characterized by two major dimensions: intervention target and degree of structure.

Intervention Target This variable refers to the focus or target of change to which techniques are directed. Techniques can be used to alter client-system processes, structures, and conditions. However, not all techniques fit each of these equally well. Techniques are selected by the way they fit the intervention target. For example, if the target of change is a communication process, techniques used by Satir (1967) might be selected. If the target is a system member's cognitions, techniques for this target should be selected. Where the target is interpersonal, a role playing technique might be selected. If the issue is to modify a group process such as decision making, techniques should target this process.

Workers must examine the origins and uses of techniques to determine intervention targets. We discover origins and uses by examining the theories on which they are based, the *specific* actions that comprise them, and where and under what conditions they have been used. In order to decide whether to use the technique of modeling, for example, we need to know what theory it is based on, what the theory proposes about how change occurs, and what the technique is supposed to achieve and how. Only with such understanding can the worker determine whether or not modeling is appropriate for the specific learning objective and circumstances in the immediate practice situation.

Degree of Structure Degree of structure is the extent to which a technique determines what information is presented and how persons interact about this information. We determine degree of structure imposed by examining precisely what the technique requires people to do. A paper and pencil test has different behavioral requirements than watching a film or participating in a discussion or role playing. Materials developed for structured groups such as assertion training and parent education identify content to be introduced and prescribe how this is to be done. Clients who are not highly verbal will have difficulty achieving their goals in groups with minimal structure, which rely primarily on members to introduce content. However, prepared materials that highly structure group process may not fit experiences of some members and should be modified. Programs and activities differ in the extent to which they impose a structure on a group and its members. Greater structure is introduced when we constrict the range of behaviors permitted and narrow the range of information examined. In selecting techniques we need to consider what will be most helpful to system members to improve role performance.

EVALUATING OUTCOMES

Evaluating in the educator role requires the worker to examine the results of change efforts in relation to goals sought. Two general goals were identified earlier in this chapter—improvements in problematic role performance and preparing for role changes and preventing future role performance problems.

Role Performance Problems

The worker and client system monitor and evaluate changes to determine whether or not existing role performance problems have diminished or disappeared. Data sources are personal observations, audio or video tapes, diaries, charts, and client notes that record observations of specific role performance issues. A social worker's progress notes of group meetings and individual conferences are reviewed regularly to note presence or absence of improvements in target behaviors. These observations may lead to reassessment or to change of strategy and techniques.

Data collection methods for evaluating client-system outcomes in a group context are provided by Rose and Tolman (1985). This summary includes a description of role play tests developed and standardized for a variety of social situations. Since role playing often is used in the educator role, procedures to measure outcomes such as these are needed. Rose and Tolman also describe specific techniques client-system members can use to monitor their own progress.

Evaluation focuses on the extent to which client systems experience fewer or no role performance problems in real life. Effort should be made to evaluate transfer of learning and not just progress noted within the change context. Verification of stabilization of change should be obtained by collecting data after the formal helping period terminates. This can be facilitated by provisions in the contract for periodic return visits, mailing in self-reports, or completing questionnaires.

Evaluating should provide for discovery of factors beyond the client system's control, which may impede or prevent successful outcomes. Others in a role relationship may contribute to the difficulty and may not be a part of the client system. On occasion these difficulties cannot be resolved and system members may choose to leave the social situation in which the role performance issue is located.

Anticipation of Role Change

The key question to evaluate with systems anticipating role changes is whether or not problems developed when role changes occurred. This requires specifying anticipated problems and determining whether or not they occurred. In parent education programs, for example, we should be clear about standards of acceptable and desirable behavior against which outcomes are evaluated. Prepared instructional materials often provide information about standardized outcomes. For example, some materials used in assertiveness training suggest what assertive behavior looks like. This information can be used to determine whether client-system members are more or less assertive after training than before.

When client systems acquire new information and skills for later use, the initial contract should include a plan for contacts to evaluate outcomes. For example, these contacts may be return personal visits, telephone calls, or mailed questionnaires to parents after the birth of a baby, to persons who changed jobs, or to persons after marriages or separations. However, we must avoid assuming a problem would have developed without social worker assistance! Our evaluation cannot conclude assistance prevented problems from occurring unless we also assess a control group. Nevertheless, some other outcomes such as feelings of greater assurance or self-confidence when a role changed may be sufficiently important to justify our help.

Emphasis is placed on evaluating data which show the *absence* of future actions or problems. Little attention has been paid to these outcomes for client systems (Bloom, 1981). Too often we collect data only about the process of helping such as participants' satisfaction, convenience of program arrangements, and content covered. Planning for evaluation must occur throughout problem solving.

Client systems often seek our help because of a community climate that supports preparing for new roles. This climate is created in a variety of ways, including the influence of national news media, magazine articles, and wire service stories in local newspapers. Local efforts also are undertaken to address local problems; some agencies have community education positions for this purpose. Community education activities also should be evaluated (Kurtz, 1982). Since we know that prevention is less costly than intervention after problems develop, we should focus on determining the most effective community education strategies for a range of role performance issues.

Chapter Nine

CLINICAL ROLE

Social worker activities designed to alter internalized effects of system stress.

The clinical role is that set of social worker behaviors designed to alter internalized effects of system stress. We present this definition and a role conception with caution approaching trepidation because developments in our field have shown how controversial any work in this area can be (Minahan, 1980). Nevertheless, we hold firmly the conviction that social workers should assist individuals to modify attitudes, feelings, and coping behaviors that interfere with their functioning. Social workers provide such assistance in the settings of agencies and private practice for many client systems. This role has been an integral part of social work's history, and we expect it to reflect the profession's central concerns and values in the future. This chapter narrows some clinical role conceptions and broadens others to distinguish it from other roles. The origins of contemporary clinical practice can be traced to early social casework. Often the terms "social worker" and "case worker" were used synonymously. The clinical role is not all of social work, but it is an essential part and is the role of choice for many client-system problems.

CONCEPTS AND DEFINITIONS

Goldstein (1980) termed clinical social work "the individualizing practice role." Workers assist individuals who hurt, who are confused, whose behavior gets them or someone else into difficulty, or who are trying to live relatively peaceful and productive lives. The individual theme was central in Richmond's definition of social casework: "Social casework consists of those processes which develop personality through adjustment consciously effected individual by individual between men and their social environment'' (Richmond, 1922; 98, 99). This definition represented the near culmination of Richmond's work and greater conceptual clarity than her earlier definition, ''the art of doing different things for and with different people by co-operating with them to achieve at one and the same time their own and society's betterment'' (Cited in Bowers, 1950; 101). As these definitions suggest, Richmond increasingly became concerned about the personal and social adjustment of individuals. Those who followed later shared this concern.

Some writers distinguish clinical practice from other social worker roles, in part, by a goal of individual change necessitated by environmental stress. Simon (1977) explicitly focused on personal change necessitated by environmental stress that results in emotional and psychological effects. Perlman (1957) and Meyer (1976) also were concerned with how social workers could respond effectively to the effects of environmental influences on individuals.

Other social workers have described the change arena as personal adjustment (Bowers, 1950); emotional disorders and mental illness (Kentucky Revised Statutes, 1982); threats to functioning from psychological stress and health impairment (NASW Register of Clinical Social Workers, 1982); and intrapsychic or interpersonal functioning difficulties (Chestang, 1980). Still other definitions focus on psychological resources (Ewalt, 1980), problems of life (Cohen, 1983), personality deficits (Lurie, 1980), psychosocial dysfunction (NASW, 1984), and problems of living (Reid and Epstein, 1972).

Historically, however, primary emphasis has been on a method or procedure for doing something where the something has been given much less attention than the doing. Thus, clinical practice has been defined and described as the casework method (Hamilton, 1951; Hollis, 1964), treatment (Turner, 1979; Frank, 1980; Briar and Miller, 1971) and therapy (Siporin, 1985). Some social worker activities in this method include evaluation, diagnosis, and helping (Chestang, 1980); processes in treatment (Frank, 1980); a relationship process (Smalley, 1967); and a form of psychotherapy (Strean, 1978).

Clinical practice descriptions occasionally have substituted a list of services for a definition or conceptualization. The Kentucky Society for Clinical Social Work, for example, provides no definition but lists a number of services: psychotherapy, marital counseling, consultation, treatment services, rehabilitation services, and mental health consultation. Cohen (1980) referred to psychosocial services; the NASW Register of Clinical Social Workers includes persons qualified to provide preventive and clinical services. Early casework definitions referred to giving expert or special services (Bowers, 1950).

Definitions that depend on methods, procedures, and services pose certain difficulties in the clinical role. First, practice activities should be based on the client system's needs and goals, not on a set of procedures the worker can use. To the extent that methods are used to conceptualize a practice role, the risk is to think first of the method and not the purpose or goal for which it is to be used.

This may lead to a mismatch between what the client system needs and what the worker does.

Second, method labels are shorthand ways to convey meaning that may not be understood similarly by those using them. If the label "casework" means a broad range of interventions not limited to individual change when used by one social worker, but means something more like individual psychological counseling to another, the label causes confusion and has little utility. Recent efforts among social workers in clinical practice to define their arena more precisely (Ewalt, 1980) represent an important attempt to clarify labels and give consistent meaning to clinical work.

Third, no professional practice is defined adequately as a method, whether the concern is social work, engineering, or nursing. Persons in each of these engage in similar general problem-solving activities. They are distinguished by the change arena, their goals, some values, and the *constellation* of activities they design to respond to issues in the change arena. A method alone cannot serve as a definer or distinguish among professional activities.

Most recent attempts to delineate the clinical role arena have centered on identifying environmental stressors and their effects on individual functioning. The *social* dimension of clinical practice is emphasized repeatedly and Germain (1979), for example, shows some ways environments affect individual functioning. This helps move the change arena away from problematic dichotomies such as health/disease, resources/deficits, and problems/normality. We think the consensus among social workers (those who call themselves clinicians and those who do not) is that all social work is about both positives and negatives in human endeavor. While social workers may be called upon to assist more often where some problem exists than where some opportunity for enhancement exists, our concern is to prevent and remedy in a *social* arena.

It is critical to retain this social focus in defining clinical activities. However, a definition that does not distinguish this role from others is not helpful. Many persons who identify themselves as clinical social workers also use other roles. Defining the clinical role broadly enough to include these other roles results in defining social work and clinical practice synonymously—the profession does not need that again! It is important to narrow the clinical role sufficiently to distinguish its central features from other roles and yet retain its focus on interactions and environments.

Students probably come to graduate or undergraduate social work study hoping to learn how to help people in some kind of trouble. As they are introduced to where social workers practice and what they do, they discover many different kinds of social workers. Or, it seems to be so because they have different titles, talk about their work in different ways, and appear to do different things. There may be an impression that clinical work is better than some other kind because clinical workers practice where complex emotional difficulties are the focus of attention. These problems may seem more important, inviting, or challenging than providing basic necessities or income maintenance.

The clinical role is appropriate any time and any place certain conditions exist. Engaging in the clinical role is not a function of a place or client-system population. It is appropriate for and needed by client systems in most if not all settings and often is used simultaneously with other roles. Selecting this role depends upon having determined that it is appropriate for and needed by a client system. It is selected when the goal is to *alter the internalized effects of system stress.* If the client-system goal is to obtain an entitlement, the social worker selects the advocate role; if the goal is to establish an entitlement, the social action role is appropriate. Where the client system has internalized stress from one or more sources that disrupts social and psychological functioning, the clinical role is needed.

CENTRAL ASSUMPTIONS

The clinical role rests on four assumptions. First, individual growth, development, and behavior are the complex interaction of an individual's endowment and all his or her internal and external environments. Second, potential stressors that interfere with growth, development, and behavior are complex and, to some extent, still unknown. Third, we do not expect all individuals to incorporate or respond to environmental stressors in the same ways. Fourth, the arenas in which to examine social functioning and the effects of stress must include the individual, intimate support networks, work and/or school, the neighborhood, and the larger community. No one of these alone is a sufficient focus of concern.

The clinical role focuses on any factor or set of factors that interferes with individual social and psychological development to impede system development and functioning. The sources of potential stress on human systems seem endless. Some are well known such as lack of proper nutrition and inadequate emotional nurturing. But the effects of other stressors such as environmental pollution either are identified tentatively or only suspected.

Stress may result from factors both internal and external to an individual. As youngsters grow and develop, their own growth patterns may place stresses on them. An individual who suffers an incapacitating stroke or is diagnosed as having Alzheimer's disease or who undergoes major surgery may perceive varying amounts of change within their own biological systems to which they respond and adjust. As individuals progress through normal aging processes, they attempt to adjust to declines in energy, strength, eyesight, hearing, and/or memory they experience.

All persons experience stress in their human and physical environments. Human environments consist of the networks of significant others on which we all depend. These sometimes are supportive and provide a consistent base for intimate, peer, and colleague relationships. At other times they are not supportive and do not provide a stable basis for relationships. As support decreases and instability increases, we perceive and attempt to adjust to the stresses placed on us by all the human systems that form significant portions of our environments.

The physical environment is as important as our biological and human relationship systems. Physical environments may or may not provide for physical and emotional needs. They may be sources of stress to physical or biological systems and to the network of human relationships upon which we depend for nurturing, work, and play. Workers examine whether or not an individual's physical environment provides protection, nurturance, more or less isolation, and more or less support for a vision of opportunity to achieve.

The effects of stress are as complex as their sources. We know that persons may be exposed to apparently similar stressors, yet respond in very different ways. One person may react negatively to geographic isolation while another does not. The capacity of one person to adapt to complex and difficult family problems is not matched by the same capacity for adaptive response in another person with similar problems. Workers must be able to recognize a high degree of variability across individuals and tolerate considerable uncertainty when making predictions about possible effects of stress. Social workers look for *possible* effects in an individual's biological system, emotional makeup, and social functioning.

The complex nature of stresses on individuals is understood not only in terms of variations across individuals. It also is understood as denoting a set of variables in interaction. This means we do not expect a particular stressor to have a single direct line effect upon only one aspect of functioning. We expect stressors to interact with many variables including other stressors and internal and external resources. If we drew a picture of probable connections among variables in an individual and her or his environment, we would depict few direct causal relationships. We expect lack of proper nutrition, for example, to affect physical growth and to have cognitive and emotional meaning as well.

All workers are concerned about all potential stresses on individuals from their biological systems, emotional makeups, and external environments. The special concern of the clinical role is to account for and, if possible, alter effects that are internalized by the person and subsequently interfere with functioning. Although we do not know which stresses will result in specifically what types of reactions, we expect some to be internalized. That is, we expect individuals to incorporate the effects of stresses in such ways that their attitudes, feelings, and learned reactions either cause them or others difficulties or prevent them from functioning at their maximum levels.

There is disagreement about how internalization occurs. The explanation given by a particular social worker depends upon which psychological theory is used to explain human growth and development. We do not argue here for one theory over any others. Many different theories purport to explain this process. Social workers need to understand the major concepts and assumptions in the theory they use, assess its empirical support, and recognize whether or not it gives directions for change. The clinical role does not require adopting any particular theoretical foundation to understand individual psychological development and functioning.

Some social workers prefer to use learning theories; others prefer a theory that describes certain psychological processes. Both groups attempt to understand what happens when an individual responds to perceived stresses. Both assume that once feelings, attitudes, and behaviors are affected as a result of individuals' interactions with their environments, the potential exists for future development and functioning to be disrupted. The goal of the clinical role is to assist individuals to respond differently so that disruptions are eased, modified, and prevented.

Social workers usually examine several arenas of social functioning to note actual or potential disruptions. These include intimate support networks or systems, work for adults, school for children and youth, and various neighborhood and community systems with which the individual interacts. A youngster engaged in normal developmental tasks may experience stress in peer relationships at school as a result of which relationships with parents and siblings are disrupted. A worker's assistance may help change feelings about relationships with peers so that the difficulty and pain are eased at home.

Another youngster's family network may be disrupted by divorce, with the result that academic performance slips and peer relationships become tangled. A worker may help such a youngster gain some perspective about his or her anger and loss, and school performance and relationships may be improved. For a single parent attempting to cope with a job, nurturing children, and maintaining a family, several social work roles may be appropriate. Where a critical issue is lack of success in parenting, which results from confused feelings about having been deserted, the clinical role may assist in changing such feelings and assisting the parent to cope better.

It is important to repeat what has been noted earlier: A thorough assessment is needed to determine all client-system goals so that not only the clinical role is used, but any others that also are appropriate. The clinical role does not stand alone as the only way to respond to disrupted social functioning. It is a critical one when attitudes, feelings, and behaviors impede maximum social functioning.

PROBLEM IDENTIFICATION AND ASSESSMENT

The purpose of problem identification and assessment is to locate the source of issues confronting client systems and to understand the relationships among facts that describe these issues. The worker begins with whatever client-system members identify as difficulties and explores, in ever larger concentric circles, the networks of system relationships where these are located and influence functioning. Because client-system members initially may identify the difficulty as some tangible deficit, we also assist them to focus on feelings about and responses to such difficulties as lack of employment or illness of a family member.

Nature and Location of Problem

Stresses that may affect functioning originate in three sources or the interaction of some or all of these. These are the system member, the system, and the system's environment. Each of these and their interactions should be examined to locate and describe the problem.

System Member Although many difficulties people experience originate outside themselves in their environments, one source for stress is the individual. All persons experience growth, development, and decline over their lifetimes, each of which places demands upon response systems. Some persons are unprepared for changes in themselves or experience physical and emotional changes, which require adjustments. When this adjustment process is uneven or is interfered with by events, such as health problems, a system member's functioning may be affected.

A social worker may be assisting a male stroke patient with a history of highly productive and remunerative work. Among other arenas the worker examines, he or she determines whether the man's responses are consistent with the severity of his medical problem. We expect a stroke patient might be angry, possibly depressed, and confused. He also may not yet understand how much progress he can expect to make, what his limits may be, and how others will respond to his health problem. The worker examines whether his reactions are approximately consistent with the problem's severity and/or are confounded by unrealistic, fearful responses, which are inconsistent with his situation.

When we ask whether some part of a problem originates with the system member, we are not blaming the victim. We attempt to understand what part, *if any,* the person has in initiating, maintaining, or prolonging the problem. We want to know what part of it he or she owns. We explore this possibility because, if we do not, we risk missing a potentially significant portion of the total client-system picture.

The System A second source of problems is in the system itself. This may involve family members or the most significant immediate relationships the member identifies. We ask such questions as: Who comprises the system? What do they think about the problem? What is the quality of relationships among persons in the system? Where is the power? Who decides what? How are decisions made? Who carries out what tasks? Who holds the system together? What are the feelings of system members about the problem? Does the problem seem to start with system members or their interactions with each other?

We may identify problem sources in attitudes of rejection, hostility, passivity, or anger. We also may observe behaviors that appear to be dysfunctional. Where one parent not only has usual family responsibilities but also the additional burden of care for an aged family member, we might observe that the spouse continues to make the same demands as always and does not share any of the increased burden for family management. Often such situations are not confronted directly and resolved with the family. When this occurs, the physical and mental health of the parent may deteriorate unless a more satisfactory resolution is reached. The worker examines how the system usually handles difficulties, whether this one has been handled differently, and whether or not the current problem is substantially different from others the system has confronted.

System Environment Beyond the immediate system, individuals have many important relationships, which may be the source of problems. For adults these include relationships at work, in neighborhood groups, with peers, and any other system with which they have ties. For children and youth these relationships are at school, with peers, the extended family, the neighborhood, and any other community organization with which they have direct ties or indirect ties through their families.

The worker examines any of these that may initiate, maintain, or prolong the problem. Usually the assessment proceeds logically along lines suggested by system members as they talk about what they do and where the live, work, and go to school. It is important to explore systems such as service or social clubs, church memberships, neighborhood groups, and formal organizations including other social agencies.

The worker's concern is the stress, if any, these systems place on client-system members. We ask how a classroom teacher responds to the hyperactivity of a child, what pressures exist at work for increased productivity, what is the level of understanding and acceptance of a person's emotional problems among peers in clubs, at church, and personnel in other service agencies. Teachers who make hyperactivity worse, supervisors who have unrealistic production expectations, or unaccepting peers may not initiate some stresses we observe. However, they may maintain or prolong them or make them more difficult to resolve.

Social workers fill in as much relevant detail as possible about the wider but still significant networks of which the client system is part. The relationship network and its substantive qualities are important to assess. We may determine the relationship's significance from the way system members talk about it. Some system members may not mention a significant relationship either because it does not seem relevant or because they have not decided how to approach it with the worker. The worker uses a framework for analysis that casts a wide net in searching for potentially important relationships and sources of problems. As parts of this framework do not reveal relevant material, they are discarded.

Interactions It is the unusual situation where any one problem source stands alone. Given our concern about parts, wholes, and relationships, we assume that one or more interactions within or among systems best explains our observations. In the example about a hyperactive child, we expect that classroom events involve the child, the child's peers, and the teacher. To understand those interactions, we need to observe what sets off bouts of hyperactivity and how these are sustained by the child, the teacher, and the child's peers. A person's report of work pressures needs to be understood in terms of what a supervisor said and how it was said and in terms of what members of the work group said and did and how these peer reactions affected the system member.

Impact of Problem

The impact of system problems is observed throughout a system's relationships and interactions. The assessment should focus on several questions: What does the problem mean to the system and its members? How has the problem changed system functioning? How severe or serious is the problem's impact?

Meaning of the Problem The question of what a problem means is important because apparently similar difficulties mean different things to different systems. Some categories of meaning include but are not limited to: social stigma in relation to reference group norms, failure to meet personal and significant others' expectations, and changes in relationships.

Client systems may ascribe meaning to problems in terms of norms of reference groups or larger society. Certain difficulties are defined by society as more or less acceptable and more or less the person's fault. Unmarried parenthood is a significant social stigma in parts but not all of society. Both fear and social stigma are associated with persons diagnosed as having AIDS. Mental illness is a problem of great concern to some client systems because of family and friends' attitudes. Being laid off work may be associated with a high level of social stigma for some client systems.

Strong social stigma may be associated with public assistance. However, AFDC recipients may view their situations differently based upon the extent to which they accept or reject traditional middle class values (Goodban, 1985). These different responses of women who shared a common welfare status confirm social workers' need to discover and understand the particular (and occasionally unique) effects of problems in terms of their meaning for a particular client system. We discover meaning from system members' problem descriptions, their feelings about it, and their perceptions of significant others' reactions. Clients who perceive pressure to conform to others' expectations may respond with feelings of diminished self-esteem, worry, and anxiety about their value and worth. Where realistically there is little that can be done to avoid the stigma, persons may feel trapped, angry, and anxious.

Client systems also have expectations and standards for member performance. These are reflected in what they hope to do, become, achieve, and experience. These are rooted in cultural and ethnic identities and have special meaning for each system and how system members carry out their activities. Where system problems are interpreted in a cultural context of fatalism, for example, members may appear uninvolved in exploring the problem or engaging in change.

Membership in all human systems constantly changes through birth, maturity, leaving home, job demands, and death. As these changes occur, system members are confronted with the need to change in response. Not all changes signal negative meaning to client systems. Difficulties may arise, however, when a change is interpreted as a significant loss or when the system's functioning is disrupted significantly.

Changes in Functioning The worker assesses how the problem and its meaning changed client-system functioning. This requires comparing current functioning with the way the system functioned before the problem developed and its impact became apparent. It may be difficult to obtain valid information about previous system functioning. But this picture should be filled in as carefully as possible to avoid over- or underestimating changes associated with the present problem.

This content area consists of all the ways systems manage and cope with daily life activities. We ask how the system solves problems, makes decisions, and acts on decisions. A particular concern is whether or not personal functioning of one or more system members has deteriorated to the point that she or he is unable to contribute to system tasks such as nurturing, management, protection, and intersystem relationships. If so, our concern is whether or not other system members can carry out these tasks.

Severity of Impact The worker's first concern is protecting and maintaining the integrity of the system and its members. We want to know that system members will not harm each other or be harmed by outside systems, either physically or psychologically. A seriously emotionally disturbed parent usually cannot provide adequate physical protection for a small child. A less disturbed parent may not be able to provide adequate psychological nurturance over time even though no immediate threat is noted.

Severity of impact is assessed in terms of two dimensions—the extent of threat and the immediacy of threat. Extent of threat requires a judgment about who is affected by changes in system functioning, what these effects are, how they interfere with functioning of others or prevent meeting normal life needs and development. Immediacy of threat is the degree to which changes in system functioning are likely to result in immediate, near-future, or long-term impact.

The worker may use several resources to assist in estimating degree of severity. These include diagnostic manuals (such as DSM-III), which provide categories of content to be assessed and suggest ways to consider severity of behavioral problems. On occasion evaluation by other professionals is used to supplement the worker's assessment. In the future we may have a social work schema for different client systems. For example, the California NASW Chapter is preparing a manual to classify social functioning problems (NASW News, 1985; 13).

Client-System Characteristics

The worker's assessment includes all system characteristics outlined in Chapter 4. Two of these are given particular attention—system resources and system vulnerability.

System Resources The worker assesses system strengths and weaknesses to make inferences about supports to and constraints on change. Since change will involve the system's resources, the worker estimates what these are and what level of changes the system can sustain. The worker infers commitment to change from system members' descriptions of the problem, its effects, what they want to do about it, and how they solved previous problems. The worker avoids making inferences from her or his own cultural perspective. In general, it seems wise to avoid using psychological explanations from which commitment to change might be inferred. Many system members can tell us what their statements mean and we can observe the extent to which their behavior is consistent with their statements.

System Vulnerability The worker assesses the extent to which system resources provide barriers to assaults which threaten it. If there is an immediate threat which cannot be met by system resources, we usually delay change that focuses on attitudes, feelings, and dysfunctional behaviors and use another role (such as broker) to provide system protection. When immediate threats have been resolved, we can attend to internalized aspects of system functioning, which are the focus of the clinical role. If the threat is not immediate or the system has resources to deal with it, the worker can attend to the longer term impact of the problem.

Summary

The worker's assessment is formalized in a statement that summarizes all relevant information and identifies hypotheses on which action is taken. Areas where further information is needed are identified.

PLANNING AND ENGAGING IN CHANGE

Planning is comprised of two major activities—identifying specific objectives and selecting appropriate and effective change strategies.

Objectives

Identifying objectives for the clinical role is carried out in much the same way as for other social worker roles. As noted in Chapter 4, goals are general statements of ends sought. Objectives are more specific statements of outcomes of the change effort or activities that facilitate reaching outcome objectives.

Selecting Strategies

A host of strategies, techniques, and procedures exists from which the worker may choose. Choices are made on the basis of three criteria. First, the strategy should be consistent with the objective. It should address the type and level of intervention the objective represents. Second, evidence should exist that it is an effective way to achieve the objective. Third, it should be consistent with professional values.

Social workers face three major problems in sorting among available strategies and making choices. First, social work does not have a fully developed typology of client-system problems, which specifies objectives as the basis for selecting strategies (Goldstein, 1980). Hamilton's (1951) classification of treatment strategies is quite general and, although focused on casework, covers more than the clinical role. Hollis' (1964) classification was not based on outcomes to be achieved but a framework for explaining problems. She explicitly chose not to connect means and ends but connected general strategies to hypotheses about how change occurs. This leaves the worker unclear about whether or not a relationship should exist between the objective and how to achieve it. Reid and Epstein's (1972) typology represented a major advance in social work and evidence exists that some strategies in this typology are effective (Rubin, 1985). This typology is broad and inclusive of problems and techniques in other social work roles and is not limited to the clinical role.

Second, many technique and procedure labels mask important similarities and differences in explanations social workers use and actions they take. Turner (1979) listed nineteen explanatory systems for clinical practice. These systems overlap and are not distinctly different from each other yet their similarities often are hidden behind differences in foci, assumptions, and change techniques. The worker must ask: What are the theory's assumptions about how problems develop? What are its hypotheses about how change occurs? To what phenomenon is the theory addressed? Only by answering these questions can the worker determine whether or not the explanation fits the client system level represented in his or her change objective. If the objective focuses on a pattern of family structure or a communication process, an explanation which deals only with individual psychological processes does not fit.

Third, many theories consist only of explanations without specifying change strategies. Thus, the worker may mix contradictory explanatory theories and change strategies. Some of social work's favorite problem explanations do not include change strategies. Therefore, we often find ourselves in the extraordinary position of rejecting learning theory explanations but using learning theory techniques (Jayaratne, 1978)!

Social workers can ask and answer some questions that help resolve these three issues. Specifically what is the client-system problem? What theory best explains how this problem came about and is maintained? What is the specific objective of change? What theory best explains how change occurs for this problem and objective? At what system level is social work assistance needed? What explanation best fits that level? What is the logical connection between problem, objective, and strategy? What is the most effective strategy among those which fit?

The worker designs a strategy which matches the objective by selecting specific techniques and procedures and combining these in actions in which she or he and client-system members engage. Techniques and procedures can be classified in terms of a general purpose and system level.

Behavioral Techniques When internalized stresses result from and/or are maintained by dysfunctional behaviors, the goal is to modify these behaviors. Techniques and procedures that provide system members opportunity to change behaviors are those that suggest alternatives, examine antecedents and consequences, and modify behavior repertoires. Many techniques were developed and tested in other fields (e.g., Rosenthal and Bandura, 1978; Leitenberg, 1976; Wolpe, 1969). Many of these have been used in social work (Gambrill, 1977; Rose, 1977; Schwartz, 1982; Stuart, 1971).

Affective Techniques When internalized stress results from and/or is maintained by feelings and emotions, the goal is to modify them. Techniques for this purpose permit and encourage system members to recognize, accept, and change problematic feelings and to visualize, anticipate, and experience alternative emotional responses. Although there are conflicting explanations about how affective change comes about, social work has a long tradition of attention to feelings and emotions. For some social workers this change arena is the most important since it is the basis for insight and subsequent changes in personal adjustment and performance (Cohen, 1983). Others do not give a central place to affect as the basis for change, but assume cognition and behavior are change arenas (Berlin, 1983).

Cognitive Techniques When internalized stress results from and/or is maintained by faulty cognitions, the goal is to modify them. Techniques for this purpose provide new and different information, confront system members with alternative definitions of their worlds, and give the system the opportunity to practice using alternative explanations for events and experiences.

Several theorists have suggested techniques for cognitive change. Some techniques are available in rational-emotive therapy (Ellis, 1962), reality therapy (Glasser, 1965), Adlerian procedures (Nikelly, 1971), and Werner's (1965, 1970) approach to social work with individuals. Techniques aimed toward cognitive change have been used in social work (e.g., Berlin, 1980; Middleman, 1983b).

Summary

Selecting change strategies and engaging in change requires the worker to identify goals and objectives and to establish a plan for working to achieve them, which explicitly connects a strategy with the problem and the outcomes sought.

Workers may choose from many different theories which purport to explain how problems come about and how change may be effected. But, care should be taken to be specific about outcomes sought, procedures to be used, and the helping context, including system characteristics. The worker is responsible to understand this context and to design strategies that match the objective and have been shown to be effective.

EVALUATING CHANGE

Social workers engage in evaluating for three purposes: (1) to determine progress toward achieving objectives; (2) to determine whether or not the total intervention is successful; and (3) to explore conditions under which various strategies are related to goal achievement.

Change Effort Progress

The worker continuously examines whether or not there is progress toward achieving client-system objectives. An outcome might be reduced anxiety about establishing discipline for the youngest child in a family. The process of achieving this usually involves instrumental and facilitative objectives. One instrumental objective might be for the parent's negative feelings about how he or she was disciplined as a child to be reduced. The worker and parent examine progress toward achieving this instrumental objective. If progress occurs, no change in strategies or work plan is needed. If progress is stalled, the worker examines the sources of this issue with the parent, other system members, relevant literature, and possibly supervisors and consultants. The strategy may be changed, or different techniques selected within the same strategy.

A facilitative objective with this parent might be for the parent to complete a regular homework assignment related to discipline. The worker may discover in evaluating that: (1) the parent seldom, if ever, completes the assignment; (2) the parent carries out the assignment, but it seems to have little effect on reaching the objective; or (3) the parent carries out the assignment, and it appears to assist in learning how to set limits for the child's behavior.

The social worker evaluates progress by examining activities, difficulties (if any) in carrying them out, and what seems to have happened as a result of these activities. A progress evaluation may result in changes in the assessment which, in turn, may lead to strategy changes.

Change Effort Success

A change effort is successful if the internalized effects of the system stress have been modified. This evaluation requires the worker and system members to specify a criterion of success. System members can and do tell us what it means to feel less anxious or less worried or more effective. In establishing the criterion, much depends upon how client-system members define their problems and how they define successful problem resolution.

Our change efforts fail for various reasons, including worker ineffectiveness. The worker may choose an inappropriate change strategy or lack skill in engaging in change. Some client systems do not respond to any available strategy. When the worker confronts intransigent problems where nothing seems to work, experimenting and innovating are needed.

What Works When

Evaluating also refers to contributing to the profession's knowledge of what works when. The worker maintains records of client systems served, specific problem areas, strategies chosen, and the success of specific clinical efforts. These are reviewed to develop tentative hypotheses about strategies that appear to work in specific kinds of problem situations.

Systematic case comparisons conducted by many different workers using their own case load information contribute to our profession's knowledge by developing questions and answers about successes and failures. So that information gleaned from case comparisons can be transmitted and shared, it is important for workers to clearly specify goals and objectives in client-system terms (not worker activities) and to specifically identify strategies used. It is desirable to avoid general labels (e.g., rational-emotive therapy) and instead describe what was done more specifically.

GENERAL PRACTICE PRINCIPLES

Several issues arise in the clinical role, which need careful attention. Some general practice principles are suggested as ways to deal with these.

First, since the clinical role involves client systems of various sizes and characteristics and the worker focuses upon different units of analysis, the worker must be clear about whether he or she is attending to process, structure, and/or interactions. The unit of analysis may change during the period assistance is provided, and the worker should consider what changes need to be made in concepts, assumptions, and strategies when this occurs. The worker initially may focus on problematic communication patterns in a family and subsequently shift focus to one or more psychological processes of a family member. As this shift occurs, the worker should move from concepts and assumptions about communication structure to concepts that describe and explain emotions and feelings of individual members.

Second, workers recognize some stresses experienced by client systems arise in their broader social contexts, which should be the focus of change. These should be examined and accounted for as the worker selects goals and plans change. For example, members of minority groups frequently experience discrimination in many different arenas. The worker should not plan a course of action which assumes all change (or even most of it) comes from the client system. To do so blames victims and assumes that system members should adjust to inappropriate social practices and norms. In addition to helping alter the effects of stress from discrimination, the worker considers other appropriate roles that may change stressful conditions.

Social work has recognized and occasionally tried to shake itself of a social control function often imposed on it by society. Some groups want us to control behavior of unmarried parents, food stamp recipients, abusive parents, and prison inmates. Some groups expect us to change values, attitudes, and preferences of some client systems whose behavior and life styles are different and threatening. Such control may be exerted through drug therapy in hospital and mental health settings. The worker should examine the assumptions about social control that exist in the community and practice setting and the procedures used to achieve such control. Where these are inconsistent with social work values, the worker should analyze how to promote a more positive social climate and effect new ways of assisting client systems.

Third, the clinical role often is used in settings where professionals from other disciplines practice. In these settings workers need to be clear about their position rights and responsibilities *and* role conceptions that help them gain influence on a client system's behalf. The worker may have prescribed tasks in a psychiatric hospital, but the worker should not limit his or her influence to these tasks alone if professional commitments suggest other tasks need to be carried out. Extending one's influence is not easy but often is possible if the worker is creative and flexible in using her or his knowledge and skills. Often the worker can develop critical positions in communication networks by the quality and quantity of information he or she possesses about client systems and the ways this information is used to influence decision making.

SUMMARY

The clinical role is selected when the social worker discovers a client system has internalized stress which results in cognitive, affective, and/or behavior difficulties. A careful assessment of these, their possible sources, and factors that maintain them form the basis for designing change strategies. As with all other social worker roles, problem solving always includes attention to other problems the client system experiences and other roles which may be needed.

Chapter
Ten

MEDIATOR ROLE

Social worker activities designed to reduce or resolve inter- and intrasystem conflict.

The mediator's purpose is to assist systems in conflict to reach agreements voluntarily about the issues that form the basis of their conflict. In contrast to the advocate role where the social worker identifies with and takes the side of the client system as a partisan to secure and protect entitlements, the social work mediator places himself or herself between conflicting systems as a neutral but interested third party who has no vested interest in the particulars of the conflict or agreements made.

Mediators in Social Work

Recent literature, particularly in practice with families, identifies the importance of social work mediation and some procedures and techniques to be used. Divorce mediation has become a significant role in private practice and family agency programs. One study reports 72 percent of mediators in public sector divorce mediation programs were social workers while 42 percent of those in the private sector were social workers (NASW News, 1984). Barsky (1984) and Pruhs and others (1984) examine the importance of this role in practice with families.

PL 94–142 opened the mediator role to social workers in educational settings. Gallant (1982) described procedures and techniques for mediators in special education disputes and training for educational mediators. Her work was based upon mediation experience in Connecticut and a collaborative project with NASW in eight states and the District of Columbia to train social work mediators for special education conflicts.

The due process regulation of PL 94–142 provided for parents' appeals of the childrens' educational programs. The regulations identified mediation as an alternative or intervening step before holding a formal due process hearing. Gallant reported a better than 75 percent success rate in mediation in Connecticut special education conflicts where disputes were resolved without need for formal due process hearings.

These uses of mediation reflect continuing interest in a role that has many historical antecedents in social work. Social workers have engaged in mediation in community work, practice with small groups and in inter- and intraagency conflicts (Schwartz, 1976).

Other Professional Mediators

Mediation is important in other fields as well as social work. These include law, psychology, education, business management, labor relations, international diplomacy, environmental affairs, and public administration. Several examples illustrate the range of conflicts for which mediators have provided important services.

The Camp David Accords between Israel and Egypt represented agreements reached through the mediation efforts of President Jimmy Carter in the late 1970s. Indian fishing rights in Washington State were mediated by the Office of Environmental Mediation at the University of Washington (Fanning, 1979). Labor and management teams negotiate issues of pay and working conditions with the assistance of mediators. Designation of wilderness areas in Western states has been mediated when environmental groups and governmental entities were in conflict about boundaries and rules for use of such land (Fanning, 1979). Lawyers use mediation as an alternative to formal litigation of disputes. Former Chief Justice Warren Burger urged use of alternative procedures, including mediation, to reduce court caseloads and improve the quality of client outcomes (Folberg and Taylor, 1984).

A number of mediation services and programs have been developed and formalized. Folberg and Taylor (1984) provide a selected list of a dozen organizations that either specialize in or spend a significant portion of their efforts in mediation. These include the Academy of Family Mediators, the American Bar Association's Special Committee on Alternative Means of Dispute Resolution, The Conservation Foundation, the Federal Mediation and Conciliation Service, the National Peace Academy Campaign, and the Society of Professionals in Dispute Resolution. Folberg and Taylor argue for establishing mediation as a separate and identifiable profession through development of appropriate standards and ethics.

Finally, considerable academic work has begun in an effort to develop theories, describe techniques, and conduct research about mediation as a conflict resolution strategy. Kochan and Jick (1978) analyzed mediation using observations of labor-management negotiations between fire fighters and government units in

New York State. A special issue of *American Behavioral Scientist* (Susskind and Rubin, 1983) presents summaries of theoretical perspectives, concepts, research, and issues in mediation. The *Journal of Conflict Resolution* includes theoretical material, research, and practical suggestions about mediation. It represents one systematic effort to promote development of this role. One journal, *Mediation Quarterly,* is devoted entirely to this area.

ELEMENTS OF MEDIATION

In this section we define terms used in mediation, identify significant assumptions, and conceptualize the mediator role for social work practice. Some of the issues in mediation that have special relevance for social workers are examined.

Definitions

"Mediating" is the act of intervening in a negotiating process involving at least two systems for the purpose of assisting them to settle differences. "Negotiating" is the act of conferring, discussing, and bargaining about differences for the purpose of reaching a settlement. In social work mediation, the negotiators are the systems directly involved in the conflict or dispute. As noted in Chapter 6, social workers may select a strategy of negotiating in either case or class advocacy, which involves the worker as one of the negotiating parties who represents a client system or class of client systems in negotiations about entitlements. When the worker takes the mediator role, however, she or he is not one of the contending parties, but a neutral and nonpartisan third party whose role is to assist the systems in conflict to reach agreements.

A "mediator" is one who interposes himself or herself between contending parties, usually at their invitation, to assist them in resolving conflicts. The mediator is neutral and nonpartisan although she or he is interested in agreements as outcomes. He or she is *not* responsible for agreements reached, only for intervening in the negotiating exchanges between contending parties. In contrast to mediators, arbitrators have the authority to decide the merits of a dispute and impose a settlement. While social workers may serve as arbitrators or be involved as negotiators in an arbitration process, we focus here only on the mediator role.

Susskind and Ozawa (1983) report an example of mediation in human services, which illustrates these definitions. Prior to the beginning of the 1984 fiscal year for state expenditures in Connecticut, the governor referred a dispute about distribution of Block Grant funds to mediation. A significant loss of funds was expected to result in conflicts among human service providers about which programs would sustain cuts and in what amounts. Representatives of eighteen groups and programs negotiated these budget cuts with the assistance of a mediation team. In this example, mediation was the process used by the mediation team to assist the program representatives to reach agreements. Representatives of service providers negotiated agreements about funding levels with the mediators' assistance.

Assumptions

Several assumptions underlie the mediator role, which are important to recognize and understand:

First, inter- and intrasystem conflict is not, in and of itself, a negative phenomenon. Conflict and disputes occur because people do not always completely share similar goals, objectives, values, and resources. Conflict can be destructive and lead to negative system outcomes if it paralyzes decision making and system functioning. It also can spark creativity as system members confront their conflicts and try to find mutually agreeable resolutions. Often the outcome of this discovery and resolution process is a creative solution that leads to more positive system functioning than would have been possible without the conflict resolution process.

Second, people have the capacity to examine facts, problems, feelings, attitudes, and issues and make decisions about their choices in relation to the choices of others. Mediation depends on an assumption that people can choose and that their choices can be modified on the basis of rational examination, assisted by a neutral party. This appeal to rationality does not negate our understanding that people may act and think in irrational ways, but mediation deals with the rational choices people can make and their strengths and opportunities for change through conflict resolution.

Third, the goal of mediation is *not* to bring about personality or behavior change, but to modify an interaction and the choices made by participants in that interaction. Participants in mediation may learn, change their behavior, and have feelings and attitudes modified. But, if so, this is secondary to an outcome of agreement seeking based upon an assumption that changes in interaction and choices in that interaction can improve significantly the quality of life for participants.

Fourth, mediation is a conflict resolution approach that helps preserve the social fabric of families, communities, and nations. It represents a social striving toward harmony, community, and conciliation in contrast to disagreement, friction, competition, and conflict. It may be one of the few conflict resolution strategies in a time of scarce resources and excessive competition, which can improve significantly the quality of life for large numbers of people (Carlisle and Leary, 1981).

There is some support for this assumption that mediation helps preserve our social fabric. Folberg and Taylor (1984) show the extent to which mediation has formed a central part of social systems in China, Japan, and parts of Africa; of Jewish, Christian, and Confucian religious systems; and more recently, of smaller social systems such as courts and business and labor groups. In these societies and small groups, mediation appears to play a significant role in preserving kinship ties, in promoting social harmony in inter- and intrasystem relationships, and in restricting the extent to which destructive conflict limits the capacity of systems to survive.

Fifth, systems experiencing internal conflict or conflict with other systems can benefit from the assistance of a neutral party skilled in mediation processes. A neutral third party presumably brings objectivity to mediation and since he or she has no personal, vested interest in the outcome, the mediator's energies and skills are used to find creative solutions rather than defend the current conflict situation.

There is some disagreement about this assumption of neutrality. Gallant (1982) describes the mediator as neutral in the conflict between parents and schools but also identifies the mediator's concern as the best interest of the child and the educational plan and program that best meets the child's needs. This suggests neutrality exists insofar as the immediate dispute between the negotiators is concerned, but a specific value commitment to the child's welfare, which is not neutral.

Compton and Galway (1979) seem to suggest some deemphasis on neutrality. They define mediation as helping to resolve disputes between client systems and other systems. This suggests the social worker's main relationship and concern is with the client system rather than with all parties to a dispute. If this is so, then it is unclear where neutrality fits.

Susskind and Ozawa (1983) argue that neutrality is inappropriate in public sector mediation. Their argument rests on the special character of public sector mediation where the outcome should be in the best interests of the community or public. They note: "While it may be necessary for mediators to be perceived as nonpartisan, the claim of neutrality . . . is misleading" (Susskind and Ozawa, 1983; 269). At issue is not only whether a mediator can be neutral but whether she or he *should* be neutral.

It is unclear how this issue of neutrality might affect the mediator's activities. It is important for social workers to consider how they can be neutral in the sense required by mediation yet reflect their concern for critical professional values that require us to protect persons whose interests may not be represented adequately. One means of resolving the problem of community representation might be to design a representation procedure in the mediation process so that minority groups in the community are not omitted systematically from negotiation. This might require developing new representation groups or structures or selecting advocates for minority groups.

Sixth, mediation is based on an assumption of voluntary selection of a mediator and voluntary participation in the mediation process. Although we shall note later that more or less voluntary choice actually occurs in some instances of mediation, the importance of this issue is in the way it distinguishes the process from arbitration. For example, in some states disputes between public school teacher organizations and school boards *must* be arbitrated. In these instances, state law requires an arbitrator to be appointed and the parties to submit to arbitration.

The arbitrator's decision about the merits of the parties' positions is final and is imposed on the teachers and school boards. The participants in mediation choose either completely voluntarily or with a modicum of choice whether to negotiate, who will mediate their negotiations, and what they finally agree to. This element of voluntariness is thought to enhance both the process engaged in and outcome agreements.

Finally, mediation rests on an assumption that negotiators rather than the mediator are responsible for the agreements made. While responsibility for decision making rests with client systems in most social work practice, the emphasis on the negotiator's responsibility is highlighted in mediation, through some procedures that will be examined later. Responsibility for one's choices may help ensure that agreements made are kept later.

These assumptions distinguish the mediator role from other roles. While system conflict may exist as issues in which the social work advocate or clinician also is concerned, the worker's goal, strategies, and position vis-a-vis client systems differ for the social work mediator. The critical distinction is that the mediator intervenes in a *process of interaction* between systems as a nonpartisan helper whose purpose is to assist systems to reach agreement about disputed issues. There is no attempt to negotiate for a system or to assist a system to make significant changes in the way it functions.

The choice of this role and subsequent selection of change strategies are based upon the goal sought and how the negotiating process is conceptualized. These elements of practice are developed in greater detail in the sections which follow.

PROBLEM IDENTIFICATION AND ASSESSMENT

The mediator role is selected as a social work intervention when the worker is invited by two or more systems or subsystems to assist in resolving disputes or when the worker perceives the need for conflict resolution within or between systems, offers to serve as mediator, and is selected by the parties to mediate. The mediator role should not be selected when the systems have another goal such as securing an entitlement, creating a new entitlement, or altering internalized effects of system stress.

The content of problem identification in mediation differs from that of most other roles. Since the worker intervenes in a negotiating process, problem identification emphasis is entirely on this process and factors that influence it. The focus is not on individual participants, their past histories or personalities, except as these impinge on the negotiating process. Negotiating problem are barriers to agreements, which arise in the negotiating interaction. While barriers may develop from problems in social functioning experienced by one or more participants or from a previous history of interaction among participants, this history is not the concern of the mediator. The concern does not extend to assisting participants to achieve change in personal or social functioning except as these are manifest specifically in the negotiating process and impede reaching agreements. As Chandler (1985) noted, mediators assess but do not diagnose in the sense of establishing a basis for in-depth psychological change.

Mediators often do not collect any data prior to the first mediation session. Gallant (1982) specifically notified potential users of educational mediation that no information other than a joint request for mediation was to be sent prior to the session. The mediator begins to identify the nature of the negotiating process and the content of the dispute at the start of a mediation session.

Problem identification and assessment are affected by the anticipated length of the negotiation. Some mediation efforts last only a few hours, others a day or so, and still others may involve several sessions of an hour or more each. Gallant's (1982) mediation of education disputes were expected to last about three hours. Folberg and Taylor (1984) reported divorce mediation sessions over a period of weeks until all disputes are settled (or cannot be settled) and a written agreement is signed. Wall (1981) described negotiating sessions as one shot, repeated, sequential, serial, multiple, or linked. When mediation lasts just a few hours, the mediator needs to identify negotiating problems or issues and develop an assessment quickly. This problem-solving step occurs repeatedly in longer mediation sessions.

Three areas should be examined in problem identification and assessment: characteristics of negotiating process, characteristics of participants, and characteristics of the negotiating situation. Each of these is described below.

Negotiating Process Characteristics

The negotiating process is the interaction of negotiating participants. This process is characterized in terms of its content and pattern.

Content Because the content of negotiation varies as a function of the type of dispute, mediators need to be knowledgeable in the specific content area. Divorce mediators need a framework of concepts usually covered in these disputes, such as child custody issues and property settlements. A mediator in race relations disputes needs to be familiar with the special concerns of minority groups such as discrimination, prejudice, equal access, and stereotyping behavior. When an agency supervisor or administrator mediates conflicts among employees, the content of the negotiating process is different from either divorce or race relations disputes.

The range of potential negotiating content in social work is very broad. Social work mediators should become familiar with the particular content areas they are most likely to need. This knowledge is formalized in a conceptual framework which the mediator uses to organize observations about the content of negotiations.

The mediator identifies content barriers to agreements and assesses the need for particular content to be the focus of negotiation. The mediator examines content for areas of agreement and disagreement and characterizes the salience of these to participants.

Process The mediator observes the interaction pattern in negotiations, which either impedes or facilitates reaching agreements. Relatively few conceptualizations of this interaction process are available and none has been tested sufficiently to confirm its descriptive and predictive usefulness. Interactions in mediation have been explained using exchange concepts (Wall, 1981), elements of manager/supervisor behavior (Pruitt, 1983; Barsky, 1984), system concepts (Schwartz, 1976; Shulman, 1979), field theory (Lewin, 1947), and negotiation stage concepts (Carlisle and Leary, 1981).

Pruitt (1983) identified two dimensions of negotiator behavior: negotiators are more or less assertive (focused on their own outcomes) and negotiators are more or less cooperative (focused on the others' outcomes). Pruitt derived four strategies negotiators use. Those with high concern for others' outcomes and low concern about their own *yield.* Negotiators are *inactive* when they have low concern for both their own and others' outcomes. Negotiators *contend* with others when they combine high concern about their own outcomes with low concern about others' outcomes. *Problem solving* is used when negotiators are high on both dimensions (Pruitt, 1983; 166).

This model of negotiation process may be useful in social work mediation if it is modified to focus on patterned interactional behaviors for which a framework is designed to connect mediator assessments with outcome objectives and worker strategies. The remainder of this chapter presents a proposed social work mediation framework. It includes suggestions about identifying patterned behaviors, which the worker assesses in negotiators' interactions, outcome objectives, and worker strategies that fit assessments. Although many assertions about social work practice still must be tested, the mediation model proposed here is highly tentative and subjected to further refinement and extensive research.

An ideal negotiating process might be one where both parties engage in problem-solving behaviors since these seem most likely to result in agreements about disputes. The most problematic process is one in which both parties demonstrate inaction since movement toward agreements in absent or limited. If one participant constantly yields, we might expect that agreements will have either little or low salience and will not be carried out. A participant may contend not only on the issue of child visitation in a divorce dispute, but on all or almost all other issues as well. An employee in a dispute with a supervisor about working conditions may yield on a specific dispute about caseload size and almost all other matters as well.

Participants may engage in contending behaviors so that agreements are difficult to reach on disputed points. This behavior is observed in statements such as, "No, I won't agree to that; it has to be my way;" or "I always gave in before and I won't give in now;" or "If I give in on this point, I'll be expected to give up more later.'' Problem-solving behavior can be inferred from statements such as, ''What if we both tried a different way such as . . . ?'' or ''How about trying it both ways for a while to see if it works?'' or ''Another solution might be . . . '' or ''If you will try it my way on this issue, I'll agree with you on another issue.''

Inaction behavior is observed in statements such as, ''I really don't care how any of this comes out;'' or ''We don't need to discuss any of this;'' or ''Trying to agree won't help anything.'' Yielding behavior is inferred from a pattern of statements such as, ''I see your point and agree;'' or ''We can do it your way;'' or ''I don't have any preference so your suggestion is all right with me.''

Assessment

Participants' negotiating behavior is observed and classified to assess whether or not a match or mismatch exists between behaviors used by participants in a mediation process. The worker determines barriers or impediments to movement toward reaching agreements in the process. A schema of movement in the negotiating process based upon match and mismatch of negotiating participants' behavior is shown below:

	MOVEMENT	NO MOVEMENT
Behavior Match	Yielding/Yielding Problem Solving/Problem Solving	Inaction/Inaction Contending/Contending
Behavior Mismatch	Yielding/Problem Solving Yielding/Contending	Inaction/Yielding Inaction/Contending Inaction/Problem Solving Problem Solving/Contending

Movement in negotiations occurs when participants' behaviors match, that is, all parties engage in yielding behavior or all engage in problem-solving behavior. Movement also occurs when there is a mismatch in negotiating behaviors, that is, when one engages in yielding behavior and the other contending behavior or when one engages in yielding behavior and the other problem-solving behavior. While movement toward agreements under conditions of mismatch is not problematic automatically, the mediator is concerned that some balance should exist in agreements. The mediator may need to act to alter highly disproportionate achievements of one negotiator over the other. In regard to a specific disputed item, then, the mismatch may not be problematic. However, if the pattern exists across all or almost all items in the dispute, disproportionate and possibly unfair advantage would go to the negotiator who consistently used contending or problem-solving behavior when the other negotiator engaged in yielding behavior.

Movement is unlikely to occur in negotiations when both engage in inaction or both engage in contending behaviors. Several conditions of mismatch may occur which impede movement: (1) Inaction occurs with yielding, contending, or problem-solving behaviors; and (2) problem solving occurs with contending behavior. The worker's strategies in these instances need to be powerful enough to move one or the other negotiator toward interactions more likely to result in movement and ultimately to agreement.

The worker examines the content and process of negotiating interactions in terms of the specific item at dispute and the pattern of interactions across the total dispute. The worker identifies areas of agreement and disagreement, the salience of the latter for each participant (how important the issue is to the participant), characteristic ways participants interact about a specific issue or across all issues, and impediments to movement in the match or mismatch of participants' negotiating behaviors. The worker's assessment contains hypotheses that explain impediments and predict how movement toward agreements can be generated.

Participants' Characteristics

Both the content and pattern of negotiating interaction are influenced by the participants' personal characteristics. Problem identification and assessment should focus on characteristics related to the success of negotiations for a given participant and for the general goal of resolving as many issues as possible. All client-system characteristics outlined in Chapter 4 should be assessed with special consideration to the following:

Experience The participants' experience is important. This refers to their prior formal negotiating experience and experiences in interactions that are similar to negotiating. Some participants may have been socialized in ethnic, cultural, or religious groups where negotiating is used to settle disagreements. This experience may have given a participant opportunity to learn skills used in formal negotiations. The worker identifies participants' experience level and the extent to which they share approximately the same level of negotiating skill. Extreme differences in experience and skill are important in strategy selection since the worker stresses agreements that are fair to both sides and not biased inadvertently.

Verbal Ability Since discussion is the major vehicle for negotiating, participants need at least basic verbal ability. They need to be able to say what the issue is from their perspectives, why it is important, what agreements they want, and what alternatives they might be willing to accept. If the worker finds a participant cannot participate verbally, he or she should suggest a representative or advocate negotiate on this person's behalf.

Lack of verbal ability may result from language differences, neurological deficits, or low basic intelligence. The worker's concern, in part, is the balance or approximate evenness of participants' verbal ability. The worker uses an assessment of deficits and their probable effects upon negotiating in selecting specific techniques and overall mediating strategies.

Personal Functioning Personal functioning is assessed for two purposes: First, possible negative effects on participants should be examined. Second, this assessment is used to limit the focus of an ongoing mediation effort to the issues it is designed to handle. Persons with serious mental health problems that significantly interfere with reasoning capacity should not be expected to negotiate agreements on their own behalf. Mediation should be delayed and the participant referred to an appropriate resource for other services. If a participant attempts to solve functioning problems in negotiating, which are not properly a matter for conflict resolution, the worker should refer him or her to an appropriate resource. Mediation may occur concurrently with such assistance, be delayed until help has been sought, or involve a representative or advocate.

Status Negotiating parties may not have equal status. When they do not, their negotiating behavior may be affected with more yielding behavior or inaction observed in the behavior of low status persons. The worker should observe status to assess whether or not these differences seem to be reflected in the participants' behavior. In an education dispute involving parents, principal, supervising teacher, and special education teacher, the principal might be perceived by all others as having the highest status and the most power. Since power may be exerted in negotiating, the worker determines whether or not and how it affects progress toward agreements. Power derived from status may make it difficult for other participants to pursue vigorously their side of a dispute or may interfere with their perception of their own power.

Commitment to Objectives Participants vary in the degree to which they are committed to their own outcomes in negotiating. Some behave in ways that suggest strong commitments while others have less strong commitments. Commitments are reflected in choices about agreements and in negotiating behavior.

A participant with a strong commitment to the objective of having her or his child visit for a particular holiday will fight harder for that outcome in divorce negotiations than another objective to which she or he is committed less strongly. When a participant's objectives are held strongly, mediation efforts may be more difficult than where they are less strongly held. A participant with relatively weak commitments, either to a specific objective or to protecting his or her outcomes in the total negotiation effort, may demonstrate lack of concern for or involvement in the process.

The worker assesses strength of these commitments to estimate: (1) the extent of participants' involvement in the process, (2) the degree of participants' flexibility in seeking agreements, and (3) the participants' probable interaction patterns or behaviors.

Flexibility Participants vary with respect to the extent of their flexibility in achieving their outcomes. If a participant sees only one or very few ways her or his outcomes can be met, she or he is less flexible than participants who consider a range of alternatives to reach agreements. Degree of flexibility extends or limits the range of alternative agreements workers can use in resolving conflicts.

Context Characteristics

The content and structure of negotiation are modified not only by participants' characteristics, but also by the negotiating environment or context. The negotiating environment directly influences the content and structure and indirectly influences these through interaction with the participants' characteristics. Four environment characteristics should be assessed.

Time Constraints This variable is the extent to which a deadline exists independent of the negotiators and limits the period during which they interact to reach agreements. Time pressure may exist, for example, in a deadline for program implementation. If agency staff members and community representatives are negotiating a dispute about program emphasis and direction, a deadline for agreement frequently is beyond the control of either group and is not subject to negotiation. It comprises a pressure under which all participants act and may serve to push them toward agreements or may be used by participants as a reason for not reaching agreement.

Some negotiating environments impose no time constraints. In these situations, only the participants' perceived pressure to conclude or the interjection of time pressure by a mediator are time constraints. It is unclear how lack of time constraints influences a negotiating process. It might free participants to explore a range of alternatives or it might reduce incentives to achieving agreements.

Constituent Representation This variable is the extent to which a participant negotiates only for himself or herself or for a group as its representative (cf. Carlisle and Leary, 1981). The worker assesses the amount of influence on negotiators, which originates in their reference groups. The least amount of influence on a negotiator exists where she or he does not represent a system formally. In divorce negotiations, for example, some negotiators can make agreements without approval of others such as grandparents, neighbors, or friends. These other system members may have varying amounts of influence on agreements, but this does not always mean strong influence or veto.

At a stronger influence level, the negotiator's reference group and system precisely and specifically define the area within which agreements can be made without the group's approval. The negotiator's behavior is flexible within the defined area but cautious and noncommittal on issues outside the area. When a negotiator must return to a community group for instructions, the negotiating process and/or content may be altered.

At a third and still stronger influence level, the reference group receives regular reports from the negotiator, discusses issues, chooses goals and strategies, and instructs the negotiator. The negotiator's latitude is circumscribed and his or her behavior is cautious and inflexible when issues and alternatives arise for which the group has not prepared.

The worker assesses this variable by answering such questions as: (1) Does the negotiator represent a group and system? (2) If so, what is the negotiator's area and extent of latitude in making agreements? (3) How strong is the system's influence on the negotiator? (4) What types of influence constrain the negotiator? (5) How comfortable is the negotiator as the group's representative? (6) Where the negotiator is not a formal representative, do significant others influence his or her behavior?

Some types of agreements are subject to outside approval by a system, which was not party to negotiations. For example, some mediation agreements must be approved or ratified by a court or other institution. When this occurs, the worker may be influenced by precedents or agreements in earlier mediation and temper suggestions about agreements or interject caution about agreements yet to be ratified.

Nature of Participation Mediation is distinguished from arbitration, in part, by the extent of voluntary participation and agreement making. Nevertheless, participation in mediation varies from being completely voluntary to being set up by courts and other agencies as a step in a more formal judicial or administrative process.

Some domestic relations courts, for example, expect all couples to meet with a mediator and attempt to resolve such matters as child custody, visitation, and support agreements as the basis for a final decree. While participation is not, strictly speaking, entirely voluntary because of the court's authority, agreements are voluntary and not imposed by the mediator. In other instances, participation is voluntary but the possible losses from not participating are so great that system members conclude they must participate (Susskind and Ozawa, 1983).

History of Interaction This context variable is the nature of participants' previous interactions. Historical data are sought only to estimate how previous interactions may influence present negotiations, not to identify problems in long-term system functioning. Nevertheless, a history of prior problematic interactions should be identified and assessed. Kressel and others (1980) noted that couples' histories of marital conflict and decision making about whether or not to divorce were factors in their attitudes about and behavior in divorce mediation. For example, where there had been a high level of conflict and disagreement about divorcing, the negotiating process was difficult for them and the mediator.

Community residents and the police may have long histories of poor relationships, which influence resolving a specific conflict. Other disputes occur where the participants' prior interactions were positive and supportive. The worker assesses the nature of this interaction history, disputes in general, and the present dispute in particular to understand better what happens in a negotiation and to select strategies.

Summary

Problem identification and assessment give the worker a picture of the negotiating process for which strategies will be selected. Problems may arise and differences among negotiating interactions are observed in three arenas: content and pattern of negotiating interaction, participants' characteristics, and characteristics of the negotiating context. The assessment consists of statements about the dispute, participants, influences upon them, anticipated negotiating patterns, and barriers to reaching agreements.

PLANNING AND ENGAGING IN CHANGE

Social work does not have a typology of mediator strategies. Most literature refers to techniques or procedures but not strategies as constellations of worker behavior differentially selected on the basis of negotiating process characteristics (Gallant, 1982; Wall, 1981; Kochan and Jick, 1978; Raiffa, 1983; Colosi, 1983; Barsky, 1984; Folberg and Taylor, 1984). A tentative typology of mediation strategies is proposed later, which focuses on the negotiating interaction in which mediators intervene. It needs to be developed further and tested in a range of social work practice arenas.

A typology of mediation strategies should meet several criteria. First, it should identify the outcome of change. Second, it should identify the negotiating process rather than individual participants as the change arena. Third, it should account for the types of impediments observed in the negotiating process. Fourth, it should identify constellations of behaviors, not single techniques.

Mediation Goals and Objectives

The goal of mediation is voluntary agreements about disputes between participants. Susskind and Ozawa (1983) suggested agreements should be acceptable to negotiators, fair to the larger community, maximize all participants' gains, and be consistent with earlier precedents. In addition, the process should not expend excessive time, effort, and money and yet improve relationships between participants. These qualifications are value judgments about successful mediation. It is unlikely all participants share these judgments and it has been noted that it is "perfectly appropriate for some relationships to end not with a bang, a whimper, or a negotiated settlement but with a farewell" (Rubin, 1983; 136)! This view does not emphasize improved relationships as an important mediation outcome.

The goal of mediation is defined here as voluntary agreement *conditioned* by the worker's value that all participants' outcomes are maximized as equitably as possible. The instrumental objective in mediation is movement toward agreements. Strategies are selected because they are: (1) likely to result in movement where none or little exists or (2) because they promote and support movement where it already exists and/or (3) because they modify existing movement which is likely to result in disproportionate, unfair participant outcomes.

Major impediments to agreement and the instrumental objective of movement toward agreement arise from three major sources: (1) a mismatch in negotiators' behaviors, (2) negotiator characteristics, particularly lack of skill in negotiating, strength of commitment to negotiators' own outcomes, and status differences between negotiators; and (3) characteristics of the situation, particularly a problematic interaction history and strong system influence on negotiators.

Change Strategies

Strategies are chosen on the basis of extent of match in negotiator behaviors. Specific techniques and procedures are selected on the basis of negotiator and context characteristics.

NEGOTIATING PROCESS	STRATEGY
Inaction occurs with inaction, yielding, contending, or problem solving	Teaching
Problem solving occurs with problem solving, yielding occurs with yielding	Maintaining
Yielding occurs with problem solving or contending	Moderating
Contending occurs with contending or problem solving	Compromising

Teaching A teaching strategy is selected to help negotiators learn alternative interaction styles or behaviors. The worker provides information about negotiating and how it works, negotiating ground rules, and what the process will involve. Opportunity is provided for inactive participants to acquire negotiating skill, test out alternative behaviors, express concern about making agreements, and practice contending or problem-solving behaviors. This strategy also is used when participants appear to fear change, when there is a problematic prior history of interaction among participants in other disputes, and when negotiators lack trust in the worker.

A facilitative objective of a teaching strategy is to give participants the opportunity to express feelings about negotiating and prior negotiating experiences (if any) with the other negotiating party. The worker supports and encourages learning new and alternative negotiating behaviors and does not focus at this stage on the specific content of disputes or reaching agreements.

Maintaining This issue-focused strategy is used when a match of behaviors exists between negotiating parties that results in movement toward agreements. The worker focuses upon disputed issues and is not concerned about the particular behavior sets of negotiators since these do not impede movement. The purpose of a maintaining strategy is to narrow the area of issue difference by identifying areas of agreement and disagreement, proposing and testing alternatives, identifying similarities in positions hidden by different terms, and proposing trade-offs or compromises. The worker focuses directly on content of the dispute when using this strategy.

Moderating The purpose of moderating is to achieve a more fair or equitable distribution of agreements among participants. It is focused upon the participants' styles of negotiating as well as disputed issues. Although movement is observed, it is likely to lead to disproportionate outcomes. Moderating is appropriate when one participant consistently yields and the other is either problem solving or contending.

Disproportionate outcomes may not always occur, but the worker should determine whether they might and, if so, use a strategy that is aimed toward more fair outcomes. An effect of this strategy is to slow down or halt movement toward agreements until the consistently yielding participant increases attention to his or her own outcomes and contends more strongly for these.

Since yielding may be mismatched with contending in an unequal status context, the worker should explicitly identify this factor in the progress, suggest how it may influence behavior, and how it can be resolved. The content focus is on whether or not and how a specific issue may be important to participants and alternative ways they may contend for it. The interaction focus is upon identifying and testing new behaviors.

Compromising The goal of this strategy is to modify the negotiating pattern so that participants increase attention to and concern about other participants' goals. It is selected when both participants engage in contending behavior or one in contending and the other problem solving. Because contending negotiators have high commitments to their outcomes, it will be difficult to reach agreements unless they moderate their commitments and consider others' outcomes. The worker identifies alternative solutions, distinguishes areas of agreement, suggests compromises, and asks contenders to focus on others' outcomes.

EVALUATING CHANGE

Social work mediators engage in evaluating for three purposes: (1) to determine progress toward reaching agreements; (2) to determine mediation success; and (3) to explore the conditions under which various mediation strategies are related to successful mediation.

Mediation Progress

The worker continuously examines whether or not progress is being made toward reaching agreements about disputed issues. The outcome objective in education disputes might be to agree on a child's grade or school placement. The process of achieving this objective may involve instrumental objectives such as parental support for transportation. If agreement on this objective is stalled, the worker reassesses and may choose a different strategy depending on what impedes agreement. An objective in a community dispute about toxic waste disposal might be that all key decision makers are involved. The worker evaluates whether or not such persons are participating. If not, mediation may be delayed until this objective is met.

Mediation Success

The ultimate goal of mediation is a resolution of conflict that is acceptable and fair to all parties. Mediation concludes when all disputed issues have been resolved or when participants agree to disagree about one or more disputed points. Some mediation fails to achieve agreement on all points for various reasons. These include failure to negotiate, worker ineffectiveness, and participant characteristics that impede negotiating.

Social work mediators contribute to the profession's knowledge of this role by keeping records of mediation activities and reviewing these to develop tentative hypotheses about what strategies seem to work in what kinds of situations. Workers' records should include the following information for analysis: the nature of dispute, the characteristics of participants, the strategies used, and the outcomes. Follow-up contacts are used to determine whether or not the agreements were kept. In reviewing mediation records, the worker asks questions such as, "In discrimination disputes with participants of particular characteristics and negotiating styles, what strategies were used and was mediation successful?" While these comparisons do not prove a strategy caused an outcome, they assist us to develop further speculations and tentative hypotheses about successful mediation practice.

General Practice Principles

Several issues arise in mediation that need careful attention; some practice principles are suggested to deal with these. First, similar to some other practice roles involving small and large groups, mediation requires focus on a process, not on an individual client state or behavior. The worker always thinks about, pictures, and describes this process. It is insufficient to identify and describe individual participants; what they do in interaction is the issue.

Second, mediators must balance professional values and the requirement of neutrality. Our commitments to protect persons who cannot protect themselves, to avoid discrimination, and to protect rights and entitlements require us to examine how others use our mediation efforts. We must avoid, for example, serving as mediators where basic rights and entitlements are being given away and advocacy is needed.

Third, we should consider how to maintain neutrality when we work in settings where it might be easy to impose a settlement, given the institution's power to decide issues. The worker should evaluate how she or he uses power as the institution's representative.

Fourth, mediation requires a combination of concern and detachment, which is difficult to achieve. The worker does not own the dispute and has no personal stake in its resolution, yet needs to convey confidence in participants' capacities to reach mutually agreeable solutions. Finding the balance of involvement needed to achieve this objective requires evaluation of the worker's style and approach.

Finally, the worker needs to assess all client-system problems and refer participants to other services when mediation is not appropriate. Since mediation often is used where difficult intra- and interpersonal problems may exist and interact with the specific dispute being negotiated, the worker constantly is alert to the possible need for other services in addition to mediation.

Chapter Eleven

GENERALISTS AT WORK

Chapters 5 through 10 introduced the general goals and strategies for six social worker role sets. More than one role set may be appropriate in practice with a single client system. A worker may need to use only one or two or as many as all six role sets across a total work assignment. This chapter presents client-system examples in various settings.

These examples illustrate: (1) how two or more role sets may be appropriate for a single client system; (2) how several role sets may be appropriate across a social worker's total assignment; (3) the complexity of generalist practice; and (4) generalist practice principles and issues. Each example includes a brief client-system description, social worker–client-system goals, major social worker activities, and discussion of principles and issues. All names used are fictitious.

CLIENT SYSTEM #1

Description

The setting is a psychiatric hospital where the social worker is part of a professional team to plan and carry out patients' treatment programs. The client system is comprised of elderly parents, Mr. and Mrs. Ellis, and their thirty-five-year-old son, Sam. Sam is diagnosed as chronic paranoid schizophrenic and has a fifteen-year history of hospitalizations. His present hospitalization was precipitated by increased aggressive behavior toward his parents. After most previous hospitalizations he has returned to live with his parents. He cannot return home this time because of his parents' increased age and decreased ability to care for him.

Goals and Objectives

Three general social work goals are evident: Link the client system with needed resources (broker role), reduce internalized system stress (clinical role), and increase information for effective role performance (educator role). Some outcome objectives might be:

1. Sam will be stabilized on appropriate medication.
2. Sam will have an appropriate community placement.
3. Sam's parents will feel less guilty about their inability to care for him.
4. Sam's parents will learn about and use support services.

Roles and Strategies

In order to achieve these goals, the social worker engages in several different strategies from broker, clinician, and educator roles. The team psychiatrist selects and prescribes medication. The social worker helps observe Sam's behavior and contributes these findings to Sam's changing assessment during his hospitalization. The social worker also uses these observations to help choose an appropriate alternative placement for Sam. How Sam achieves this first objective serves as an indicator of placement readiness and type.

The second objective usually is the responsibility of the social worker who works with Sam and his parents to locate and use a placement. Achieving this objective may require engaging in three roles sets. Using broker activities, the worker identifies the kind of placement needed, matches Sam's characteristics and needs with placement resources, and refers him to the resource.

In some instances the community may not have an appropriate placement resource. If not, the worker uses the case of Sam and any others with similar placement problems as data to support arguments for new entitlements in social action strategies. Engaging in broker activities in Sam's case might involve strategies of referring and creating resources. Where creating is used, it leads naturally to work in the community on behalf of client systems with similar needs.

Assessment of this client system might have noted that Sam's parents expressed concern and distress about their inability to provide care. If so, one goal would be to reduce the effects of this internalized stress. We might also wish to help them better understand the problems they and Sam face so that they can proceed with life tasks more realistically and confidently.

The clinical role set directs the worker to a more detailed assessment of the sources of system stress. If we discover Sam's parents appear concerned because they have developed and maintained a set of personal and family expectations they no longer can meet, we might choose both cognitive and affective strategies. We would assist them to revise their expectations, talk about their feelings, affirm the significant care they previously have provided, and support them in their present circumstances.

Finally, the educator role directs the worker to providing Mr. and Mrs. Ellis new information about Sam's illness, groups of persons with similar problems, and activities in the community from which they also may learn. The purpose of providing such learning opportunities is to offer information for new perspectives about mental illness and support in and confidence about performing different parental roles.

Practice Principles and Issues

This example illustrates both possibilities and problems a worker might confront with one client system. The worker recognizes and responds to at least three sets of expectations: those of the hospital and treatment team, those of the community, and her or his own professional and personal expectations. The worker may experience limits imposed by the team. Many workers are fortunate to work on teams where decision making is shared and responsibilities for carrying out a plan are assigned appropriately considering team members' knowledge and skills.

In other instances, workers are brought into planning late, told what the plan is, and expected to carry it out without regard to their assessments. It is difficult for the worker to feel a part of this process and to contribute information needed for a thorough assessment and realistic plan. The worker's activities are compromised, her or his potential effectiveness is reduced, and his or her responsibility to serve and protect clients is hampered. The worker engages this problem directly in discussions with team members, seeks outside mediation to assist negotiating the conflict, and/or seeks administrative intervention to change team procedures. Effective generalist practice is constrained by role expectations, which the social worker seeks to modify consistent with his or her ethical commitment to put client systems rather than institutional structures as his or her primary focus and concern.

The goals identified in this example combine strategies from three role sets. The choice of strategies results from a comprehensive client-system assessment and contracts made between worker and system members. It is *not* sufficient for the worker only to serve as broker and connect this family with placement resources. A multifacetted assessment, which includes all issues and problems client system members identify, usually requires other activities. Even when a worker might be prevented by agency policy from offering clinical and educational strategies, he or she is responsible to serve as broker and refer the family to appropriate resources.

CLIENT SYSTEM #2

Description

The social worker and client-system members meet in the psychological services division of a prepaid health program agency. The client system is comprised of parents, Mr. and Mrs. Johnson, and three daughters, Karen, age ten, Betty, age fourteen, and Joan, sixteen. Mr. Johnson is employed as a maintenance man and Mrs. Johnson works part-time as a department store sales clerk. Three years ago the Johnsons moved away from their extended family in a rural farming area about sixty miles away to a modest home which they are purchasing in a recently developed neighborhood. Karen, Betty, and Joan attend school regularly, are at grade level, and have average academic achievement. During the past two years, conflict between Mrs. Johnson and her two older daughters has become pronounced with arguments about school, boyfriends, and chores. One report says Mrs. Johnson strikes Joan during these arguments. Mr. Johnson appears to ignore these conflicts. Mrs. Johnson requested assistance to relieve the conflict between herself and her daughters.

Goals and Objectives

Two different approaches might be taken with this system. As the worker gathers more information and makes a differential assessment, she or he might discover the family's conflict is of long duration and the current mother-daughter conflict represents more serious stress and adjustment problems. Some indicators of this might be an earlier history of significant conflict between parents and/or children, emotional disturbance of any family member, and/or evidence of significant failure to cope with family, social, and personal life tasks. Let us assume we find Mr. Johnson has a history of depressive episodes with which Mrs. Johnson and her daughters cannot cope. During such episodes Mrs. Johnson expects support from Joan and mother-daughter conflict is increased. Given the goal of reducing internalized system stress, the outcome objectives might be:

1. Mr. Johnson's depressive episodes will be stabilized, reduced, or eliminated.
2. Mrs. Johnson and the daughters will resolve interpersonal conflicts without verbal battles.
3. Mrs. Johnson will not strike daughters.
4. The level of family life satisfaction will increase for all members.
5. Karen, Betty, and Joan will accept limits set by parents most of the time.

To achieve these outcomes the worker and client system need to identify both instrumental and facilitative objectives. Some instrumental objectives might be:

1. Mr. Johnson will acquire an understanding of his depressive episodes.
2. Mrs. Johnson will feel less threatened and more confident with her responses to her husband.
3. Mrs. Johnson will not use her daughters for support they cannot be expected to provide.

Three important facilitative objectives that make it possible to work to achieve instrumental and outcome objectives are:

1. Mr. Johnson will participate in psychological and psychiatric evaluation.

2. The parents will participate in counseling as appropriate after a complete assessment of family problems.
3. Karen, Betty, and Joan will participate in groups focused on reducing parent-child conflicts.

Problem identification and assessment, however, might indicate this is a strong, generally well-organized family without physical abuse by the mother. The main source of difficulty results from two stresses that taxed its knowledge and interpersonal adjustment skills. The first is the move from a rural to urban area with its attendant loss of significant extended family support. The second is the new school for the daughters with loss of long-time friends and the need to make new friends just as Betty and Joan try to manage normal teenage developmental tasks. If this were our assessment, the goal would be for the Johnsons to learn new skills for effective role performance. The outcome objectives might be:

1. The parents will establish limits and provide consistent discipline for Betty and Joan.
2. Verbal battles in the family will be eliminated.

Instrumental objectives to achieve these outcomes are:

1. The parents will acquire knowledge of life tasks confronting teenagers.
2. The parents will learn appropriate expectations for teenagers.
3. The parents will acquire skill in setting consistent limits for their daughters.
4. Karen, Betty, and Joan will learn how to make new friends.

Facilitative objectives might be:

1. The parents will participate in a parents-of-teenagers educational group.
2. Betty and Joan will participate in a teenagers' group, the content of which is learning to know yourself and how to get along with parents.
3. All family members will participate in occasional discussions focused on improving family communication skills.

An alternative goal is to reduce or resolve intrasystem conflict. This goal is chosen when the assessment shows a quite strong family, no significant defects in knowledge for role performance, and little likelihood that the present difficulty represents conflict that already has influenced functioning negatively. Given this goal, the outcome objectives might be:

1. Mother and daughters will not fight.
2. Father will participate in family life.

Instrumental objectives might be:

1. The parents will form an effective subsystem.
2. Parent and teenage subsystems will identify their conflicts.
3. Parents and children will learn how to negotiate.

A facilitative objective is that parents and teenagers will participate in negotiating sessions with the worker as mediator.

Roles and Strategies

If the worker and client system have chosen the first goal, altering internalized effects of system stress, the worker chooses the clinical role. It is likely that all three clinical strategies may be used—affective, cognitive, and behavioral. The choice depends on the sources and effects of stress as noted in the assessment. Specific techniques or procedures are chosen based upon the worker's knowledge of effectiveness research, his or her skills, and available resources.

If the worker and client system choose the second goal, learning more effective role performance, the worker uses the educator role. The worker may choose to include family members in on-going, already available agency sponsored groups for parents and teenagers, refer the family to such groups and/or form groups for this purpose. An alternative is to engage in educational sessions with family members to teach them by providing specific information and designing practice sessions in which they can acquire new skills.

Finally, if the goal is to reduce or resolve intrasystem conflict, the worker chooses the mediator role. Depending upon subsystem (parents' and daughters') negotiating skills and styles, the worker selects teaching, maintaining, moderating, and/or compromising strategies. For example, the teenage subsystem might persist in a contending approach to negotiating while the parental subsystem remains essentially inactive in negotiating. If this occurs, the worker engages in teaching to provide both subsystems, but especially the parents, information and skill for negotiating.

Practice Principles and Issues

An inductive approach is illustrated in which the worker does not foreclose too quickly in problem identification and assessment. As patterns of parts and relationships become clearer, the worker tests out which theoretical explanation best describes the whole. Since theoretical explanations guide searches for more information, we should not start out labeling this an abusive family, or a multiproblem family, or a family with communication problems. We may discover later one or more of these labels fit. If we can avoid them as starting points, we may discover none fits.

This example also illustrates an occasion when we might choose two goals simultaneously—both relieving effects of system stress and educating for improved role performance. Some social workers suggest clinical strategies also meet an educational objective such as improved role performance. Others suggest educator strategies also meet the objective of reducing internalized effects of system stress. It seems logical that some effective role performance is blocked by ineffective cognitions and that some internalized effects of system stress may originate in poor role performance. Research may show both statements are valid in specific circumstances. Why, then, should a worker distinguish these goals and strategies from each other?

There are three reasons for distinguishing goals and choosing strategies on the basis of a particular goal. First, workers should be clear about what they intend to do and avoid selecting goals based on strategies they prefer to use. Second, such clarity assists workers to engage in practice outcome research. Third, such distinctions help workers think about the profession in more inclusive ways. Workers are asked to think of themselves as professional social workers skilled in differential assessment, clear and precise goal selection, and careful in matching strategies to fit goals rather than to think of themselves as clinicians who use selected techniques.

CLIENT SYSTEM #3

Mrs. Harrison, a fifty-six-year-old black woman, was referred to the hospital social service department by an outpatient nurse. Mrs. Harrison came to the clinic for routine medical care of an upper respiratory infection. A chest x-ray showed some abnormality and the physician recommended hospitalization for further tests. Mrs. Harrison is employed three days a week as a child care aide in a community center. Her husband, who was a day laborer, is deceased and her two children live in distant states. Even though her income and assets are meager, she does not qualify for the state medical assistance plan and she has no private or employee insurance. Because her medical situation is not considered life threatening, she cannot be admitted on an emergency basis. No hospital will accept Mrs. Harrison without assurance there is a source to pay her medical bill. Mrs. Harrison has a grade school education and relatively little experience in dealing with formal social agencies. Her support system is comprised of neighbors in her low-income neighborhood, her church where she has been active many years, and her colleagues at work.

Goals, Objectives, and Strategies

One goal is apparent immediately, another may be needed, and a third goes beyond this client system to others like it. The worker begins by trying to find a resource to pay for medical tests, matching need with resources, and uses the broker role. This may involve using an existing resource or creating a resource. In the discovery process, the worker may learn that a resource to which Mrs. Harrison is entitled exists but it has been withheld. This involves the worker in case advocacy. Although the outcome objective is the same as for the broker role—obtain medical care—instrumental and facilitative objectives are different. An instrumental objective is that Mrs. Harrison and the worker will discover the probable reason the entitlement has been withheld. A facilitative objective is that Mrs. Harrison will participate in assessing the risks, if any, in an advocacy strategy needed to secure the entitlement.

Let us assume the resource agency and Mrs. Harrison's worker share the goal of providing health care and a minor administrative mix-up has occurred regarding Mrs. Harrison's eligibility. The worker helps Mrs. Harrison provide needed data and/or persuades the resource agency worker to reinterpret available data. In this instance the social worker uses problem solving and persuading strategies.

Most workers with clients like Mrs. Harrison have more than one client system in need of resources. They are in a position to move to a third goal—creating entitlements for groups of actual or potential client systems without access to medical care. This might take several directions.

The worker might choose to focus on one or more social agencies (such as the community center where Mrs. Harrison works) to develop medical insurance plans for part-time employees. While this will not solve the medical care problem for all marginally employed persons, it reaches part of the problem. The outcome objective is to increase the number of part-time employees with health insurance coverage. Instrumental and facilitative objectives might be stated in terms of the worker's specific work plan. For example:

1. In three months the local NASW Chapter will choose this problem as its social action focus.
2. In six months a coalition of interested community leaders, social workers and persons employed part-time will exist.
3. At the end of the first year, a plan of action based on a needs assessment will be developed by the coalition.

As the worker begins to work toward these objectives, she or he develops more specific outcome, instrumental, and facilitative objectives at each step. The worker selects appropriate social action strategies based on assessments and how well objectives have been met.

Practice Principles and Issues

The Harrison example illustrates a dual focus in practice. The profession's history includes a focus on specific client systems in need of immediate help and the broader social policy tasks they represent. This dual focus is carried out best through many different efforts. If policy issues (such as entitlements for medical care) are left entirely to state or national NASW programs or to interested citizens, they may be left undone. Who knows more about the extent and type of need that form the basis for policy initiatives than social workers directly involved with client systems? No one.

The Harrison example also illustrates the importance of identifying and understanding community networks that provide significant client system supports and how these may differ for certain ethnic and cultural groups. Mrs. Harrison's church membership and standing may be very important. It may represent a network similar to an extended family that supports its members who live away from

Appalachia in Northern industrial centers. The culture that grounds and orients a Native American woman who lives away from but near her tribal home in Arizona or New Mexico must be recognized and understood. The advice of tribal leaders, particularly those who are healers, may continue to influence significantly how persons participate in the search for medical resources. The patterns of network aid, support, and constraint in a barrio may play a critical part in the way a Mexican-American woman with health problems participates in problem solving.

Appreciating and affirming the importance of such cultural and network influences is a critical social work task. The worker adjusts her or his expectations to reflect client-system experiences. The worker also is alert to ways institutions mold people to their images of acceptable problems and appropriate solutions.

The profession and the institutions in which we work tend to devalue broker activities and relegate them to the least experienced and lowest paid social workers. We save rewards and status for feelings, attitudes, and relationships! But for Mrs. Harrison and others like her, there may be nothing more important than obtaining medical evaluation and care. To suggest by actions, if not words, that helping her is unimportant and takes little skill misrepresents the competence effective broker activities require.

CLIENT SYSTEM #4

Description

This example is comprised of the total work assignment of a social worker in a community center. Approximately one-third of the worker's assignment is work with residents in a twelve-block neighborhood to identify and solve neighborhood problems. Another third of the time goes to organizing and coordinating the center's after school program. The remainder is the worker's assignment to a community task force examining complaints of drug use in public schools.

The agency's immediate neighborhood is racially integrated and comprised of low-income families most of whom have lived in the area many years. Some housing has deteriorated; city services have not kept pace with neighborhood needs when revenue sharing funds were used primarily in outlying, newly developed areas to build fire stations, parks, lighting, and sewers. The nearby downtown area has changed from small shops to large office buildings and parking garages. Major department and grocery stores moved out to malls around the city and the neighborhood has become isolated from the mainstream of services and activities. There is one elementary school in the neighborhood; all children are bussed out to junior high and high school. There are three churches in the neighborhood.

Neighborhood leadership consists mainly of older white residents considered by some younger and black neighbors to be out of touch with neighborhood problems. The agency has a neighborhood advisory group comprised of residents who have been active in agency programs. Some of these are neighborhood leaders, but most are younger persons who participate in sports leagues held at the center in the evening and on weekends.

The three broad purposes for the worker in this assignment are to: (1) assist neighbors to improve the quality of neighborhood life; (2) provide socialization activities for neighborhood children after school; and (3) assist the broader community to solve drug use problems. Each of these involves the social worker in problem-solving activities and the more specific goals in each part of the assignment may require the worker to engage in several different role sets. Some possible directions for social worker action are described below.

Goals, Roles, and Strategies

Neighborhood Improvement Assume that complaints about neighborhood problems occasionally have been heard from parents who pick up children from the after school program. Reports include such matters as safety, housing deterioration, lack of police patrols, and poor garbage pick up and street cleaning services.

Problem solving begins with the worker inviting interested persons to a neighborhood meeting at which problems are discussed and a plan of action, beginning with a needs assessment, is formulated. The worker is alert at this stage to encourage broad participation of recognized community leaders, advisory group members, and persons who express interest whether or not they participate in center programs. The worker assists this group to organize, choose leadership, and plan a course of action. Many different tasks may be required of the worker. One goal that might emerge from the needs assessment is to match resources with needs for which the broker role is appropriate. One of the neighbors' first concerns might be to install a stop sign at an intersection used by many children going to and from school. No crossing guard is provided, and attempts by a few parents to get something done several years ago was not successful.

The group's outcome objective is to increase safety for children at this intersection. Two instrumental objectives might be:

1. A stop sign will be installed.
2. A crossing guard will be assigned to the intersection.

Objectives that might facilitate these outcomes are:

1. Neighbors will marshall effective arguments to present to officials.
2. City and school officials will meet with neighborhood representatives.

Something that seems so easy to obtain as a stop sign may turn out to be difficult. The worker may discover that linking neighbors with the proper resources and helping them present their case in an effective way results in no change. The group might find that although crossing guards are provided at similar intersections in other neighborhoods, the school system claims lack of funds prevents further service. It appears this neighborhood is entitled to similar resources despite the school system's argument of no funds. The goal, then, is protecting and securing this entitlement and the worker engages in the advocacy role. In so doing he or she assists the group to make a thorough assessment of the adversary (school system) and its own strengths and weaknesses in seeking to obtain this entitlement.

The outcome and instrumental objectives are the same as for the broker role. But facilitative objectives reflect differences in the strategies to be used. If the group chooses to use education and persuasion strategies first, a facilitative objective is that the group will select representatives who can present its case effectively to school system representatives. Another facilitative objective is that a high level of cohesion will exist in the neighborhood advocacy group.

Depending on the nature of other problems found in the needs assessment, the worker might need to use social action, mediator, and educator strategies to assist the group to meet its goals. Social action might be necessary to achieve the objective of creating a new entitlement, such as a procedure in city government for hearing neighborhood complaints about city services. Mediation might be chosen if neighborhood improvement is impaired by racial conflict. The educator role might be used if a significant problem is a lack of opportunity for younger persons to learn leadership roles. While not all of these issues might be discovered, similar issues might be present and the worker's responsibility is to be open to resolving them either directly or by securing the resources to do so.

Socialization Groups Workers in community centers and other agencies often are responsible to organize groups for the purpose of assisting members to acquire knowledge and skill in growing up to become productive citizens. The context for such learning may involve participation in many different activities (recreation, solving tasks, or working on projects).

Let us assume this group is comprised of eleven boys ages ten through twelve who meet each weekday afternoon. The group is racially integrated; eight or nine boys attend regularly. Most of their time is spent playing basketball, soccer, and baseball. They have a formal meeting at least once a week and more often depending upon what is happening in the group. They are typical for their ages—lively, boisterous, and sometimes sensitive to real or imagined failures to achieve. They all go to the same school and, except for two members, all grew up in the neighborhood.

While the worker's general purpose may be to keep them occupied in constructive after school activities, suppose John, age eleven, and his family have just moved to the neighborhood. Another worker refers John to the group because both parents work all day. John wishes he were good at sports but he is small and uncoordinated. The group is working to learn soccer and John cannot pass the ball, block shots, or "anything," the boys say. Some members tease John occasionally and he leaves the playground crying. He wishes others would accept him but he cannot contribute to their usual activities so they will have reason to accept him. Two or three times, Pete, who is a quiet but effective group leader, tries to bring John back to the playground but cannot figure how to do so.

There are two immediate foci for the worker—help the group learn to accept differences and assist John to participate. There might be a third depending upon an assessment of John in the group. If John has significant adjustment problems not appropriate for this group, assistance to him outside the group is sought. Two goals might be: (1) the group will learn new social skills, and (2) John will learn new coping methods. The educator role is appropriate for the first goal; the second goal might involve either the educator or clinical role depending on the assessment.

One social skill we assume all persons need is the capacity to tolerate and accept others who are different. Youngsters can learn not everyone plays soccer well and not everyone needs to. One outcome objective for this group is that members will accept John despite his lack of soccer playing ability. To achieve this objective the worker and group might identify these instrumental objectives: (1) group members will not tease John; (2) the group will select some alternative activities John is good at; and (3) the group will identify other differences among members not based on sports.

Several facilitative objectives might be identified: (1) the group will discuss alternative activities, (2) the group will choose a sanction for teasing John; (3) the group will talk about what difference means and give examples.

The second objective, that John will learn new coping methods, probably could be achieved along with the first unless he is a very disturbed youngster whose behavior problems are exacerbated by participating in the group or who is so disruptive that the group cannot function with him as member. If the worker approaches the second objective in the group, two instrumental objectives are: (1) John will practice talking about his hurt rather than crying and (2) John will make suggestions about alternative activities he likes. If it developed that John simply does not have sufficient skill or psychological strength to make it in the group at this time, he might be referred to one more appropriate to his needs or to a source where the clinical role is available.

Community Drug Task Force Workers often are asked to assist in exploring and solving broader community problems. All roles except the clinical role might be used depending upon the community, the task force, and the problem. Possibly the most important knowledge and skills the worker uses are systematic problem-solving steps. These include leadership skills and knowledge of the community—its structure, problems, and people. In this example the client system is the community and the task force's work focuses upon discovering the nature and extent of the problem, proposing solutions, and possibly (but not always) assuming responsibility to carry out some proposed solutions.

The worker participates as a member who helps carry out group tasks. Where he or she has special skills others do not, these are used to achieve instrumental as well as facilitative objectives. For example, one instrumental objective might be that a survey of drug use in schools will be completed by the end of the first six months. Several conditions are necessary to facilitate achieving this objective including cooperation of the school system, access to data, and cooperation of parents and students. The worker might serve as chairperson of a subcommittee to do the survey. In this capacity the worker assists in establishing objectives, procedures, and assignments as he or she ordinarily would in any problem-solving process. The worker might need to find resources (broker role), arrange and provide opportunities for committee members to learn new skills (educator role), and mediate disputes between task force and community members.

Practice Principles and Issues

If a worker had an assignment similar to this illustration, his or her work would not be easy. But it would not be boring or dull either! Developing the knowledge and skills needed to practice in these different arenas requires more than collecting a bit of information and some hit-or-miss experience.

This example also illustrates some of the information a worker needs to have about research. The worker needs to know enough to answer some or all of the following questions: What assessment procedures will be most effective (give the most accurate picture) in this neighborhood for this problem? What trade-offs need to be made between accuracy and thoroughness of assessment and practical problems such as funds and neighborhood involvement? How do assessment tasks fit group members' skills? What do they need to be taught? What techniques and procedures can be used to maintain neighborhood "ownership" of this research and its findings? For research to be integrated adequately into problem solving, the worker treats the needs assessment (research) just like all other activities which engage her or him in solving a problem with system members.

Although this example is set in a community center, work assignments with this breadth of problems and tasks also occur in other settings. The typical day for a social worker in a domestic violence center might include many different activities and several roles. A worker in a family agency, school, or medical hospital is likely to work on many different problems with diverse client systems and use several roles.

CLIENT SYSTEM #5

The worker in this example works in a manufacturing plant employee assistance program. Most of the worker's tasks involve referrals by supervisors of employees with problems of alcoholism, excessive absenteeism, and family difficulties. Edith Smith, a worker in the shipping department, appeared at the worker's office in tears at the end of her shift. Their conversation revealed that several male employees made derogatory and sexually explicit remarks to Ms. Smith during the day.

Although this has occurred since she was hired six months ago, Ms. Smith did not report it until after her probationary period ended. Harriet Jones, with whom Ms. Smith occasionally rides to and from work, told Ms. Smith she has been sexually propositioned by her supervisor in an assembly line work unit. Ms. Smith heard a rumor that a woman in the accounting department made a similar complaint to the personnel office about her supervisor.

About a year ago the company began hiring women in nontraditional jobs under pressure from the state civil rights commission and some women's organizations. The total work force of 287 includes 43 women. Of this group, 29 work in clerical positions such as receptionists, telephone operators, secretaries, typists, and housekeeping for administrative offices. The remaining 14 work in nontraditional jobs. The company has a record of generally good labor relations including an excellent benefit package. As a family-owned company with long ties in the community, it has a positive image of significant contributions to community life over 25 years. Company officials resisted hiring women in nontraditional jobs because they thought women could not operate heavy equipment safely.

Goals, Objectives, and Strategies

The worker is expected to go directly to the heart of the complaint—the right of all women to work in a harassment-free environment. Do not stop with support to Ms. Smith; do not take a detour into whether or not she is telling the truth; do not wander down the path of explaining masculine responses to sharing their workplace with women on women's provocative clothes or behavior! Go directly to class advocacy.

The social worker's goal is to protect an existing entitlement. The outcome objective is that harassment will be eliminated. Initially, the problem-solving process involves Ms. Smith. Ms. Jones is invited to participate immediately. Any others who also are interested in or affected by the problem are invited to participate. This group discovers the nature and extent of the problem. After a thorough assessment involving as many women employees as possible, the worker and advocacy group choose and engage in advocacy strategies.

There are several possible approaches depending upon what the assessment reveals. Strategies are selected on the basis of the extent to which the advocacy group and management share the same outcome goal and how much change is needed to achieve the goal. At each step, the worker assists group members to assess risks.

A negotiating or bargaining strategy might be used if instrumental or facilitative objectives are not shared. The former implies compromise might be possible and that the group has power derived from the entitlement. The latter assumes the group is willing to give up something to get something and has sufficient power to persuade management to bargain. The implicit or explicit threat might be to go public with the problem. The worker helps members to understand differences between these strategies, make decisions about what to give up if bargaining is chosen, learn how to negotiate and bargain, and choose negotiators and bargainers.

Pressure tactics may be necessary if management does not share the goal of a harassment-free workplace or says it does but will not take steps to bring it about. Whether they are chosen depends upon the group's assessment of potential job-related risks members might experience. An examination of how the company responded to and involved itself in earlier encounters with civil rights agencies might provide clues about what would happen with additional public disclosures. The group might examine any residue of ill-will toward or support for the company in the community that can be traced to this earlier encounter. Such information might help predict the amount and kind of public reaction to expect from disclosures as a pressure tactic.

Practice Principles and Issues

Although risks do not always occur in advocacy, the potential exists precisely because the worker stands on the side of a client system against another subsystem or system. Often the worker stands with one subsystem against a subsystem that holds the power of worker dismissal. It might be less risky to take a mediator role where the worker stands between the two subsystems as a neutral party. But, then one must assume rights are negotiable!

What may be negotiable is *how* the right will be protected—the circumstances under which it is secured and how management (in this case) proposes to protect the right. Social work advocates might use negotiating and bargaining *strategies* to establish some of the conditions under which rights are secured and protected. The worker may negotiate for a group or teach members to negotiate. It does *not* involve the neutral *role* of mediating between negotiating subsystems.

The social worker's job, professional reputation, and/or work effectiveness may be risked in advocacy. But, more often the issue is our degree of commitment to conflict strategies (Epstein, 1970). The profession needs to know more about how workers develop commitments to conflict strategies and how they use them where needed.

Keith-Lucas' (1975) assessment of social work's reluctance to join alliances with disenfranchised groups and/or our inability to take leadership in such alliances still is valid: "It has become clear that such a revolutionary alliance . . . will not be looking to social work as a major participant. . . . There is probably only one way this new alliance could become a reality. That would be if social work's knowledge and values could infuse radical movements with real expertise about methods and . . . fuse its values with the energy and indignation of the radical groups." (Keith-Lucas, 1975; 95–96).

Six years later Miller (1981) incensed some social workers and rallied others with dirty sheets, dirty words, and a reminiscence of our commitments in the 1960s. Those years may or may not have been among the profession's best, but our values were apparent in our commitments to rights!

Chapter Twelve

ISSUES FOR THE FUTURE

The purpose of this chapter is to examine selected issues that will shape the future of practice and its social role. Although social work's agenda is broader than the issues discussed here, we consider these critical to practice effectively. Each issue needs the concerned, thoughtful attention not only of professional associations but individual social workers as well.

PRACTICE RESEARCH

How social workers resolve the issue of whether or not research holds a central place in practice will help determine our future effectiveness and capacity to frame important social questions. Research is one thread tying our most important concerns and activities together.

Whether we recognize it or not, social workers practice on the basis of probability statements and, as hypotheses, they should be confirmed or rejected through systematic investigation. When one strategy is chosen over another, the worker hypothesizes it is more likely to be helpful than the other. When she or he emphasizes certain facts in an assessment, the implication is that they have more meaning and relevance in an hypothesis than others do. When social workers choose to promote a particular cause in a legislative hearing, it is because that cause is seen as contributing in a significant way to solving a social problem.

One impediment to research progress is our confusion about facts and values. Facts are statements that have been confirmed and that may or may not also contain values. Values are statements of preferences: they influence the ends we wish to achieve and the means to achieve these ends. We should not use value statements as facts unless they have been confirmed (Gordon, 1965).

Although we may prefer a particular program, we must be clear that other programs, which might be consistent with our values, may be more effective. This also may be true for specific techniques, and we are expected to use those which are value consistent and effective. We need to subject our instrumental value statements to research so they can be confirmed or disconfirmed. Research is not *the* solution to all social ills. It is one tool that helps us to explore our society in systematic ways. We still must be clear about our values and make choices consistent with them.

Research techniques have been used by social workers to answer two types of questions. One type helps us to find out how big a problem is, who experiences it, and in what ways it is experienced. Answering such questions usually is called descriptive research because the answers describe something and because we ask these questions without making cause and effect predictions. Early medical social workers at Massachusetts General Hospital obtained descriptions of industrial injuries and illnesses—who was affected, where they worked, their illnesses and medical progress, and what their families and environments were like. Among many recent examples of descriptive research is Wyers and Kaulukukui's (1984) study of social services provided by selected employee assistance programs.

We also ask and answer questions that predict something. These studies are important because some of them attempt to discover whether or not our practice is effective. They help answer questions about whether or not providing services in certain ways has a positive (and predictable) impact on a problem. One example is a study of the effectiveness of milieu therapy in improving mentally ill young adults' skills (Velasquez and McCubbin, 1980).

The evolution of practice research demonstrates increasing sophistication in using measurement and evaluation tools to answer significant questions. Several research efforts since the early 1950s illustrate important practice research. Social workers learned much from each of these about the role of research in practice.

Significant Early Research

Social Movement Scale An early attempt to evaluate practice utilized a movement scale to examine case records for client progress (Kogan and others, 1953). Although a small amount of positive change was found, which appeared to persist after termination of social worker assistance, this research was important because it represented willingness to answer the hard question—do our services make a difference? This study is not considered an adequate way to evaluate client improvement by current standards because no comparison group was used. Nevertheless, it was a beginning which later studies built upon.

Services for Delinquents Some succeeding studies resulted in heated controversy among social workers. One examined whether or not selected social worker services reduced the incidence of social adjustment problems in teenage girls (Meyer and others, 1965). Many criticisms of this research blamed researchers for selecting the wrong service and irrelevant indicators of change even though these were the responsibility of program workers and not evaluators.

This study was important for two reasons. First, it used a comparison group and, if the results had been positive, social workers could have said with some assurance that their efforts made a difference. Second, this study required us to clarify the role of researchers vis-à-vis program planners and staff. Social workers did not like the findings but began to learn they should not be blamed on the evaluator.

Multiproblem Families A second controversial study hit social work where it hurt most when Brown (1968) discovered that professionally educated caseworkers did no better with multiproblem families than untrained public assistance workers. Few social workers wanted to believe the findings much less use them. Even the researcher appeared to back away from his findings (Briar, 1971). The Chemung County study, nevertheless, taught us two important lessons.

The first lesson was that practice research depends, in part, upon saying precisely what the worker does. A label such as casework or therapy or learning approach will not suffice. To say casework service (in this study) was offered says almost nothing or everything. The central behavioral elements of helping activities must be identified and distinguished from no assistance or from an alternative way of helping.

The second lesson was that good research always holds the possibility (threat!) of disconfirming our favorite assumptions. Some social workers were not prepared for this and proceeded to argue before Congressional committees that we needed funds to educate more professional social workers who would make a significant impact on public welfare problems!

Fischer's Conclusion By the early 1970s sufficient practice studies existed for some tentative conclusions to be drawn about the outcomes of our work. The first review of outcome studies concluded that casework services were not effective in achieving selected client-system goals (Fischer, 1973). Although some social workers were distressed and defensive about this finding, others pointed to its conclusions to support the need for research and, in particular, studies that specified more precisely practice objectives and activities. Social work began to face the issue of accountability more directly.

Learning from Research While Fischer had answered a question about outcomes of some practice, Wood (1978) examined studies to discover what they might teach us about good quality practice. Although her conclusion about effectiveness was similar to Fischer's, she asked, What aspects of practice can (and should) be improved? Her discoveries reaffirmed accepted tenets of competent practice and suggested research findings might have been more positive if practice had been carried out more competently.

This review highlighted the need to recognize that helping strategies occur in a process and context. Although it is unlikely that a truly ineffective strategy can be improved significantly by competent practice, the absence of competence may reduce the impact of otherwise effective strategies. Wood's review served to focus social workers' attention on what we need to do to improve practice quality.

Has Effectiveness Improved?

Recent effectiveness reviews suggest a more optimistic picture than Fischer's and Wood's conclusions. Reid and Hanrahan (1982) found that studies after 1973 resolved many of Wood's criticisms. Practice had become more standardized with problems, goals, and procedures more clearly stated and less all-encompassing. There was evidence that some techniques were effective in particular practice situations even though this conclusion was criticized (Fischer, 1983; Epstein, 1983). Rubin (1985) supported the conclusion that recent practice appears to be more effective and social workers' activities more clear and focused than earlier in our history.

Research Issues

Despite a more optimistic assessment about some social work achievements, there is concern this knowledge will not have its needed impact on practice. It is not easily disseminated and utilized. Research competes with other urgent social worker tasks, and social workers disagree about how to answer practice questions.

If making research central to practice rests with individual social workers, then several problems exist. First, social workers do not know enough about statistics to make sense of research reports (Witkin and others, 1980). Second, although social workers can distinguish good from poor research designs, the nature of the findings tends to interfere with this judgment (Kirk and Fischer, 1976). Third, social workers use relatively little research (Kirk and others, 1976) but appear to participate in more research than might have been expected given the generally gloomy assessment of their knowledge (Connaway and others, 1985; Gentry and others, 1984).

If the issue about practice research relates less to the worker and more to the profession's research models, we shall need to examine again the purposes of practice research and the procedures needed to achieve them. We want research to help us answer three general questions: What characterizes our client systems and their problems? What characterizes our helping activities? What helping activities are effective in what circumstances?

While social workers may agree about these purposes, we do not agree on research models and techniques that help answer them. On the one hand a heuristic model is proposed, which guides discovery of answers in general rather than rigorously systematic ways (Pieper, 1985; Heineman, 1981). The second model, which has equally strong adherents, is a traditional scientific (logical positivism) model (Hudson, 1982; Mullen, 1985). These models start from different assumptions and draw contrasting pictures of the discovery process. The issue of objectivity is at the center of these differences.

More than once in social work's history we have cornered ourselves in searches for the *one right way*. The same will happen in searching for ways to increase the centrality of research in practice unless we focus first on the purpose of a particular research question or problem, then match a research technique to that purpose. Traditional case studies, ethnographic and naturalistic field studies, single system designs, surveys, and other descriptions, and experimental designs all have a place in social work. None is inherently better than another, but each fits particular purposes and questions.

Practice Questions

We need to answer two general types of practice questions. The first might be called insight questions. These questions are not about what strategies are effective. Rather, they focus upon nuances of meaning, which enable us to describe more fully what client systems are like and our difficulties and possibilities in helping them. They might be called questions about our practice wisdom.

Unfortunately, many social workers look for information from outside experts to answer difficult practice problems. What if we placed more value on what social workers already know by assisting them to draw out their insights and collate and share these with the profession in more formal ways? New formats, arenas, and mechanisms will be needed for building and testing this part of our knowledge base. Current social work journals emphasize more formal studies and may not be read widely enough to serve this purpose. Professional forums are useful but do not include any mechanism for systematically following up issues, questions, and information. Forum themes are selected for national policy and practice timeliness, not as ways to consider knowledge development issues. What we do not need is an accumulation of case studies in journals or more workshops! We need a research agenda and mechanisms to work on it that include ways social workers can contribute their practice insights, suggestions, and observations. NASW is the logical group for this task, but whether it can and will do so is not clear.

All social workers expect NASW to be all things to its members. Striking a balance between membership services, national policy concerns, and knowledge development is not easy. One (probably outrageous) suggestion is for NASW to declare a two or three year moratorium on all activities *except* developing a research agenda, designing mechanisms to pursue it, and putting these into place. With all NASW resources focused on this issue we might make progress. But would the membership tolerate such a radical departure from services to itself? Maybe it would if it were convinced of the task's urgency and assured of meaningful participation.

The second set of questions we need to answer requires traditional scientific methods. We need to ask questions that test practice wisdom by asking what strategies work with what specific client systems under what conditions. This book is full of potential questions because it represents one way to organize certain instrumental values, facts, and unconfirmed practice wisdom, which have been accumulated, repeated, and promoted in social work for many years.

Summary

If research is to hold a central place in social work's future, at least four things are needed. First, social workers should distinguish carefully ultimate values from their preferences about ways to practice based on unconfirmed practice wisdom and knowledge. Second, practice wisdom, including, most especially, assertions about effectiveness, must be examined systematically. Third, research methods should be chosen to fit our research purposes and problems, not our preferences. To accomplish these tasks, we need social workers who know how to engage in and use research and effective ways to communicate research developments and outcomes.

A DUAL FOCUS

A second issue is strengthening social work's dual focus. The profession's mission has been and is to reconcile society's social policies with the problems and needs of particular client systems. Our success in living up to our commitment is uneven.

While social work alone is not responsible for this issue, we often find ourselves at the center of controversies about how to meet significant human needs. This may be an uncomfortable position but it also gives social work opportunities to influence policy development and implementation. An example illustrates this issue and our dilemmas.

When large numbers of mental hospital patients were deinstitutionalized, transitional care programs were not funded adequately. Many patients could not make a gradual and effective adjustment outside hospitals, and many communities experienced significant increases in the number of persons who lived on the streets. While social workers agreed deinstitutionalization was appropriate for many patients, we were concerned about what would (and did) happen to patients where planning and funding transition programs were inadequate. This policy shift involved us at many different levels—helping client systems, working with community planners, and bringing the problem to the policy makers' attention. In the end we had to adjust to a new state of affairs that was better in some ways than inappropriate long-term hospitalization, but worse in others for persons who slept in abandoned buildings and under railroad overpasses. Making this adjustment did not mean liking it and social workers continue solving problems brought about by the policy change. Social work's values and our potential practice effectiveness are abrogated and threatened regularly by policy changes such as this one.

Our ultimate concern is the social contract that binds members of society together and how adequately it reflects our values and knowledge about human needs and possibilities. Social work's values contain basic elements of this contract. The contract includes the idea of equity or evenness in the distribution of resources based upon one's contributions. However, we practice on the basis of exceptions to this principle and do not confront the problems behind our categories of exceptions or the conflicts that arise from them.

Social workers constantly ask their communities and larger society for exceptions to the prevailing social contract. But our communities must often be confused about why we ask for some exceptions and not others when we seldom make our underlying assumptions and values explicit. We ask for exceptions to the idea of equity, which claims that our social fabric is held together because everyone except the youngest and most feeble carries a share of the load.

We have been selective in recognizing the place of responsibility in the give and take of human exchange and its relevance to certain groups. We accept that a juvenile restitution program, if it is not harsh and does not discriminate against categories of youngsters, may have value both to juvenile offenders and to society. But we usually reject workfare programs, which require work in return for public assistance, because problems of human dignity and near servitude may result in some communities. Both programs, however, contain elements of the equity idea—if a person steals from a record shop or depends on the public treasury, some form of restitution must be made. The teenage offender and welfare recipient are both part of our social fabric and are responsible to help keep it intact.

The issue for practicing social workers is not simply one of public relations and persuasion. We shall need to rationalize our exceptions first within the profession and examine what they cost to make as well as the costs if they are not made. We may discover that the equity idea is flawed seriously and should be replaced with an alternative view of social responsibility.

Whether social work can or will follow the implications of its dual focus to the issue of social justice is not clear. But if it does not, practice will be caught in a tangle of exceptions most of which lead us only to residual functions and not to opportunities for proactive practice. Social action will continue to be a dirty word and social action strategies needed to establish rights in a just society will be ignored in favor of some catch-all, poorly distinguished advocacy idea.

PROFESSIONAL STATUS

A third issue is how social workers respond to our status in society. Depending upon one's view, social work is a profession or a semiprofession or an occupation. As noted in Chapter 2, social work has expended much effort to establish, maintain, and promote its status. We have done so not only for our own benefit but also to increase our power on behalf of others.

One correlate of social work's position may be the status of groups with which we work. Since we help disadvantaged and disenfranchised persons who occupy marginal social positions, our status may reflect our client system's marginality. Our dilemma is: Shall we increase status by working increasingly with less marginal groups or ignore status issues and maintain identification with marginal groups? Can we acquire more power without leaving our mission and values behind?

Numerous individual social workers choose politics and elective office as influence arenas where they can maintain professional commitments. Others take appointed governmental positions for similar purposes. Social workers in small and rural communities often hold positions of influence because of educational attainments, social ties, family networks, and community size. Still others choose social work education as their influence arena. But not all can or wish to make such choices. And what of the profession as a whole and its choices?

If we assume the primary purpose is to acquire power for its use on behalf of others, there are three ways our power might be increased. First, we need to examine our practice systematically, including practice wisdom and effectiveness. This will aid in gaining power based on knowledge. Second, we need to improve our competence as practitioners. This means developing greater clarity about client-system problems, distinguishing their goals and objectives from our activities, and selecting strategies consistent with client-system goals.

Third, we need to use the power we have more consistently and effectively. Traditional analyses of professions and their status use somewhat arbitrary criteria. Professions that control their own work and are subjected to little social control are thought to have more status and power than those over which more extensive control is exercised. By these criteria and most others used in traditional sociological analysis, social work has little status and not much power. While we might prefer to control more of our work, this seems unlikely unless we become a private practice profession. To do so would cut us off from some of the most significant assistance we can give to groups with greatest need.

Social work's pivotal position between client systems and resources gives us power which we have not exploited fully. We usually know more about social systems than any other profession or occupational group. Our skill in making systems work is one of our most important characteristics. But we seldom advertise it, often overlook it in favor of higher status activities, and prefer not to be identified as system experts but as therapists or counselors. Making systems work is no inconsequential skill, and we should consider what it means for social work as well as our client systems. It gives us a unique storehouse of information about society and social institutions, what works and does not work, and how to help not only client systems but consumers of all types of services. This knowledge and capacity to help generalizes beyond traditional social agencies and usual client systems. We might exploit this source of power in several ways.

First, we need to recognize and appreciate what we can do. We should not let anyone tell us the knowledge we acquire of our communities and skills we develop in getting some of its social institutions to work for people are not as important as some more prestigious activity. To make the most of our knowledge, it must be known outside social work. We might form public interest groups to collate and distribute information about social institutions where special issues and problems exist in obtaining services and what can be done about these. What could we do with a community telephone hotline containing the latest update on food stamp rules and procedures, the utility company's winter care program, a mental health center's waiting list, or the most effective way to request assistance from the Small Business Administration Office? Such a plan puts our knowledge and skill to work for the whole community and places us in a crucial information giving position.

We can teach more people in our communities the essential features of what we do in problem solving. The purpose of such education is not to transform them into mini-social workers (although that might not be a bad idea!), but to empower more persons than we can serve directly. It also helps advertise and promote one of our most important skills.

Finally, our knowledge of social institutions and their effects on people should be used in advocacy and social action. In five minutes at any gathering of two or more social workers, one can learn of at least one client system's difficulties in obtaining a service. If one system experiences difficulty, we can be almost certain others do also. Using this knowledge on behalf of others and increasing our power is not simply a matter of joining some cause. We must recognize where our allegiances are and how divided they become between loyalties to client systems and to agencies where we work.

Because some of us may not be able to take class advocacy and social action risks without protection, we may need to seek alternatives. We might form privately funded advocacy and social action groups. NASW chapters can develop coalitions and alliances with other interested groups. Our special contribution to these is providing information about what happens in the community that hurts and jeopardizes its citizens. Making our knowledge work will take us into some nontraditional places where we need to be advocates without taking differences as attacks on our professional status.

Social workers have significant sources of power. We either have been reluctant to use them or have not figured out how. We depreciate what we know, even to ourselves. Having done so, we sometimes look for power where others seem to get it—high status positions and nonmarginal client systems—rather than exploit what we know and can do.

SPECIALIZATION

Briar (1974) identified social work's dilemma about practice specializations. Knowledge is expanding at such a dramatic rate none of us can keep up. Although social workers do not need each new piece of information as soon as it is available, much new information is relevant to practice. One approach to this issue is to identify practice specializations that social workers can enter and for which they develop, maintain, and change their knowledge base as new information becomes available.

Social work has spent almost thirty years identifying its common core for a unified profession. This concern has yielded somewhat to recognition that we cannot all keep up with and use all relevant developing knowledge. The idea of specialized practice, however logical and reasonable, still threatens some because of fear that it will fragment social work into dysfunctional divisions and reduce our effectiveness. How we resolve this issue will tell us much not only about social work's unity but also its creativity and maturity.

This book is about things we think are central to social work as a whole—its historical commitments, a framework for approaching any practice situation, and general strategies for solving client-system problems. It is one way to identify basic or core social work values, conceptual frameworks, and processes. Although it is not about specialized practice, the way social work practice was formulated contains suggestions about specializations.

This formulation and our biases lead us to conclude specializations should not be developed in traditional ways. First, because social workers are concerned about wholes, parts, and relationships, specializations based on partializing *problems* has limited utility. We have seen what happened in medical care when relationships among different problems were ignored.

Second, specializations based on *size of client system* makes arbitrary assumptions about practice knowledge and actions. We always practice with groups and their size is not how we come to know them and is not central in distinguishing what we do. Third, specializations should not be based on constellations of *program services.* This concept is so broad that it hides important distinctions across practice. Our client systems are groups of various sizes with particular characteristics who experience one or more problems for which particular outcome objectives and helping strategies can be identified. How can this understanding be captured for a practice specialization framework? Two suggestions are made below.

Practice Objectives

One approach is to organize specializations by broad outcome categories. One specialization might be practice for provision of resources: another would be practice for acquiring knowledge and skill for improved role performance. Specialization in resource provision requires the worker to become expert about a full range of resources and all the detailed knowledge of systems providing those necessary to make these systems work for people. The worker needs to know common as well as unique or special characteristics of client systems usually needing resources. The social worker also would be expected to develop expert skill in broker role strategies. Specialized practice for knowledge acquisition and improved role performance requires the social worker to have expert knowledge of learning theories, usual client system characteristics, information from other fields about how people learn, and particular techniques and procedures in educator strategies. A problem with this approach is its similarity to our former specializations by practice methods. While it focuses on common themes and characteristics of systems, social work might slip too easily into designating specializations by role and strategy concepts without giving sufficient attention to client systems' characteristics.

Populations

A second approach to identifying specializations is to design them on the basis of certain assumptions and knowledge about populations. Populations are groups of persons who share common characteristics some of which, for social work purposes, are defined as threats to their well-being. The term has been used by several disciplines including geography, demography, sociology, and epidemiology. Each uses the term to identify a unit of analysis in which common characteristics, issues, or problems may be examined. Professionals in public health, community medicine, community mental health, and public health nursing use the term "population at risk" to denote groups thought to be threatened by various health problems.

We may share concern about a population with other professionals but social work's focus or concerns are on different functions or purposes. Ordinarily our function is *social* rather than medical or judicial, for example. We make this *social* function operational in the strategies we use to meet population groups' problems in resource acquisition, protection, and establishment of entitlements, role performance, internalized stress, and system conflict. While theoretically all populations may experience or be at risk to experience any or all of these problems, most social work practice is focused on persons currently experiencing difficulties. The concept of risk, however, allows us to consider social work assistance where timely help may prevent difficulties.

Identifying and characterizing populations (and populations at risk) is one way to define specializations. It will not be easy for several reasons. First, we need to identify the critical features or dimensions that distinguish populations. Often used terms such as "poor," "low income," "disadvantaged," "ill" and "delinquent" are not very discriminating and probably will not serve to distinguish populations from each other. Second, it is not clear whether broad and general population groups or more narrow and specific distinctions should be made. The former probably would result in large and conceptually unwieldy specializations. The latter might result in so many specializations that the idea loses its conceptual power.

Third, populations should be distinguished from each other in ways that capture important social work concerns. We should not make distinctions only on the basis of concepts that capture our concern for remedies but also those that express our concern for prevention. We need concepts that capture the essence of social work's value commitments—concepts that refer to wholes, parts, and relationships, our understanding of basic human needs, and our commitment to diversity.

Finally, one area of specialization is the generalist as specialist. Although such a designation seems to be a contradiction in terms, the idea is that a social worker who focuses his or her knowledge and skills broadly rather than more narrowly to one client-system population also must develop practice competence and, therefore, can be said to have specialized in generalist practice (Gentry, 1977).

NEW PRACTICE ARENAS

Future social workers will have the opportunity to develop new practice arenas. Those discussed here represent arenas where some social workers have or are practicing but where the profession has yet to take full advantage of the challenges required to become visible and influential.

Rapid Response Practice

Social workers historically have responded to many different types of community emergencies. Some of these were discussed in Chapter 5. The more general challenge is to prepare for a broad range of community problems characterized by the need for rapid response. These needs may require social workers' assistance in one or more roles. Although major disasters such as airplane crashes, floods, and tornadoes are emergencies that occasion social worker help, there are other community needs of less dramatic or far-reaching magnitude where social workers also might provide assistance.

When facilities of a significant social institution, such as a church or community center, are damaged or destroyed, community residents might need assistance in rebuilding. When violence develops between persons striking a factory and those crossing picket lines, mediation services might be helpful. Social workers might assist students, parents, and school personnel to resolve discord that develops when a significant number of students are displaced from one school to another. Occasionally hostages are taken during family and community disputes; terrorism is occurring at an increasing rate in modern society. These life threatening incidents involve public protection personnel such as police, but may need social workers' services as well. The sudden death of a high school student under unusual circumstances might require immediate professional assistance to classmates. Where a major store or factory closes and displaces workers for whom no employee assistance program is available, social workers might help.

We need to think about our communities. Has anything happened in the past six months that displaced people, resulted in unusual stress for a group, or highlighted the possibility that social workers might have assisted had they responded quickly? To answer this question, it is important *not* to start from knowledge about services offered by existing agencies. We should begin from an understanding of human needs and all the things that might interfere with meeting these. Our assessment includes whether or not an existing service is available to meet the need.

Second, we *do not* begin by expecting persons in need to find their way to whatever resources currently exist. Our task is to help them get there and/or to take the service to them. Social work has been concerned too long with the unproven assumption that help seeking behavior represents motivation that must be assessed before help is given. What high school student will go to the principal's office and ask to be excused to attend the mental health clinic for social worker assistance when a distressing event occurs at school? Which striking coal miner will consider that an area social worker might help mediate a dispute? When a group of employees is laid off work, will they think first of the range of services our practice can offer?

The challenge is to design rapid response models, which make it possible to offer assistance quickly in many types of community situations. Groups of social workers might identify the kinds of services they can offer and advertise these to community groups most likely to need them. Certain agencies such as mental health clinics and family service providers might form rapid response units comprised of team members who are competent to engage in several different roles depending upon an initial assessment of system status. We can learn much from the Red Cross and Salvation Army about how to proceed as well as offer our services directly to these two groups. NASW Chapters might organize such teams, advertise them, and assign coordinating responsibility to members on a rotating basis so that services can be offered quickly when needs develop.

The challenge is not to decry lack of recognition, but to organize and offer assistance quickly, decisively, and effectively. Such assistance requires competent, knowledgeable social workers. It means we accept responsibility to seek out those who may need our help rather than hoping they find their way to our offices.

Connecting Private and Public Enterprises

There is increasing opportunity for work in an arena which bridges private enterprise and public service. Many for-profit organizations that provide critical public services, such as banks, savings and loan companies, and public utilities, serve those who are able to handle their own affairs but also those who cannot do so. Some of this latter group are mentally incompetent, others do not understand complex institutions, and still others do not have adequate resources to participate in expected ways. Practice has emphasized broker and advocacy strategies designed to provide or secure resources or entitlements for individual clients. There are other opportunities, however, and the examples below may suggest still others.

Some elderly persons cannot manage their personal financial affairs adequately. These include incompetent persons, frail elderly, and those without family or other support networks. Financial resources of some of these persons are managed by bank trust departments or offices. Those with more limited resources usually are not managed this way and some portion of this group is at risk of exploitation. Social workers might organize services for this latter group to protect financial resources and assist in other areas.

For example, several social workers might design a program that offers the following services: (1) competency assessment for the court, (2) social assessments to determine all needed services, (3) referral to services, (4) management of monthly incomes and (5) reporting to the court or designated trustee. These services might be housed in banks or other financial institutions with social workers providing services to some bank customers along with services to nonbank customers. A program like this ties together some services and goes beyond what any one institution or agency may be able to do alone. It requires competent social workers who know how to engage in several roles, who are skilled in assessment, and who can design a program consistent with relevant laws and regulations and community needs. This practice arena uses private institutional resources and connects them with knowledge about and resources in public social services to meet significant community needs and extend social work practice.

Some public utilities such as electric and gas companies have winter care programs designed to help low-income residents meet heating bills. Usually the funds are solicited from other utility users when they pay utility bills. This income is placed in special funds to help persons identified by public assistance agencies as needing financial help. The funds generally help cancel unpaid bills and reduce whatever deficit the company experiences. Although these programs are important for the recipient and helpful to the company, the general public seldom knows how the programs work, how much income is generated, and how it is managed. What place might there be in public utilities for social workers?

If social workers organized and managed such programs, we could educate the public about community needs, refer persons not currently using other resources, and engage in social action to obtain resources. If we remember that utilities often are "public" only in the sense of certain federal and state regulations, we might be able to think of more ways to make them truly public. To do so requires us to design services that are accepted by these institutions and from which they also benefit.

Social workers will need to think differently about client systems than we sometimes have in the past. We must identify our functions and services as relevant to the community—not just those persons in need because they are named as our clients. Building partnerships with important private institutions is not achieved by pronouncing our worth, but by recognizing needs and responding to them in nontraditional ways.

Private Services

Many social workers are finding employment in for-profit social services. An increasing number of hospitals, day care facilities, home health programs, and prisons are owned privately and operated for profit. Many of these hire social workers for positions similar to those they hold in publically funded programs. The special challenge for social work in these arenas is two fold.

First, practice effectiveness may be challenged more easily in private than public services. The burden to produce will be great since a for-profit organization cannot tolerate a deficit. This challenge is a welcome one since it places responsibility for effective practice squarely where it belongs. We will be expected to demonstrate outcomes in relation to system goals rather than processes or activities. We will no longer have the luxury of reporting only numbers of persons served or number of interviews conducted as indicators of our productivity. Although this may be threatening, it also can spur more thoughtful, critical practice, which does not claim more than it can justify on the basis of client-system improvements.

The second part of the challenge is more problematic. Do we wish to see a society where there are two classes of service—one for those who can pay the for-profit rate and one for those who cannot? If the public arena includes only the most difficult problems of basic necessities and if social work finally abandons groups who use such services, we shall have lost or forfeited one major reason for our profession. A significant future challenge is how to take advantage of new service opportunities, including those in the for-profit service arena, while maintaining our social commitments.

Robert Stewart wrote about a recent conservative social trend:

> If social work abandons its traditional commitments, there will be no ethnically pluralistic professional group in society concerned with poor and disadvantaged populations. . . . If social work abandons its commitments to its values, I will abandon social work. My . . . primary reasons for being a social worker would be gone (1981; 273).

It is important to consider Stewart's words as we think about and plan for social work's future. We have the opportunity to become an effective profession, which combines compassion for individual people in trouble and larger social issues by practicing where we can make a difference. To do so without leaving behind those for whom we exist will require us to remember why social work began and what it has tried to do. It will require strong value commitments, less concern about status and more about knowledge and competence and a vision of what our society can become—a society where justice is the norm.

REFERENCES

Ad Hoc Committee on Advocacy. The Social Worker as Advocate: Champion of Social Victims. *Social Work 14*(2), 1969; 16–22.

ADAMS, DAVID. The Red Cross: Organizational Sources of Operational Problems. *American Behavioral Scientist 13*(3), 1970; 392–403.

ALINKSKY, SAUL D. *Reveille for Radicals.* Chicago, IL: The University of Chicago Press, 1946.

———. *Rules for Radicals.* New York: Random House, 1971.

ALISSI, ALBERT S. AND MAX CASPER (eds.). Time as a Factor in Groupwork: Time-Limited Group Experiences (Special Issue). *Social Work with Groups 8*(2), 1985.

ANDERSON, JOSEPH. Social Work with Groups in the Generic Base of Social Work Practice. *Social Work with Groups 2*(4), 1979; 281–294.

ANNAS, GEORGE J. *The Rights of Hospital Patients.* American Civil Liberties Union Handbook Series. New York: Avon Books, 1975.

APGAR, KATHRYN AND JENNIFER COPLON. New Perspectives on Structured Life Education Groups. *Social Work 30*(2), 1985; 138–143.

AUSTIN, DAVID M. The Flexner Myth and the History of Social Work. *Social Service Review 57*(3), 1983; 357–377.

BALES, ROBERT F. *Interaction Process Analysis: A Method for the Study of Small Groups.* Cambridge, MA: Addison-Wesley, 1950.

BALGOPAL, PALLASSANA AND THOMAS V. VASSIL. *Groups at Work.* New York: Macmillan Publishing Company, 1983.

BANDURA, ALBERT. *Principles of Behavior Modification.* New York: Holt, Rinehart and Winston, 1969.

———. *Social Learning Theory.* Englewood Cliffs, NJ: Prentice-Hall, Inc., 1977.

BAROZZI, RONALD L., DANIEL PARK, JR., AND EUNICE L. WATSON. A Family Agency Integrates Advocacy, Counseling and Family Life Education. *Social Casework 63*(4), 1982; 227–232.

BARSKY, MONA. Strategies and Techniques of Divorce Mediation. *Social Casework 65*(2), 1984; 102–108.

BARTH, RICHARD P., STEVEN P. SCHINKE AND JOSIE S. MAXWELL. Coping Skills Training for School-Age Mothers. *Journal of Social Service Research 8*(2), 1984/85; 75–94.

BARTLETT, HARRIETT M. Toward Clarification and Improvement of Social Work Practice. *Social Work 3*(2), 1958; 3–9.

BECK, BERTRAM M. Professional Associations: National Association of Social Workers. In John B. Turner (ed.), *Encyclopedia of Social Work.* Washington, D.C.: National Association of Social Workers, 1977; 1084–1093.

BECKER, DOROTHY G. Smith, Zilpha Drew (1852-1926). In John B. Turner (ed.), *Encyclopedia of Social Work.* Washington, D.C.: National Association of Social Workers, 1977; 1272–1273.

BEHLING, JOHN, CAROLETTA CURTIS AND SARAH FOSTER. Impact of Sex-Role Combinations on Student Performance in Field Instruction. *Journal of Education for Social Work 18*(2), 1982; 93–97.

BELL, BILL D. Disaster Impact and Response: Overcoming the Thousand Natural Shocks. *Gerontologist 18,* 1978; 531–546.

BERLIN, SHARON. Cognitive-Behavioral Approaches. In Aaron Rosenblatt and Diana Waldfogel (eds.), *Handbook of Clinical Social Work.* San Francisco, CA: Jossey-Bass Publishers, 1983; 1095–1119.

———. Cognitive-Behavioral Intervention for Problems of Self-Criticism Among Women. *Social Work Research & Abstracts 16*(4), 1980; 19–28.

BERNARD, L. DIANE. Education for Social Work. In John B. Turner (ed.), *Encyclopedia of Social Work.* Washington, D.C.: National Association of Social Workers, 1977; 290–300.

BERREN, MICHAEL R., ALLAN BEIGEL, AND STUART GHERTNER. A Typology for the Classification of Disasters. *Community Mental Health Journal 16*(2), 1980; 103–111.

BLACK, TERRY R. Coalition Building—Some Suggestions. *Child Welfare 62*(3), 1983; 263–268.

BLOOM, MARTIN. *Primary Prevention: The Possible Science.* Englewood Cliffs, NJ: Prentice-Hall, Inc., 1981.

BOWERS, SWITHUN, O.M.I. The Nature and Definition of Social Casework. In Cora Kasius (ed.), *Principles and Techniques in Social Casework: Selected Articles, 1940–1950.* New York: Family Service Association of America, 1950; 97–127.

BRAUN, LINDA A., JENNIFER K. COPLON, AND PHYLLIS C. SONNENCHEIN. *Helping Parents in Groups.* Boston, MA: Resource Communications Inc., 1984.

BRETON, MARGOT. A Drop-In Program for Transient Women: Promoting Competence Through the Environment. *Social Work 29*(6), 1984; 542–546.

BREUL, FRANK R. AND STEVEN J. DINER. *Compassion and Responsibility: Readings in the History of Social Welfare Policy in the United States.* Chicago, IL: The University of Chicago Press, 1980.

BRIAR, SCOTT. Clinical Judgment in Foster Care Placement. *Child Welfare 42*(4), 1963; 161–169.

———. Welfare From Below: Recipients' Views of the Public Welfare System. In Jacobus ten Broek (ed.), *The Law and The Poor.* San Francisco, CA: Chandler Publishing Co., 1966; 46–61.

———. Family Services and Casework. In Henry S. Maas (ed.), *Research in the Social Services: A Five-Year Review.* New York: National Association of Social Workers, 1971; 108–129.

———. The Future of Social Work: An Introduction. *Social Work 19*(5), 1974; 514–518.

BRIAR, SCOTT AND HENRY MILLER. *Problems and Issues in Social Casework.* New York: Columbia University Press, 1971.

BROVERMAN, INGE K., DONALD M. BROVERMAN, FRANK E. CLARKSON, PAUL S. ROSENKRANTZ, AND SUSAN R. VOGEL. Sex-Role Stereotypes and Clinical Judgments in Mental Health. *Journal of Consulting and Clinical Psychology 34*(1), 1970; 1–7.

BROWN, GORDON E. *The Multi-Problem Dilemma.* Metuchen, NJ: Scarecrow Press, 1968.

BROWN, STEPHEN M. Male Versus Female Leaders: A Comparison of Empirical Studies. *Sex Roles 5*(5), 1979; 595–611.

BRUNO, FRANK J. *Trends in Social Work.* New York: Columbia University Press, 1948.

CALDER, NIGEL (ed.). *Nature in the Round: A Guide to Environmental Science.* New York: The Viking Press, 1973.

CARLISLE, JOHN AND MALCOLM LEARY. Negotiating Groups. In Roy Payne and Cary Cooper (eds.), *Groups at Work.* London: John Wiley & Sons, Ltd., 1981; 165–188.

CATTON, WILLIAM R., JR. AND RILEY E. DUNLAP. A New Ecological Paradigm for Post-Exhuberant Sociology. *American Behavioral Scientist 24*(1), 1980; 15–47.

CHANDLER, SUSAN MEYERS. Mediation: Conjoint Problem Solving. *Social Work 30*(4), 1985; 346–349.

CHESTANG, LEON W. Competencies and Knowledge in Clinical Social Work: A Dual Perspective. In Patricia L. Ewalt (ed.), *Toward a Definition of Clinical Social Work.* Washington, D.C.: National Association of Social Workers, 1980; 1–12.

CHIN, ROBERT. The Utility of System Models and Developmental Models for Practitioners. In Warren G. Bennis, Kenneth D. Benne and Robert Chin (eds.), *The Planning of Change.* New York: Holt, Rinehart and Winston, Inc., 1969; 297–312.

CHIN, ROBERT AND KENNETH D. BENNE. General Strategies for Effecting Changes in Human Systems. In Warren G. Bennis, Kenneth D. Benne and Robert Chin (eds.), *The Planning of Change.* New York: Holt, Rinehart and Winston, Inc., 1969; 32–59.

The Christian Science Monitor (Boston), May 5, 1986; 3 & 12.

CHURCHILL, SALLIE R. Prestructuring Group Content. *Social Work 4*(3), 1959; 52–59.

COELHO, GEORGE V., DAVID A. HAMBURG AND JOHN E. ADAMS (eds.). *Coping and Adaptation.* New York: Basic Books, 1974.

COHEN, JEROME. Nature of Clinical Social Work. In Patricia L. Ewalt (ed.), *Toward a Definition of Clinical Social Work.* Washington, D.C.: National Association of Social Workers, 1980; 23–32.

———. Insight Development. In Aaron Rosenblatt and Diana Waldfogel (eds.), *Handbook of Clinical Social Work.* San Francisco, CA: Jossey-Bass Publishers, Inc., 1983; 252–265.

COLLINS, ALICE H. AND DIANE L. PANCOAST. *Natural Helping Networks: A Strategy for Prevention.* Washington, D.C.: National Association of Social Workers, 1976.

COLOSI, THOMAS. Negotiation in the Public and Private Sectors: A Core Model. *American Behavioral Scientist 27*(2), 1983; 229–253.

COMPTON, BEULAH AND BURT GALWAY. *Social Work Processes.* Homewood, IL: Dorsey Press, 1979.

CONNAWAY, RONDA S., MARYRHEA MORELOCK AND MARTHA E. GENTRY. Research Productivity of Women and Men in Selected Social Work Positions. *Administration in Social Work 9*(1), 1985; 81–91.

COOLEY, CHARLES H. *Social Organization: A Study of the Larger Mind.* New York: Charles Scribner's Sons, 1920.

COULTON, CLAUDIA J. Developing an Instrument to Measure Person-Environment Fit. *Journal of Social Service Research 3*(2), 1979; 159–174.

The Courier-Journal (Louisville), June 14, 1985a; A 5.

The Courier-Journal (Louisville), September 5, 1985b; B 1 & B 2.

CURRAN, JAMES P. AND PETER M. MONTI (eds.). *Social Skills Training: A Practical Handbook for Assessment and Treatment.* New York: Guilford Press, 1981.

Curriculum Policy for the Master's Degree and Baccalaureate Degree Programs in Social Work Education. Adopted by the Council on Social Work Education, Board of Directors, May 1982.

DAILEY, DENNIS M. Are Social Workers Sexists? A Replication. *Social Work 25*(1), 1980; 46–51.

———. Androgyny, Sex-Role Stereotypes, and Clinical Judgment. *Social Work Research & Abstracts 19*(1), 1983; 20–25.

Dallas Disaster Aid, *NASW NEWS 30*(8), 1985; 1, 4.

DAVIDSON, WILLIAM S., III AND JULIAN RAPPAPORT. Advocacy and Community Psychology. In George H. Weber and George J. McCall (eds.), *Social Scientists as Advocates.* Beverly Hills, CA: Sage Publications, Inc., 1978; 167–199.

DAVIS, ALLEN F. Settlements: History. In John B. Turner (ed.) *Encyclopedia of Social Work.* Washington, D.C.: National Association of Social Workers, 1977; 1266–1271.

DAVIS, LARRY (ed.). Ethnicity in Social Group Work Practice (Special Issue). *Social Work with Groups 7*(3), 1984.

Defender (Louisville), May 24, 1979; 16.

The Denver Post, July 3, 1985.

DREW, PATRICIA. Social Work Practice: A Historical Comparison (Unpublished Doctoral Dissertation, Washington University, 1972).

DUEHN, WAYNE D. The Patterning of Stimulus-Response Congruence and Content Relevance: A Study of Client-Worker Interaction in the Diagnostic Phase of Counseling. (Unpublished Doctoral Dissertation, Washington University, 1970).

DYE, THOMAS R. *Understanding Public Policy.* Englewood Cliffs, NJ: Prentice-Hall, Inc., 1981.

EASTON, DAVID. An Approach to the Analysis of Political Systems. *World Politics 10,* 1957; 383–400.

ELLIS, ALBERT. *Reason and Emotion in Psychotherapy.* New York: Lyle Stuart, 1962.

ENNIS, BRUCE. *Handbook on Mental Patients' Rights.* New York: American Civil Liberties Union, 1973.

EPSTEIN, IRWIN. Professional Role Orientations and Conflict Strategies. *Social Work 15*(4), 1970; 87–92.

EPSTEIN, NORMAN. A Residence for Autistic and Schizophrenic Adolescents. *Social Casework 63*(4), 1982; 209–214.

EPSTEIN, WILLIAM M. Research Biases. *Social Work 28*(1), 1983; 77–78.

ERIKSON, KAI T. *Everything in Its Path.* New York: Simon and Schuster, 1976.

EVANS, ROBERT T. (ed.). *Social Movements: A Reader and Source Book.* Chicago, IL: Rand McNally, 1973.

Ewalt, Patricia L. (ed.). *Toward a Definition of Clinical Social Work.* Washington, D.C.: National Association of Social Workers, 1980.

Falck, Hans S. The Membership Model of Social Work. *Social Work 29*(2), 1984; 155–160.

Fanning, Odum. Environmental Mediation: The World's Newest Profession. *Environment 21*(7), 1979; 33–34, 36–38.

Farrell, John C., Addams, Jane (1860–1935). In John B. Turner (ed.), *Encyclopedia of Social Work.* Washington, D.C.: National Association of Social Workers, 1977; 12–13.

Feld, Sheila and Norma Radin. *Social Psychology for Social Work and the Mental Health Professions.* New York: Columbia University Press, 1982.

Fischer, Joel. Is Casework Effective? A Review. *Social Work 18*(1), 1973; 5–20.

———. Evaluations of Social Work Effectiveness: Is Positive Evidence Always Good Evidence? *Social Work 28*(1), 1983; 74–76.

Folberg, Jay and Alison Taylor. *Mediation: A Comprehensive Guide to Resolving Disputes Without Litigation.* San Francisco, CA: Jossey-Bass Publishers, Inc., 1984.

Forum 3(1), 1982; 1, 4. University of Washington, School of Social Work, Seattle, WA.

Frank, Margaret G. Clinical Social Work: Past, Present, and Future Challenges and Dilemmas. In Patricia L. Ewalt (ed.), *Toward a Definition of Clinical Social Work.* Washington, D.C.: National Association of Social Workers, 1980; 13–22.

Franklin, Donna. Differential Clinical Assessments: The Influence of Class and Race. *Social Service Review 59*(1), 1985; 44–59.

Freedman, Joel. One Social Worker's Fight for Mental Patients' Rights. *Social Work 16*(4), 1971; 92–95.

Friedsam, Hiram J. Reactions of Older Persons to Disaster-Caused Losses: An Hypothesis of Relative Deprivation. *Gerontologist 1*(1), 1961; 34–37.

Fritz, Anna. Parent Group Education: A Preventive Intervention Approach. *Social Work with Groups 8*(3), 1985; 23–31.

Galinsky, Maeda and Janice H. Schopler. Patterns of Entry and Exit in Open-Ended Groups. *Social Work with Groups 8*(2), 1985; 67–80.

Gallant, Claire B. *Mediation in Special Education Disputes.* Silver Springs, MD: National Association of Social Workers, 1982.

Gambrill, Eileen D. *Behavior Modification: Handbook of Assessment, Intervention, and Evaluation.* San Francisco, CA: Jossey-Bass, Inc., Publishers, 1977.

Gamson, William. *The Strategy of Social Protest.* Homewood, IL: Dorsey Press, 1975.

Garcia, Alejandro. The Chicano and Social Work. *Social Casework 52*(5), 1971; 274–278.

Garfinkel, Herbert. *When Negroes March.* Glencoe, IL: The Free Press, 1959.

Garvin, Charles D. Theory of Group Approaches. In Aaron Rosenblatt and Diana Waldfogel (eds.), *Handbook of Clinical Social Work.* San Francisco: Jossey-Bass Publishers, 1983; 155–175.

Geertz, Clifford. The Ultimate Ghetto. *The New York Review of Books 32*(3), February 28, 1985; 14–15.

Gentry, Martha E. Social Simulation Games in Social Work Education and Practice. *Social Work Education Reporter.* April–May 1972; 29–30, 39–42.

———. Early Detection and Treatment: Social Worker and Pediatricians in Private Practice. *Social Work in Health Care 3*(1), 1977; 49–59.

———. Consensus as a Form of Decision Making. *Journal of Sociology and Social Welfare 9*(2), 1982; 233–244.

———. Further Developments in Activity Analysis: Recreation and Group Work Revisited. *Social Work with Groups 7*(1), 1984; 35–44.

———. Coalition Formation and Processes. *Social Work with Groups 10*(3), 1987.

Gentry, Martha E., Ronda S. Connaway and Maryrhea Morelock. Research Activities of Social Workers in Agencies. *Social Work Research & Abstracts 20*(3), 1984; 3–5.

Germain, Carel B. (ed.). *Social Work Practice: People and Environments.* New York: Columbia University Press, 1979.

Gilbert, Neil. *Clients or Constituents.* San Francisco, CA: Jossey-Bass Publishers, Inc., 1970.

Gingerich, Wallace and Stuart A. Kirk. Sex Bias in Assessment: A Case of Premature Exaggeration. *Social Work Research & Abstracts 17*(1), 1981; 38–43.

Gitterman, Alex and Carel B. Germain. Social Work Practice: A Life Model. *Social Service Review 50*(4), 1976; 601–610.

Glasser, William. *Reality Therapy: A New Approach to Psychiatry.* New York: Harper & Row, 1965.

GLENN, MARY W. The Growth of Social Case Work in the United States. In Fern Lowry (ed.), *Readings in Social Case Work, 1920–1938.* New York: Columbia University Press, 1939; 67–80.

GLESER, GOLDINE C., BONNIE L. GREEN AND CAROLYN WINGET. *Prolonged Psychosocial Effects of Disaster.* New York: Academic Press, 1981.

GOLDBERG, GALE AND JOY ELLIOTT. Below the Belt: Situational Ethics for Unethical Situations. *Journal of Sociology and Social Welfare 7*(4), 1980; 478–486.

GOLDSTEIN, EDA. Knowledge Base of Clinical Social Work. *Social Work 25*(3), 1980; 173–178.

GOODBAN, NANCY. The Psychological Impact of Being on Welfare. *Social Service Review 59*(3), 1985; 403–422.

GORDON, WILLIAM E. Additional Notes on Eliciting and Stating Generalizations. Paper prepared for Medical Social Work Section, Committee on Concepts, National Association of Social Workers, January, 1959.

———. Knowledge and Values: Their Distinction and Relationship in Clarifying Social Work Practice. *Social Work 10*(3), 1965; 32–39.

———. Basic Constructs for an Integrative and Generative Conception of Social Work. In Gordon Hearn (ed.), *The General Systems Approach: Contributions Toward a Holistic Conception of Social Work.* New York: Council on Social Work Education, 1969.

GORDON, WILLIAM E. AND HARRIETT M. BARTLETT. Generalizations in Medical Social Work: Preliminary Findings. *Social Work 4*(3), 1959; 72–76.

GREEN, BONNIE L. AND GOLDINE C. GLESER. Chronic Psychopathology in Survivors of the Buffalo Creek Disaster. Presented at the Society for Life History Research in Psychopathology, Cincinnati, 1978 (unpublished manuscript).

GREENWOOD, ERNEST. Attributes of a Profession. *Social Work 2*(3), 1957; 45–55.

GUMP, PAUL AND BRIAN SUTTON-SMITH. Activity Setting and Social Interaction. A Field Study. *American Journal of Orthopsychiatry 25*(4), 1955; 755–760.

HAGEN, JAN L. Justice for the Welfare Recipient: Another Look at Welfare Fair Hearings. *Social Service Review 57*(2), 1983; 177–195.

HAMILTON, GORDON. Basic Concepts in Social Case Work. In Fern Lowry (ed.), *Readings in Social Case Work, 1920–1938.* New York: Columbia University Press, 1939; 155–171.

———. *Theory and Practice of Social Case Work.* New York: Columbia University Press, 1940 and 1951.

HANDLER, JOEL F. Justice for the Welfare Recipient: Fair Hearings in AFDC—The Wisconsin Experiment. *Social Service Review 43*(1), 1969; 12–34.

HARTFORD, MARGARET E. Socialization Methods in Social Work Practice. In John B. Turner (ed.), *Encyclopedia of Social Work.* Washington, D.C.: National Association of Social Workers, 1977; 1387–1392.

HARTMAN, HEIDI. The Family as the Locus of Gender, Class and Political Struggle: The Example of Housework. *Signs: Journal of Women in Culture and Society 6*(3), 1981; 366–394.

HASENFELD, YEHESKEL. People Processing Organizations: An Exchange Approach. In Yeheskel Hasenfeld and Richard A. English (eds.), *Human Service Organizations: A Book of Readings.* Ann Arbor, MI: The University of Michigan Press, 1974; 60–71.

———. The Implementation of Change in Human Service Organizations: A Political Economy Perspective. *Social Service Review 54*(4), 1980; 508–520.

HEARN, GORDON (ed.). *The General Systems Approach: Contributions Toward a Holistic Conception of Social Work.* New York: Council on Social Work Education, 1969.

HEINEMAN, MARTHA. The Obsolete Scientific Imperative in Social Work Research. *Social Service Review 55*(3), 1981; 371–397.

HENRY, SUE. *Group Skills in Social Work.* Itasca, IL: F.E. Peacock Publishers, Inc., 1981; 288–324.

HOLLIS, FLORENCE. Some Contributions of Therapy to Generalized Case Work Practice. In Fern Lowry (ed.), *Readings in Social Case Work, 1920–1938.* New York: Columbia University Press, 1939a; 305–318.

———. *Social Case Work in Practice: Six Case Studies.* New York: Family Welfare Association of America, 1939b.

———. *Casework: A Psychosocial Therapy.* New York: Random House, 1964.

HOMANS, GEORGE C. *Social Behavior: Its Elementary Forms.* New York: Harcourt Brace and World, 1961.

HOWARD, JOHN R. *The Cutting Edge: Social Movements and Social Change in America.* Philadelphia, PA: J.B. Lippincott Co., 1974.

HUDSON, WALTER. Scientific Imperatives in Social Work Research and Practice. *Social Service Review 56*(2), 1982; 247–248.

HUERTA, FAYE AND ROBERT HORTON. Coping Behavior of Elderly Flood Victims. *Gerontologist 18,* 1978; 541–555.

JAYARATNE, SRINIKA. A Study of Clinical Eclecticism. *Social Service Review 52*(4), 1978; 621–631.

KAHN, SI. *How People Get Power.* New York: McGraw-Hill, 1970.

———. *Organizing: A Guide for Grassroots Leaders.* New York: McGraw-Hill Book Co., 1982.

KANTER, ROSABETH MOSS. *Men and Women of the Corporation.* New York: Basic Books, 1977.

KEITH-LUCAS, ALAN. An Alliance for Power. *Social Work 20*(2), 1975; 93–97.

KELLEY, ESTEL W. Techniques of Studying Coalition Formation. *Midwest Journal of Political Science 12*(1), 1968; 62–84.

KELLY, JAMES A. *Social-Skills Training: A Practical Guide for Interventions.* New York: Springer Publishing Co., 1982.

Kentucky Revised Statutes 335.010-335.170 and 335.990; 201 KAR 23:070, Section 5. State Board of Examiners of Social Work, Commonwealth of Kentucky, 1982 Revised Edition; 14.

Kentucky Society for Clinical Social Work. The Clinical Social Worker. Pamphlet, n.d.

KHINDUKA, SHANTI K. AND BERNARD J. COUGHLIN, JR. A Conceptualization of Social Action. *Social Service Review 49*(1), 1975; 1–14.

KILLIAN, LEWIS M. Social Movements: A Review of the Field. In Robert R. Evans (ed.), *Social Movements: A Reader and Source Book.* Chicago, IL: Rand McNally, 1973; 9–53.

KIRK, STUART A. AND JOEL FISCHER. Do Social Workers Understand Research? *Journal of Education for Social Work 12*(1), 1976; 63–70.

KIRK, STUART A., MICHAEL J. OSMALOV AND JOEL FISCHER. Social Workers' Involvement in Research. *Social Work 21*(2), 1976; 121–134.

KLEIN, PHILIP. *From Philanthropy to Social Welfare.* San Francisco, CA: Jossey-Bass, Inc., Publisher, 1968.

KOCHAN, THOMAS A. AND TODD JICK. The Public Sector Mediation Process: A Theory and Empirical Examination. *Journal of Conflict Resolution 22*(2), 1978; 209–240.

KOGAN, LEONARD, J. MCVICKER HUNT AND PHYLLIS F. BARTELME. *A Follow-Up Study of the Results of Social Casework.* New York: Family Service Association of America, 1953.

KOHLBERG, LAWRENCE. *Essays on Moral Development.* San Francisco, CA: Harper & Row, 1981.

KOTLER, PHILIP. The Elements of Social Action. *American Behavioral Scientist 14*(5), 1971; 691–717.

KRESSEL, KENNETH, NANCY JAFFEE, BRUCE TUCHMAN, CAROL WATSON, AND MORTON DEUTSCH. A Typology of Divorcing Couples: Implications for Mediation and the Divorce Process. *Family Process 19*(2), 1980; 101–116.

KURTZ, P. DAVID. Using Mass Media and Group Instruction for Preventive Mental Health in Rural Communities. *Social Work Research & Abstracts 18*(3), 1982; 41–48.

KUTCHINS, HERB AND STUART KUTCHINS. Advocacy and Social Work. In George H. Weber and George J. McCall (eds.), *Social Scientists as Advocates.* Beverly Hills, CA: Sage Publications, Inc., 1978; 13–48.

LAIRD, JOAN AND JO ANN ALLEN. Family Theory and Practice. In Aaron Rosenblatt and Diana Waldfogel (eds.), *Handbook of Clinical Social Work.* San Francisco, CA: Jossey-Bass Publishers, 1983; 176–201.

LAUE, JAMES H. Advocacy and Sociology. In George H. Weber and George J. McCall (eds.), *Social Scientists as Advocates.* Beverly Hills, CA: Sage Publications, Inc., 1978; 167–199.

LAUER, ROBERT H. (ed.). *Social Movements and Social Change.* Carbondale, IL: Southern Illinois University Press, 1976.

LEE, PORTER R. Social Work: Cause and Function. In *Proceedings of the National Conference of Social Work.* Chicago, IL: The University of Chicago Press, 1930.

LEIGHNINGER, ROBERT. Systems Theory and Social Work: A Reexamination. *Journal of Education for Social Work 13*(3), 1977; 44–49.

LEITENBERG, HAROLD (ed.). *Handbook of Behavior Modification and Behavior Therapy.* Englewood Cliffs, NJ: Prentice-Hall, Inc., 1976.

LEWIN, KURT. Frontiers in Group Dynamics: Concept, Method and Reality in Social Science; Social Equilibria and Social Change. *Human Relations 1*(1), 1947; 5–41.

LEWIS, VERL S. Charity Organization Society. In John B. Turner (ed.), *Encyclopedia of Social Work.* Washington, D.C.: National Association of Social Workers, 1977; 96–100.

LIPSKY, MICHAEL. *Street-Level Bureaucracy.* New York: Russell Sage Foundation, 1980.

LITWAK, EUGENE. Organizational Constructs and Mega Bureaucracy. In Rosemary C. Sarri and Yeheskel Hasenfeld (eds.), *The Management of Human Services.* New York: Columbia University Press, 1978; 123–162.

LONEY, GLENN. *20th Century Theatre.* New York: Facts on File Publications, Inc. *1,* 1983.
LONG, NICHOLAS. Information and Referral Services: A Short History and Some Recommendations. *Social Service Review 47*(1), 1973; 49–62.
Los Angeles YWCA, Los Angeles, CA, 1981.
LOTT, BERNICE E. *Becoming a Woman: The Socialization of Gender.* Springfield, IL: Charles C Thomas Publisher, 1981.
LOWRY, FERN (ed.). *Readings in Social Case Work, 1920–1938.* New York: Columbia University Press, 1939.
LURIE, ABRAHAM. Clinical Social Work Contribution to Social Work. In Patricia L. Ewalt (ed.), *Toward a Definition of Clinical Social Work.* Washington, D.C.: National Association of Social Workers, 1980; 75–86.
MANNHEIM, KARL. *Ideology and Utopia.* New York: Harcourt Brace & World, Inc., 1936.
MAUZERALL, HILDEGARDE. Emancipation from Foster Care: The Independent Living Project. *Child Welfare 62*(1), 1983; 46–53.
MCCARTHY, JOHN D. AND MAYER N. ZALD. Resource Mobilization and Social Movements: A Partial Theory. *American Journal of Sociology 82*(6), 1977; 1212–1241.
MCKECHNIE, JEAN L. (ed.). *Webster's New Twentieth Century Dictionary of the English Language Unabridged.* Second Edition. Cleveland and New York: The World Publishing Company, 1970.
MEAD, GEORGE H. *Mind, Self, and Society.* Chicago: The University of Chicago Press, 1934.
MEYER, CAROL H. *Social Work Practice.* New York: The Free Press, 1976.
MEYER, HENRY, EDGAR F. BORGATTA AND WYATT C. JONES. *Girls at Vocational High: An Experiment in Social Work Intervention.* New York: Russell Sage Foundation, 1965.
MICHAEL, SUZANNE, ELLEN LURIE, NOREEN RUSSELL, AND LARRY UNGER. Rapid Response Mutual Aid Groups: A New Response to Social Crises and Natural Disasters. *Social Work 30*(3), 1985; 245–252.
MIDDLEMAN, RUTH R. *The Non-Verbal Method in Working with Groups.* New York: Association Press, 1968.
———. The Use of Program: Review and Update. *Social Work with Groups 3*(3), 1980; 5–23.
——— (ed.). Activities and Action in Groupwork (Special Issue). *Social Work with Groups 6*(1), 1983a.
———. Role of Perception and Cognition in Change. In Aaron Rosenblatt and Diana Waldfogel (eds.), *Handbook of Clinical Social Work.* San Francisco: Jossey-Bass Publishers, 1983b; 229–251.
MILANOF, LILLIAN C. From the President. NASW Kentucky Chapter NEWSLETTER. *11*(6), 1986; 1.
MILLER, HENRY. Dirty Sheets: A Multivariate Analysis. *Social Work 26*(4), 1981; 268–271.
MILLER, LEONARD S., ROBERT PRUGER AND MARLEEN CLARK. Referral: Technology and Efficiency. *Journal of Social Service Research 3*(2), 1979; 175–186.
MILLER, STEPHEN J. Professions, Human Service. In John B. Turner (ed.), *Encyclopedia of Social Work.* Washington, D.C.: National Association of Social Workers, 1977; 1098.
MINAHAN, ANNE. What is Clinical Social Work? (Continued). *Social Work 25*(5), 1980; 340, 420–430.
MORALES, ARMANDO. The Collective Preconscious and Racism. *Social Casework 52*(5), 1971; 285–293.
MORRISON, DENTON E. Some Notes Toward Theory on Relative Deprivation, Social Movements and Social Change. *American Behavioral Scientist 14*(5), 1971; 675–690.
Mother Jones. Frontlines, May 1983; 10.
MULLEN, EDWARD J. The Construction of Personal Models for Effective Practice: A Method for Utilizing Research Findings to Guide Social Interventions. *Journal of Social Service Research 2*(1), 1978; 45–63.
———. Methodological Dilemmas in Social Work Research. *Social Work Research & Abstracts 21*(4), 1985; 12–20.
National Association of Social Workers. *Building Social Work Knowledge: Report of a Conference.* New York: National Association of Social Workers, 1964.
———. Report of a Task Force on Labor Force Classification, *NASW NEWS 26*(10), 1981; 7.
———. Clinical Definition is Adopted by Directors. *NASW NEWS 29*(3), 1984; 12.
———. *NASW NEWS 29*(8), 1984; 5–6.
———. *NASW NEWS 30*(9), 1985; 13.
The NASW Code of Ethics. *Social Work 25*(3), 1980; 184–188.
NASW Register of Clinical Social Workers. Washington, D.C.: National Association of Social Workers, 1982.

National Senior Citizen's Law Center. *The Nursing Home Law Handbook.* Los Angeles, CA: National Senior Citizens Law Center, *29*(2), 1984; 155–160.

NELSON, JUDITH. Intermediate Treatment Goals as Variables in Single-Case Research. *Social Work Research & Abstracts 20*(4), 1984; 3–10.

NEWSTETTER, WILBUR I. The Social Intergroup Work Process. *Proceedings of the National Conference on Social Work.* New York: Columbia University Press, 1948; 205–217.

NIKELLY, ARTHUR G. (ed.). *Techniques for Behavior Change.* Springfield, IL: Charles C Thomas, 1971.

NORTON, DOLORES G. with contributions by Eddie Frank Brown, Edwin Garth Brown, E. Aracelis Francis, Kenji Murase and Ramon Valle. *The Dual Perspective: Inclusion of Ethnic Minority Content in the Social Work Curriculum.* New York: Council on Social Work Education, 1978.

NOWAKI, CHRISTINE M. AND CHARLES A. POE. The Concept of Mental Health as Related to Sex of Person Perceived. *Journal of Consulting and Clinical Psychology 40*(1), 1973; 160.

OLMSTEAD, JOSEPH A. AND HAROLD E. CHRISTENSEN. Effects of Agency Work Contexts: An Intensive Field Study. Washington, D.C.: Social and Rehabilitation Services, Department of Health Education and Welfare, Research Report No. 2, Volume 1; 1973.

OLSEN, LENORE. Services for Minority Children in Out-of-Home Care. *Social Service Review 56*(1), 1982a; 572–585.

———. Predicting the Permanency Status of Children in Foster Care. *Social Work Research & Abstracts 18*(1), 1982b; 9–20.

OPPENHEIMER, MARTIN AND GEORGE LAKEY. *A Manual for Direct Action.* Chicago: Quadrangle Books, 1964.

ORCUTT, BEN A. A STUDY OF ANCHORING EFFECTS IN CLINICAL JUDGMENT. *Social Service Review 38*(4), 1964; 408–417.

OWEN, DENIS F. *What is Ecology?* London: Oxford University Press, 1974.

PARSONS, TALCOTT. *The Social System.* Glencoe, IL: The Free Press, 1951.

PEARLMAN, MARGARET H. AND MILDRED G. EDWARDS. Enabling in the Eighties: The Client Advocacy Group. *Social Casework 63*(9), 1982; 532–539.

PERLMAN, HELEN HARRIS. *Social Casework: A Problem-Solving Process.* Chicago, IL: The University of Chicago Press, 1957.

———. *Persona: Social Role and Personality.* Chicago, IL: The University of Chicago Press, 1968.

PERLMAN, JANICE E. Grassrooting the System. In Fred M. Cox, John L. Erlich, Jack Rothman, and John E. Tropman (eds.). *Strategies of Community Organization* (Third Edition). Itasca, IL: F.E. Peacock Publishers, 1979; 403–425.

PERROW, CHARLES. A Framework for the Comparative Analysis of Organizations. *American Sociological Review 32*(2), 1967; 194–208.

PERRY, LORRAINE R. Strategies of Black Community Groups. *Social Work 21*(3), 1976; 210–215.

PIAGET, JEAN. *The Moral Judgment of the Child.* New York: The Free Press, 1965.

PIEPER, MARTHA HEINEMAN. The Future of Social Work Research. *Social Work Research & Abstracts 21*(4), 1985; 3–11.

PINCUS, ALLEN AND ANNE MINAHAN. *Social Work Practice: Model and Method.* Itasca, IL: F.E. Peacock Publishers, Inc., 1973.

POPPLE, PHILIP R. The Social Work Profession: A Reconceptualization. *Social Service Review 59*(1), 1985; 560–577.

PRICE, JULIA S. *The Off-Broadway Theater.* New York: The Scarecrow Press, Inc., 1962.

PRIESTLEY, PHILIP, JAMES MCGUIRE, JAMES FLEGG, VALERIE HEMSLEY, DAVID WELHAM, AND ROSEMARY BARNITT. *Social Skills in Prison and the Community: Problem-Solving for Offenders.* Boston, MA: Routledge & Kegan Paul, 1984.

PRUHS, ANE, MARY LOU PAULSEN AND WILLIAM TYSSELING. Divorce Mediation: The Politics of Integrating Clinicians. *Social Casework 65*(9), 1984; 532–540.

PRUITT, DEAN G. Strategic Choices in Negotiation. *American Behavioral Scientist 27*(2), 1983; 167–194.

PUMPHREY, RALPH E. AND MURIEL W. PUMPHREY. *The Heritage of American Social Work.* New York: Columbia University Press, 1961.

RADIN, NORMA. Socioeducation Groups. In Martin Sundel, Paul Glasser, Rosemary Sarri, and Robert Vinter (eds.). *Individual Change Through Small Groups* (Second Edition). New York: The Free Press, 1985; 101–112.

RAIFFA, HOWARD. Mediation of Conflicts. *American Behavioral Scientist 27*(2), 1983; 195–210.

REID, WILLIAM AND LAURA EPSTEIN. *Task-Centered Casework.* New York: Columbia University Press, 1972.

REID, WILLIAM AND PATRICIA HANRAHAN. Recent Evaluations of Social Work: Grounds for Optimism. *Social Work 27*(4), 1982; 328–340.
RICHAN, WILLARD AND ALLEN MENDELSOHN. *Social Work—The Unloved Profession.* New York: New Viewpoints, 1973.
RICHMOND, MARY E. *Social Diagnosis.* New York: Russell Sage Foundation, 1917.
———. *What is Social Case Work?* New York: Russell Sage Foundation, 1922.
ROBINSON, VIRGINIA P. *A Changing Psychology in Social Case Work.* Chapel Hill, NC: University of North Carolina Press, 1930.
ROSE, SHELDON D. *Group Therapy: A Behavioral Approach.* Englewood Cliffs, NJ: Prentice-Hall, Inc., 1977.
ROSE, SHELDON AND RICHARD TOLMAN. Evaluation of Client Outcomes in Groups. In Martin Sundel, Paul Glasser, Rosemary Sarri, and Robert Vinter (eds.), *Individual Change Through Small Groups* (Second Edition). New York: The Free Press, 1985; 368–390.
ROSEN, AARON. The Treatment Relationship: A Conceptualization. *Journal of Consulting and Clinical Psychology 38*(4), 1972; 329–337.
———. Barriers to Utilization of Research by Social Work Practitioners. *Journal of Social Service Research 6*(3/4), 1983; 1–15.
ROSEN, AARON AND RONDA S. CONNAWAY. Public Welfare, Social Work and Social Work Education. *Social Work 14*(2), 1968; 87–94.
———. Categorizing Behavior and Stimulus Boundness. *Psychological Reports 23*(3), 1969; 971–977.
ROSEN, AARON, RONDA S. CONNAWAY AND WAYNE D. DUEHN. The Patterning of Pre-Treatment Expectancies and Their Relation to Interview Content in Treatment of Sexual Adjustment Problems. In Harvey L. Gochros and LeRoy G. Schultz (eds.), *Human Sexuality and Social Work.* New York: Association Press, 1972; 102–118.
ROSENTHAL, TED L. AND ALBERT BANDURA. Psychological Modeling: Theory and Practice. In Sol L. Garfield and Allen E. Bergin (eds.), *Handbook of Psychotherapy and Behavior Change: An Empirical Analysis.* New York: John Wiley and Sons, 1978.
ROSSI, PETER AND HOWARD E. FREEMAN. *Evaluation* (3rd edition). Beverly Hills, CA: Sage Publications, 1985.
ROTHMAN, JACK. Three Models of Community Organization Practice, Their Mixing and Phasing. In Fred M. Cox, John L. Erlich, Jack Rothman, and John E. Tropman (eds.), *Strategies of Community Organization.* Itasca, IL: F.E. Peacock Publishers, 1979; 25–45.
RUBIN, ALLEN. Practice Effectiveness: More Grounds for Optimism. *Social Work 30*(6), 1985; 469–476.
RUBIN, JEFFREY Z. Negotiation: An Introduction to Some Issues and Themes. *American Behavioral Scientist 27*(2), 1983; 135–147.
SATIR, VIRGINIA M. *Conjoint Family Therapy.* Palo Alto, CA: Science and Behavior Books, 1967.
SEABURY, BRETT A. The Contract: Uses, Abuses and Limitations. *Social Work 21*(1), 1976; 16–21.
SCHULTZ, STEPHEN. The Boston State Hospital Case: A Conflict of Civil Liberties and True Liberalism. *American Journal of Psychiatry 139*(2), 1982; 183–188.
SCHUTZ, MARGARET L. AND WILLIAM E. GORDON. Reallocation of Educational Responsibility Among Schools, Agencies, Students and NASW. *Journal of Education for Social Work 13*(2), 1977; 99–106.
SCHWARTZ, ARTHUR. *The Behavior Therapies: Theories and Applications.* New York: The Free Press, 1982.
SCHWARTZ, WILLIAM. Between Client and System: The Mediating Function. In Robert Roberts and Helen Northen (eds.), *Theories of Social Work with Groups.* New York: Columbia University Press, 1976; 171–197.
SHADER, RICHARD AND ALICE J. SCHWARTZ. Management of Reactions to Disaster. *Social Work 11*(2), 1966; 99–104.
SHAFTEL, FANNIE R. *Role Playing for Social Values: Decision-Making in the Social Studies.* Englewood Cliffs, NJ: Prentice-Hall, Inc., 1967.
SHORE, JAMES, ELLIE L. TATUM AND WILLIAM VOLLMER. Evaluation of Mental Effects of Disaster: Mount St. Helens Eruption. *American Journal of Public Health. 76* Supplement, 1986; 76–83.
SHULMAN, LAWRENCE. *The Skills of Helping Individuals and Groups.* Itasca, IL: F.E. Peacock Publishers, 1979.
SIMON, BERNECE K. Diversity and Unity in the Social Work Profession. *Social Work 22*(5), 1977; 394–400.
SIPORIN, MAX. Current Social Work Perspectives on Clinical Practice. *Clinical Social Work Journal 13*(3), 1985; 198–217.

SMALLEY, RUTH ELIZABETH. *Theory for Social Work Practice.* New York: Columbia University Press, 1967.

SMELSER, NEIL J. *Theory of Collective Behavior.* New York: The Free Press, 1962.

SOSIN, MICHAEL AND SHARON CAULUM. Advocacy: A Conceptualization for Social Work Practice. *Social Work 28*(1), 1983; 12–17.

SPECHT, HARRY. Managing Professional Interpersonal Interactions. *Social Work 30*(3), 1985; 225–230.

STEINER, JOSEPH. Group Counseling with Retarded Offenders. *Social Work 29*(2), 1984; 181–185.

STEWART, ROBERT P. Watershed Days: How Will Social Work Respond to the Conservative Revolution? *Social Work 26*(11), 1981; 271–273.

STREAN, HERBERT S. *Clinical Social Work: Theory and Practice.* New York: The Free Press, 1978.

———. Worker-Client Relationships. In Aaron Rosenblatt and Diana Waldfogel (eds.), *Handbook of Clinical Social Work.* San Francisco, CA: Jossey-Bass Publishers, 1983; 266–279.

STUART, RICHARD B. Behavioral Contracting with the Families of Delinquents. *Journal of Behavioral Therapy and Experimental Psychology 2*(1), 1971; 1–11.

SUNLEY, ROBERT. *Advocating Today: A Human Service Practitioner's Handbook.* New York: Family Service America, 1983.

SUSSKIND, THOMAS AND CONNIE OZAWA. Mediated Negotiation in the Public Sector. *American Behavioral Scientist 27*(2), 1983; 255–279.

SUSSKIND, THOMAS AND JEFFREY Z. RUBIN (eds.). Negotiation: Behavioral Perspectives (Special Issue). *American Behavioral Scientist 27*(2), 1983.

TAFT, JESSIE. *A Functional Approach to Family Case Work.* Philadelphia, PA: University of Pennsylvania Press, 1944.

TARGUM, STEVEN S., ANN E. CAPODANNO, HOWARD A. HOFFMAN AND CLAIRE FOUNDRAINE. Intervention to Reduce the Rate of Hospital Discharges Against Medical Advice. *American Journal of Psychiatry 139*(5), 1982; 657–659.

TERI, LINDA. Effects of Sex and Sex-Role Style on Clinical Judgment. *Sex Roles 8*(6), 1982; 639–650.

THEODORSON, GEORGE A. AND ACHILLES G. THEODORSON. *A Modern Dictionary of Sociology.* New York: Thomas Y. Crowell Company, 1969.

THIBAUT, JOHN W. AND HAROLD H. KELLY. *The Psychology of Small Group Behavior.* New York: John Wiley and Sons, 1959.

THOMAS, EDWIN J. Selecting Knowledge from Behavioral Science. In *Building Social Work Knowledge: Report of a Conference.* New York: National Association of Social Workers, 1964; 38–47.

———. *Socio-behavioral Approach and Applications to Social Work.* New York: Council on Social Work Education, 1967.

THOMAS, EDWIN J., RONALD A. FELDMAN AND JANE KAMM. Concepts of Role Theory. In Edwin J. Thomas (ed.), *Behavioral Science for Social Workers.* New York: The Free Press, 1967; 17–50.

THURSZ, DANIEL. Social Action. In John B. Turner (ed.), *Encyclopedia of Social Work.* Washington, D.C.: National Association of Social Workers, 1977; 1274–1280.

TOSELAND, RONALD W. AND ROBERT F. RIVAS. *An Introduction to Group Work Practice.* New York: Macmillan Publishing Co., 1984.

TROPMAN, JOHN E. AND ELMER J. TROPMAN. Community Welfare Councils. In John B. Turner (ed.), *Encyclopedia of Social Work.* Washington, D.C.: National Association of Social Workers, 1977; 187–193.

TURNER, FRANCIS J. *Social Work Treatment: Interlocking Theoretical Approaches.* New York: The Free Press, 1979.

United States Code, *19,* Title 50, Section 456. Washington, D.C.: U.S. Government Printing Office, 1982 Edition; 249.

VAN MENTS, MORRY. *The Effective Use of Role-Play.* London: Kogan Page Ltd., 1983.

VELASQUEZ, JOAN S. AND HAMILTON I. MCCUBBIN. Towards Establishing the Effectiveness of Community-Based Residential Treatment: Program Evaluation by Experimental Research. *Journal of Social Services Research 3*(4), 1980; 337–359.

VINTER, ROBERT D. Program Activities: An Analysis of Their Effects on Participant Behavior. In Martin Sundel, Paul Glasser, Rosemary Sarri, and Robert Vinter (eds.), *Individual Change Through Small Groups* (Second Edition). New York: The Free Press, 1985; 226–236.

VON BERTALANFFY, LUDWIG. *General System Theory Foundations, Development, Applications.* New York: George Braziller, 1968.

WALL, JAMES A. Mediation: An Analysis, Review and Proposed Research. *Journal of Conflict Resolution 25*(1), 1981; 157–180.

WARREN, ROLAND L. *Truth, Love and Social Change.* Chicago, IL: Rand-McNally & Co., 1971.
WEISSMAN, HAROLD AND ANDREA SAVAGE. *Agency-Based Social Work: Neglected Aspects of Clinical Practice.* Philadelphia, PA: Temple University Press, 1983.
WERNER, HAROLD D. *A Rational Approach to Social Casework.* New York: Association Press, 1965.
———. *New Understandings of Human Behavior.* New York: Association Press, 1970.
WILENSKY, HAROLD AND CHARLES LEBEAUX. *Industrial Society and Social Welfare.* New York: The Free Press, 1965.
WILSON, GERTRUDE AND GLADYS RYLAND. *Social Group Work Practice.* Boston, MA: Houghton-Mifflin, 1949.
WITKIN, STANLEY L., JEFFREY L. EDLESON AND DUNCAN LINDSEY. Social Workers and Statistics: Preparation, Attitudes, and Knowledge. *Journal of Social Service Research 3*(3), 1980; 313–322.
WOLOCK, ISABEL. Community Characteristics and Staff Judgments in Child Abuse and Neglect Cases. *Social Work Research & Abstracts 18*(2), 1982; 9–15.
WOLPE, JOSEPH. *The Practice of Behavior Therapy.* New York: Pergamon Press, 1969.
WOOD, KATHERINE M. Casework Effectiveness: A New Look at the Research Evidence. *Social Work 23*(6), 1978; 437–458.
WRIGHT, JAMES D., PETER H. ROSSI, SONIA R. WRIGHT, AND ELEANOR WEBER BURDIN. *After the Clean-Up.* Beverly Hills, CA: Sage Publications, Inc., 1979.
WYERS, NORMAN L. AND MALINA KAULUKUKUI. Social Services in the Workplace: Rhetoric vs. Reality. *Social Work 29*(2), 1984; 167–172.

INDEX

R

S